Systems
Engineering

Systems Engineering

Coping with Complexity

Richard Stevens, Peter Brook, Ken Jackson and Stuart Arnold

An imprint of **Pearson Education**

London · New York · Toronto · Sydney · Tokyo
Singapore · Madrid · Mexico City · Munich · Paris

PEARSON EDUCATION LIMITED

Head Office:
Edinburgh Gate
Harlow CM20 2JE
Tel: +44 (0)1279 623623
Fax: +44 (0)1279 431059

London Office:
128 Long Acre
London WC2E 9AN
Tel: +44 (0)20 7447 2000
Fax: +44 (0)20 7240 5771

First published in Great Britain 1998

© Pearson Education 1998

British Library Cataloguing in Publication Data
A CIP catalogue record for this book can be obtained from the British Library.

ISBN 0-13-095085-8

10 9 8 7

Typeset by Pantek Arts, Maidstone, Kent
Printed and bound in Great Britain by Redwood Books, Trowbridge, Wiltshire.

The publishers' policy is to use paper manufactured from sustainable forests.

Contents

Preface

Richard Stevens is Chief Technical Officer for QSS Inc, specialising in requirements management and systems engineering work. He is responsible for innovation and methods within QSS, and has written and given a variety of courses on systems, software and requirements engineering. Previous experience includes the European Space Agency, and an author of the Agency's software standards. He can be contacted at rjstevens@compuserve.com

Peter Brook is the Director of Systems Engineering in DERA, responsible for introducing systems engineering practices across the organization. His previous experience has covered technical support, major project audit and research management in a number of system areas, including Air Defence & ATC, Communications Networks and Military Command & Control, as well as serving as the Director of Science (Land) in the MOD. Peter is currently a Director of INCOSE, representing European Government and Academia, and is contactable at pbrook@dera.gov.uk

Ken Jackson is a principal consultant at QSS Inc. specializing in enabling industrial clients to establish improved requirements management capability, both for the processes and the information to be gathered. Ken has had over three decades of experience on complex systems, often those with complex real-time software. He is a founder member of both the IEEE Technical Committee on the Engineering of Computer Based Systems and the UK Chapter of INCOSE. He was one of the developers of the MASCOT methodology. Ken is visiting professor at the University of Ulster, and can be contacted by e-mail at ken.jackson@oxford.qss.co.uk

Stuart Arnold is currently Systems Engineering Manager in DERA's Systems and Software Engineering Centre. Originally a microwave engineer at the Roke Manor Research Laboratory, Stuart has had many years of experience in industry working internationally for Philips in development, manufacture and product support. Stuart is currently joint editor of the ISO 15288 systems engineering standard and his e-mail address is sarnold@dera.gov.uk

The authors' collective experience amounts to more than ten decades of work in industry, large customer organizations and consultancy. They have been involved in system research, system specification, product development, project auditing and quality assurance across large defense, telecommunications, space and software-intensive systems. More recently, the authors have been jointly involved in the development of the DERA Systems Engineering Practices and the ISO 15288 standard, for which the material in this book is a background development. The book is shaped by all of these experiences as well as by extensive feedback from system engineers attending training courses in the USA and Europe.

Audience and objectives for this book

This book introduces the concepts of systems engineering which have evolved to cope with the complexity of modern developments. They embody a system approach which can be applied to a wide variety of developments from huge aerospace systems to mass-produced consumer electronics, pharmaceuticals, and developments of large-scale software.

Systems engineering is steadily growing more important in the increasingly globalized environment. We have to build ever more intricate products to remain competitive, and this complexity introduces difficulties which demand a system approach. The interactions between components become more difficult to manage, gradually becoming the dominant problem of development. At the same time, the pressure to cut the development cycle time is remorseless.

Theory is when you understand everything, but nothing works. Practice is when everything works, but you do not understand why

The book addresses a range of different types of development, from one-off customer developments to mass-produced products. Typically these systems are complex physical items containing significant amounts of software. The front end of the life cycle – the area in need of most attention and with most leverage on successful system creation - is therefore handled in detail. The rest of the development life cycle is then covered, gradually introducing the tailored multi-level approaches needed to cope with real-life systems. The book does not cover manufacture, operations or maintenance in any detail, except where they interact with systems engineering during the development.

This book presents a rationalization of industrial practice in product development. The emphasis throughout is on real experience of the authors and their colleagues, rather than academic theory. Most of this book is actually 'applied common-sense', perhaps imperfect but still very useful. Systems engineering is not new, and indeed the best engineers in any domain have always used the core principles, without formalizing them.

Audience for the book

The principal audience for this book are the engineers, already practising or in education, who will be responsible for producing systems for the future. Others involved in complex developments are expected to find the book useful, for example customers acquiring systems and project managers who interact with the systems engineering processes. The material presented here is targeted at graduate engineers who have been educated in a single specialist engineering discipline, hardware or software, and who wish to understand systems. It is intended to support education, for example in a Masters course, or through in-house training. Lecturers should ideally have personal experience of multiple large-scale industrial developments. The principles of systems engineering need to be understood by all engineering students, and parts of the material will be highly relevant to undergraduates. The book therefore attempts to fill a gap for general-purpose training material to convey the core concepts of systems engineering, independent of the type of product or the organizational processes.

The book contains exercises at the end of each chapter, and the accompanying Web site (www.complexsystems.com) contains proposed answers to these real-world problems. None of these exercises have 'perfect' answers, reflecting the compromises that inevitably have to be made by system engineers and their managers. The book is intended as a source of guidance material and can never substitute for the exercise of professional judgement.

The principles described in this book can be taken up within an organization, and so need to be justified in business terms. Improving the systems engineering processes requires dialog between engineers and managers, undertaken in non-technical terms. The book contains material to help make the case.

Systems engineering needs a defined process supported by procedures, heuristics, rules, training, and tools which can be used to drive and check the progress of projects. Systems engineering processes are being developed within the UK's Defence Evaluation and Research Agency (DERA), for its in-house engineering projects and to assist in its role as advisor in defense system procurement. Relevant documentation will be made available as it is developed via the Web site.

Contributors and reviewers

The contributors and reviewers of this book have brought an enormous range of experience to bear in their efforts to help improve the material. The authors gratefully acknowledge all those who have given generously of their ideas and trust they will find the final product worthy of their contribution. The sections from William Miller (AT&T), Bruce Pinnington (Barclays plc), Gary DeGregorio (Motorola), and Brian McCay (QSS) are gratefully acknowledged. Key reviewers include Jock Rader (Hughes Aircraft), Allen Fairbairn (Trans-Manche), Robin Greenwood (formerly of ESA), Ian Alexander (private consultant), Peter Robson (Siemens-Plessey), Gary Putlock (QSS) and Pert Russell (Hyper Technology). The reviewers in DERA were Peter Bottomley, Colin Boyne, Orlena Gotel, John Hinsley, John Keenan, Nick Peeling, Trevor Rickard, and David Whitaker. The authors would like to thank Martin Hicks, Siân Leetham and Jeremy Winwood of DERA for the illustrations. We would like to specially thank Jerry Lake, founder and former president of INCOSE, for his comments. The book also owes an intellectual debt to the European Space Agency Software Standards, directed over many years by Carlo Mazza[1].

The views expressed in this book are entirely those of the authors and do not represent the views, policy or understanding of any other person or official body.

Introduction

one

1.1. The importance of systems engineering

The world is currently gripped by changes more intense and rapid than those triggered by the industrial revolution more than 250 years ago. A company can think of a new product, implement it in software, and distribute it around the world in hours, or sometimes even minutes. A car manufacturer can, for example, improve the software in a diagnosis system, and then electronically transmit it to 10,000 existing service centers. These changes impose global competitive pressures on companies, and they are driven by our increasing ability to handle complexity.

The last ten years have seen an increasing concentration of the rewards from advanced technology. For many types of product, the concept of a 'local' market is disappearing. We increasingly work in distributed companies, connected by electronic mail to colleagues who may be thousands of miles away.

Don't give the public what it wants – give them something better – Roxy Rothafel from Hollywood

The factors driving these competitive pressures are:

- *increased complexity of products;*
- *globalization of the marketplace, with the erosion of national boundaries as trade barriers;*
- *reduction of product development cycles in the best industrial companies;*
- *software as the dominant force for change in almost all new products;*
- *world-wide deployment of new technology in ever shorter timescales;*
- *systems constructed from bought-in technology and components;*
- *re-use of components, information and knowledge across projects;*
- *partnerships for product development leading to world-wide teams;*
- *the transition from paper-based control to control through electronically managed information;*
- *an understanding that intellectual capital often is the major part of the assets of modern organizations.*

Systems engineering is the key technology to manage this complexity.

Time to market with the right product

Figure 1.1 shows a simple product cycle from requirements to eventual use. The first step of systems engineering is the definition of the requirements,

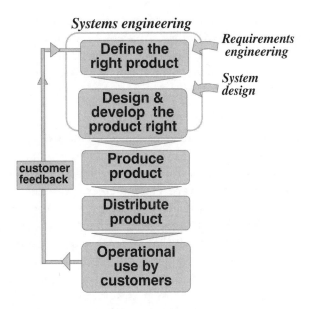

Figure 1.1: Time to market with the right product

followed by designing and developing the initial product. The role of capturing and managing requirements – sometimes called requirements engineering – helps us define what the product must do. The design then defines what will be produced. The development process then generates the initial systems, and the next steps take the product to mass-production, deployment, and operational use. Feedback from users then determines the shape of future products. Even on one-off developments like the Channel Tunnel, we learn lessons which can be applied on the next large construction project. Throughout the whole process, trade-offs and compromises are needed to reconcile requirements with what is feasible.

For many businesses, the key success factor is delivering the right product to market before competitors, and even the development cost is secondary to product timeliness. Products can be released globally and, if they are good enough, take the whole of the market. This puts a huge premium on being in advance of rivals. Typically, 50–75% of the calendar time in development is spent on the early pre-production phases. For example, developing a complex system, such as a car, aircraft, or telecommunications system, may involve several million hours of work from several thousand people over a period of five to eight years. The front-end processes of requirements and design absorb most of the calendar time of development. This is where we have to look to improve the time to market.

Supplying better products and shortening the development time therefore demand dramatic improvements in requirements engineering and system

We have great development processes – but we can't find out what the users want – U.S. telecoms engineer

design. Spending more effort on the mass-production and distribution stages makes little difference to the time to market. However, 'time to market' is not a sufficient goal, and the real objective is to achieve 'time to market with the right product'. In this context, 'right' means what users really want, affordable, and produced ahead of competitors.

The need for systems engineering

Systems engineering is therefore crucial for business success, and effective systems processes are key intellectual assets for a modern business. In a large-scale survey of several thousand engineers, the two most common reasons for project failure were incomplete requirements and lack of user involvement. Five of the eight main problems were requirements, the three others were managerial, but none was about technology[2]. Indeed, in many cases, there were systems with no formal requirements. Another survey indicated that the larger and longer the project, the more likely it is to fail[3]. The essential message is that most projects fail to deliver the right product, on time, and within budget. Putting this in more positive terms, the key factors for success are good front-end systems engineering processes, product superiority and an understanding of the market[4].

No complex system can be optimum to all parties –

Eberhart Rechtin

Case studies of real projects show unequivocally that successful projects have clearly defined criteria for success and that investing in systems engineering clearly reduces cost over-runs[5]. These results are hardly surprising – it is very difficult to build something superb if you do not know why you are building it. Even the best-implemented product is useless if it solves the wrong problem.

1.2. What is systems engineering?

What is a system?

The definition of a 'system' depends upon one's view of the world. Frequently through the text, the word system is used synonymously with a product. In this sense, a product is an artefact (a human-made entity with a distinguishing and identifiable purpose) that draws on integrated, constituent parts, each of which does not individually possess the required overall characteristics.

An end product is a valuable focus for the engineering project, but the correct response to user needs is really a full **operational capability**. While this may sound abstract, this is what provides the user with the full service required instead of just a product. This might involve a set of product(s), operational procedures, support processes, marketing material training, and disposal actions integrated into a working environment. While the customer might buy a radio transmitter, successful operation also demands electricity supplies, trained staff, support equipment, and a maintenance service. The operational environment consists of multiple external systems with which the end product interacts. These external systems range from cooperating systems (e.g.

maintenance and support) to competing systems (e.g. commercial rivals or those trying to destroy our system).

Making an end product needs development support systems (including infrastructure and a test system), and perhaps a system to install or mass-produce the product. Figure 1.2 shows the development of an end product which is then injected into an environment to interact with other systems. The end product leads the process for developing these associated systems; for example, the nature of the product drives the test or production system.

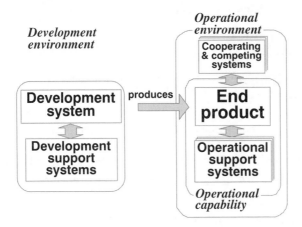

Figure 1.2: Development and operational systems

This book considers the development of a single end product, but each supporting system can be constructed using the same principles, as the subject of a potentially autonomous project. This approach bridges to the concepts underlying to the IEEE 1220 and EIA 632 systems engineering standards, which more widely define all of these derived systems.

For certain kinds of products, some of these associated systems may not be necessary. For example, we can do without a manufacturing system for a one-off development. These additional systems are sometimes hidden from the purchaser, but are nevertheless essential for success. Figure 1.3 shows the different related systems, for the case of an ambulance command and control system which is used as a running example through the book.

What is systems engineering?

Systems engineering is about creating effective solutions to problems, and managing the technical complexity of the resulting developments. At the outset, it is a creative activity, defining the requirements and the product to be built. Then the emphasis switches again, to integration and verification, before delivering the system to the customer. The later phases might involve

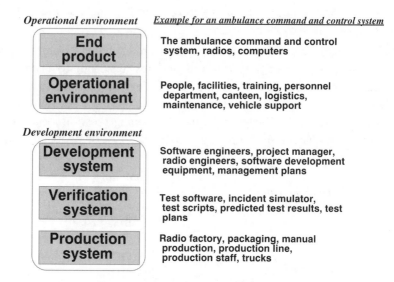

Figure 1.3: We build many systems

The whole is more than the sum of its parts. The part is more than a fraction of the whole – Aristotle

mass-production or to a single customer paying for a one-off development. Even while components are being developed, systems engineering performs a crucial role in technical management.

The systems engineering role must handle the whole life cycle in a balanced way. At all times, the role involves trade-offs between competing factors such as performance, risk and cost. Systems engineering must ensure that designs are practicable and also meet the user requirements. An holistic approach is needed without bias toward specific sub-systems or technology. The system engineer is always scouring the development for risk from end-to-end, confirming decisions only when the risks are acceptable.

Systems engineering must bridge the abstract early stages and the grimy detail of implementation. Systems engineering first establishes what is feasible, then creates the architecture for the system to be produced. It defines the requirements for components, but does not itself produce or manufacture components.

Capturing and organizing requirements is a vital systems engineering task. User requirements should act as the reference point for what users need, but most organizations handle such requirements poorly. Requirements are the foundation for any product – cars, planes, bridges, buildings, organizations or even political and financial legislation. Like all foundations, they call for early work in return for later results.

Systems engineering is different from specialist disciplines such as mechanical or electrical engineering. Technical coordination is a core element of its work. Each specialist discipline tends to think that a development will work only if it follows the philosophy of its own discipline. System engineers must provide the framework for the work of all other disciplines, remaining independent of discipline and product type. System engineers must understand the technical issues, translate them into user needs, and then negotiate with the project manager about the cost and schedule impacts. The role therefore depends upon the ability to communicate across the disparate groups involved in a development.

1.3.   Management and systems engineering

Systems engineering is inevitably both a managerial and a technical role, although some might claim it is restricted to technical issues. In practice, systems engineering decisions, however technical, have schedule and cost implications. A single poor decision or a cost estimate made without realistic information can destroy a product or even a company.

The key difference between project management and systems engineering is that the latter always defines the requirements and creates the architecture. Project management has a wider, but intrinsically less creative role. Its prime function is to ensure everything is done, but not necessarily do it. The coverage in this book emphasizes the technical view, but the two areas are inter-dependent and only partially separable.

Right now we are too busy to bother about our requirements – European Space software manager

Project management without systems engineering is meaningless. Successful management requires trade-offs between variables such as cost, schedule, quality and performance. These tasks cannot be meaningful without the information produced by systems engineering. Because time and resources are easy to measure, management sometimes attempts to control projects without the key element of requirements. What use is meeting cost and budget targets without producing a useful product?

Project managers are probably looking at the systems engineering roles and thinking 'If this is systems engineering, I do it already'. Software engineers or integrated circuit designers are thinking the same, and they are all correct. Systems engineering is not just a role for a specialist group of people, but a part of the work of every individual working in the project team. On a small project, the project manager will do the systems engineering, and perhaps the implementation as well. On large systems, it will be performed at multiple levels throughout the development by all disciplines.

1.4.   The system life cycle

Figure 1.4 shows a sequential development approach, from the user requirements to the delivery of a complete operational capability. This simplistic but revealing model consists of a sequence of processes from user requirements, through system requirements, architectural design, and component development to the testing cycle of integration, installation and

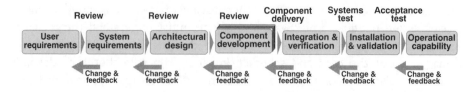

Figure 1.4: The simple system life cycle

operations. At each process boundary, a review or a test allows progress to be monitored and a commitment made to the next stage. These boundaries act as quality milestones, controlling the gradual transformation from a high-risk idea into a complete product. The life cycle defines the order in which information must be produced, and the users, developers and designers each have the responsibility for separate parts of the information.

Each component is developed as an entity, fitting within the overall design framework. The components are then integrated into a complete system, which can be transferred to the working environment.

You cannot always tell the truth by sticking to the facts – Colette

Figure 1.5 shows another view of the life cycle reorganized as a 'V-diagram', with verification occurring across the horizontal links and between the definition phases. The left-hand side of the V-diagram defines what must be built, and the right-hand side builds it from the components, and verifies the end products against the left-hand specification. Information produced to specify components is the basis of testing of those components during in the integration stage. Components are accepted, integrated and verified in stages until they are formed into a complete, tested system. The better the work on the left-hand side is done, the easier is the work on the right hand.

Here we consider validation as end-to-end verification, showing that the complete system meets its user requirements under operational conditions.

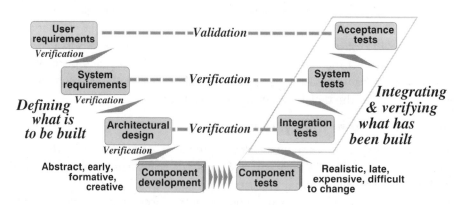

Figure 1.5: The V-diagram form of the simple life cycle

Coping with risk and complexity

Small, simple systems can be easily visualized as a single entity while evaluating the advantages of different possible solutions. For large systems, overall behavior emerges only when the complete system can be seen as an entity. Complex systems are typically formed from interacting elements, which themselves are increasingly 'intelligent' and partially autonomous. A complex system cannot be managed in the head of a single person, but it is always essential to see such systems as a single entity, and at different levels of detail. Engineers and managers must create faithful abstractions that show an overall view or allow them to explore the fine detail.

The sequential life cycle is a logical way of expressing many core concepts about development. It is not however practical for systems engineering of large-scale, realistic systems. Before committing to a project, an organization needs to be sure that it is affordable, technically feasible, acceptably 'safe', as well as providing users with the quality they need. While quality is dependent on the user requirements, we need to understand the design to obtain realistic values of cost and risk (Figure 1.6). This diagram defines the key front-end role of systems engineering, which cycles through requirements and architectural design until a consistent, practical compromise can be reached.

Every failure of implement- ation is, by definition, a failure of formulation – Henry Mintzberg

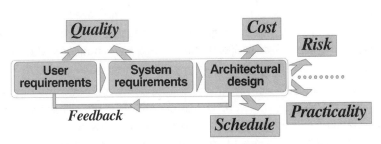

Figure 1.6: Quality, cost, schedule, risk and feasibility

Life cycles usually illustrate the steady increase in commitment during a project, but they are poor at showing the work being performed at any given time. In practice, each set of information is defined gradually through the life cycle, not fixed within a single phase (Figure 1.7). In an early feasibility study, the prime concern might be requirements, but there must also be an outline design to explore practicality. As these risks become clear through the life cycle, the information that defines the system improves in quality.

During development, we may not have enough information to be completely confident that the design really can be implemented. Risk has to be managed

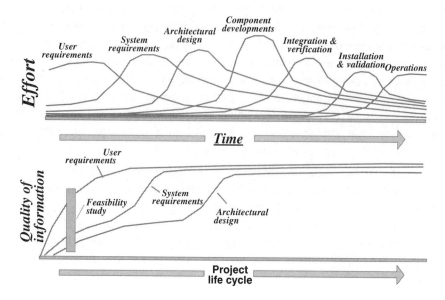

Figure 1.7: Commitment and exploration

and controlled throughout the life cycle. Some argue that the core management activity is risk management – reducing the risk of delivering a poor quality product. Most projects run late, go over-budget and do not meet their requirements[6] – if they ever had any in the first place.

The sequential life cycle demonstrates the fundamental concepts of processes and reviews. However, taken in isolation this view is illusory, because it assumes stability in requirements and the working environment. Exploration of the architecture and some of the components is essential to confirm that the requirements are both practical and affordable. Feedback from the design will therefore modify the requirements. The objective is to have a compatible set of requirements, design, costs and risks before committing to implement the system. Change and risk are inevitable and we should plan for them, not treat them as surprising.

Choosing the development approach

The basic system life cycle is inevitably tailored from project to project, because no fixed pattern is uniquely suited to develop all products. The resultant life cycle is therefore much more complicated. The elements of the sequential life cycle can be re-used to build these more realistic development approaches. Choosing a suitable development approach is a key early activity in managing risk, although the process may not need to be totally defined early on. This decision determines whether to develop (for example) incrementally or in an evolutionary fashion; how to decompose, and whether the risks demand a prototyping approach. A life cycle matched to the needs of the project will significantly reduce development risk, yet it is often chosen casually.

Information management

The choice of the development approach effectively determines a model of the information that will define the product. Traditionally this was called a 'document tree', but modern tools can transform this paper-based approach into an 'information model' held within a computer. The information model is produced early, but is usually amended during the course of the project.

Systems engineering therefore creates and organizes the key information that defines the system. A complex system is managed through information created in a suitable structure, in an appropriate order, and with traceability between different elements. Only the right people can see and change that information. This approach encourages teamwork, for example through integrated product teams, yet ensures personal responsibility.

This information defines the product, how it is developed and tested, and how it is produced. We must have tools to design microelectronics with millions of transistors and simulate how they will work before committing them to silicon. In the same way, we need methods and tools to organize the entangled information that lies behind any development. Most of the technical issues of handling this information are becoming straightforward, as long as we have the right people, processes and methods to manage it. The purpose of this information is to make decisions and define what must be built. It has to be good enough for these purposes and no more.

Software as part of the system

Complex systems contain motors, hydraulics, people, documentation and software. But most new functionality in today's products is implemented through software. The concept of a software 'system' as a separate development is, however, an illusion and software must be handled sensibly in a system context. Large software-intensive systems have a notoriously high failure rate, and the major cause tends to be weak systems engineering, not anything specific to software. In this book, software engineering is treated as a specialist discipline, implementing the requirements packaged through systems engineering. Software is a component in a system, and no more exempt from project control than any other discipline.

The project and the organization

The project always exists within a business that creates and resources it (Figure 1.8). The business normally controls the development through a product manager responsible to the customer. To do its work properly, the

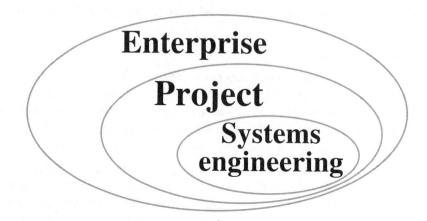

Figure 1.8: The project and its context

business also needs to apply systems engineering techniques, for example, to initiate projects successfully, to control multiple projects, or promote re-use.

1.5.   Requirements through the life cycle

It may work in practice, but the theory is quite unsatisfactory – French engineer

There is often a tendency to rush into 'cutting metal' (or code) early, in the mistaken belief that this will advance a project. It provides a comforting illusion that something useful is being done. Engineers and managers often think of requirements as a task that is completed early on. Sometimes the work is not done at all, and we work extremely hard at perfecting the wrong product. The role of the enterprise in nurturing projects and managing their introduction emerges strongly in the latter half of the book.

Figure 1.9 shows a curve of a work profile through the life cycle of a healthy project, separated into the customer-side and supplier effort. The earliest tasks are the responsibility of the customer, with then balance of effort then gradually passing to the supplier. The role of requirements is always active. Requirements are used for a variety of tasks in the life cycle, and so need to be kept up-to-date throughout the development. Initially, they define the business and user objectives, and are then used for an abstract definition of the solution. An individual design can then usually be optimized by selectively cutting out high-cost, low-benefit areas. Cost-to-completion estimates must be firmly based on deliverables linked to the requirements.

During design and implementation, potential changes are evaluated against their costs and impact on the design and requirements. Requirements should therefore be organized so that compromise is possible later. Further on in the

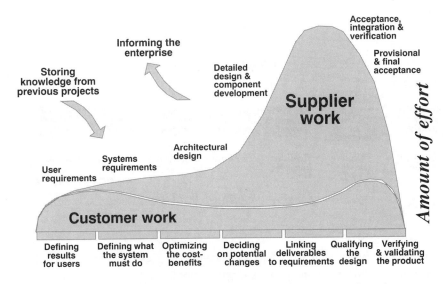

Figure 1.9: Customer-service provider effort through the life cycle

development, realistic prototypes (called engineering models) are tested against the requirements to verify the design, and so allow manufacture to start. The components, assemblies, and completed system are all tested against the requirements, as is the final product before acceptance by users.

Making wine is simple, but not easy –

Italian proverb

Requirements are also a form of retained knowledge, a set of rules extracted from experience and re-applied to the next generation of new systems. Organizational knowledge and policy can then be sensibly applied to every project. The history of industries such as railroads and aerospace illustrates that severe accidents often drive improved practices. Good design practice is therefore a form of directed evolution. Information on failures (and successes) is captured in requirements and re-applied to future design e.g.

'No single failure within the braking system shall endanger life'

1.6.   Structure of the book

The first half of the book

The first part of this book follows the steps of the sequential life cycle to introduce the basic systems engineering concepts (Figure 1.10). These separate processes, such as architectural design, are the modules of all life cycles. While this development approach provides useful concepts, it is too simplistic to reflect the reality of development. The first additional concept of tailoring the life cycle is introduced in Chapter 7, rearranging the separate processes into development approaches such as evolutionary or incremental development. The first half of the book is a compilation of the knowledge acquired through decades of experience, and while it may cause differences of

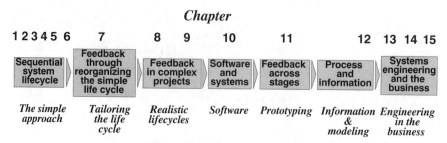

Figure 1.10: Logic of the book

opinion, it has been validated across dozens of projects. The second half covers more recent work in systems organization.

Chapter 2 describes the **user requirements** process. The discussion focuses on the capturing, structuring, and reviewing of requirements from people who will be users of the product. Business requirements and working environment are also covered.

Chapter 3 describes the **system requirements** process. The chapter focuses on the creation, organization, preparation and review of system requirements, with a coverage of management activities. Many methods used for organizing requirements information apply equally to the design processes that follow.

Chapter 4 describes the **architectural design** process. The process creates an architecture close to the components that are actually constructed, and defines their behavior and interaction. This stage defines the elements to be produced and so forms the basis for the project management of implementation phases.

The sequence of integrating the components into a complete working system is covered in **Chapter 5** on **integration to operations**. This is a multi-stage process, gradually integrating the units into a complete system, and leads to accepting the end product into its operational environment.

Chapter 6 discusses the interaction between **systems engineering and project management**, in terms of its disciplines of configuration management, verification and validation, and quality assurance. Decision-making and risk management are covered in relation to systems engineering.

In practice, every project also adopts some form of tailored life cycle to better handle complexity, risk, and change. **Chapter 7** shows the major variants of development approaches, such as incremental, evolutionary and framework architectures. Collection of feedback from operational systems is also covered. A cut-down life cycle covers the lower-risk, smaller systems that often form the bulk of an organization's work, at least in terms of numbers of projects. Each of these different life cycles is essentially a re-organization of the processes that make up the simple life cycle. For example, the process of capturing user requirements will always be needed and be similar across different projects.

The second half of the book

The second half uses these concepts to explore more realistic approaches showing the concurrency, iteration and feedback of real-world system development. The book introduces these complex concepts one at a time and separately, so that they can be seen in relation to the simple life cycle

Although it is rooted in industrial reality, the second half is more contentious, presenting results from research work of the last five years. The later chapters present the life cycles as concurrent processes, and shaped by the nature of the system and the point in the life cycle.

Chapter 8 firmly breaks the mold of sequence, by considering the interactions leading to the creation of complex systems. Even re-arrangement of the separate processes is not enough, because feedback across processes is also needed. For example, feedback is needed from design exploration before committing to a set of requirements. The complexity introduced by the size of systems demands a multi-level, multi-project approach. Systems must be partitioned into multiple components that are developed concurrently, yet work together as a complete holistic system. Life cycles that address these real-world issues are introduced in *Chapter 8*.

I read part of the book all of the way through

– Sam Goldwyn

This more realistic approach changes the nature of project management. *Chapter 9* discusses *management in multi-level projects* including the control of lower level developing components. While components are being developed, extra management processes are needed to control the interactions between suppliers. The chapter produces a generic concept of how to handle sub-projects in a complex environment.

The interaction between *software and systems* is covered in *Chapter 10*. Most systems suffer from the 'software problem' but many of the difficulties are actually due to systems engineering issues. We need to handle systems that are a mixture of software, hardware and people.

The objective of *prototyping* is to provide feedback and reduce risk as early as possible. Prototyping occurs in a variety of forms, during different stages of development. The use of feasibility studies, modeling and simulation, and prototyping to explore risk and value is covered in *Chapter 11*.

Chapter 12 describes the *information modeling* of systems to illustrate how project information is increasingly managed electronically, rather than being document-based. Although we often refer to 'documents', in practice these are now more often generated from software. Developing an information model that defines all the information relating to a product is one of the first tasks for the project team. The systems engineering process is the starting point to build such models. Once the system information has been organized, many other tasks that use that information become much easier. These include decision management and cost estimation.

Chapter 13 then covers the interactions between **systems engineering and the enterprise,** with particular emphasis on the end-to-end life cycle of a system. A project is actually created and developed through a series of stages, each followed by a gate for evaluating the project. Each stage uses the traditional life cycle to generate enough information to make decisions. These stage-gates are defined in systems engineering terms in this chapter. The business must put effort into systems engineering to control multiple projects, for technology management, handling issues such as 'systems-of-systems', interoperability and re-use, and organizational process development. Initiating new projects is a key business-level activity covered in this chapter.

Improving the systems engineering processes is primarily a managerial, not a technical problem. Systems engineering must therefore be understood and applied at the organizational level. **Chapter 14** illustrates **improving the systems engineering processes** across the business. The chapter defines the business benefits as part of selling the approach to management, who must provide the budget. Several experts have contributed 'war stories' about their efforts to improve the systems engineering processes in different businesses such as a research agency, financial institution, and the medical device industry.

Finally, **Chapter 15 summarizes the principles of systems engineering** covered in the book. References are then documented in appendices.

Through the book, examples are given for a number of different types of products, primarily reflecting the experiences of the authors. A hypothetical ambulance command and control system has already been referred to, and in other parts of the book the engineering of cars, airplanes and defense systems are discussed as examples.

1.7.   Summary

If it is so simple, why doesn't everyone do it?

Your first comment on reading this material may be *This is obvious – it is only common sense* . This should be closely followed by asking *why don t we do it?* But in practice, systems engineering may well be simple, but it is far from easy, and few businesses currently handle it well. Undoubtedly many products have been successfully produced without employing systems engineering in any formal way. But the challenge is to achieve widespread, repeatable product development. This requires discipline and dedication over an extended period.

This introductory chapter has presented the scope of the book, explained the concepts of systems engineering which are fundamental to well-managed developments, and introduced the system life cycle for a simple product development. The chapter has also introduced the concept of actively tailoring the basic life cycle to handle the problems of complexity that are common in creating modern systems. This approach turns out to be essential for dealing with large multi-level projects.

The user requirements process

two

2.1. Objectives for user requirements

What do users want?

User requirements are the first step towards defining a system. Every system needs to satisfy its end users to be successful, and so we must define who they are and what they want, expressed in their own terms. Understanding a product shows us what is dominant today, but understanding the user requirements tells us what will dominate the future. These needs can then drive all subsequent development stages from a user perspective. The user requirements process is very different in nature to the rest of the life cycle, and should be short, intensive and highly interactive. Even if the requirements are not all practical, we need to understand what the users want. Poor handling of user requirements causes severe consequences later.

User requirements should be expressed in the terminology of the problem domain, defining what the users want to do with the system. In other words, user requirements are defined from an operational point of view, not in terms of system functionality or equipment. Many development approaches fail to distinguish between user and system requirements, weakening the role of users. User and system requirements must be kept separate, with the former driving the latter. Unfortunately this rarely happens, and the 'requirements' are often a single entity, mixing up user needs with box-drawings of the solution, background material, system functions, design elements, and unverifiable wishes.

This is also the logical place to define a coherent set of business requirements. Customer commitment and the system boundaries are often unclear at the start of the user requirements process. The business objectives act as the frame for the user requirements, defining the boundaries of any proposed system.

Figure 2.1 shows how user requirements are defined, starting by defining the user types, and capturing requirements from them. These must be structured into a coherent set, which is then reviewed and agreed by users, and updated, and issued as the user requirements document (URD).

Users tend to give the fewest, most general requirements possible (e.g. 'it must be easy to use') or solutions ('I want a database'). Design decisions will

Figure 2.1: Capturing user requirements

be scattered through these generalities. System engineers have to interact with users to turn this noisy information into measurable, testable requirements, suitable for driving the rest of the project. Requirements are not generated as an end in themselves, but for use later in the project.

Different types of users

Users are defined as all of those people involved in the operation of the finished product – provided that their needs will influence that product. For a plane, the different user types would include the passengers, pilots, flight attendants, ground staff such as maintenance and cleaning staff, and also the air traffic controllers who will guide the plane. Different types of users will have different requirements, and we may prioritize those requirements differently. For example, if we accepted every requirement from the maintenance engineers, the plane may be easy to maintain, but difficult to fly! The maintenance view nevertheless provides valid user requirements about ease of access or visibility of faults. All requirements must be captured, even those that cannot be fully implemented. The fundamental user of the product is the person who really needs the end product, and not necessarily the system operator.

Example user requirement – The driver shall be informed about likely traffic blockages

The people influencing the product are sometimes called the 'stakeholders'. The term must include maintenance engineers, operators, and trainers. Other stakeholders include the production engineers, verification engineers and quality assurance staff. These different groups have different needs, responsibilities, and interests which have to be reflected in the organization of the requirements. The needs of operational users are defined in the user requirements, while those from the development environment are best included in the system requirements.

For the moment the focus is on operational users and their needs. A diagram showing the different types of users, their roles and their inter-relationships can be useful. A number of different, usually informal, 'soft system' methods have been suggested for handling the early processes (e.g. Checkland's[7] approach) but these have been applied only sporadically. Figure 2.2 shows the case of an ambulance command and control system, and we can quite clearly see that call dispatch, patient diagnosis and transport allocation will be

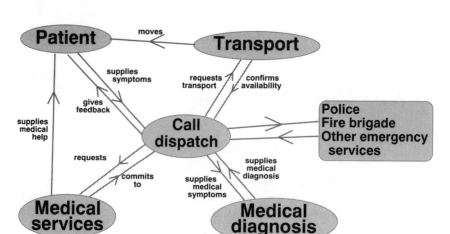

Figure 2.2: Links between different kinds of users

needed. The diagram shows the flows of information between these various user types. No 'job positions' have yet been decided, nor do we know where these skills will be placed.

User requirements must be organized into a coherent set, always linked back to the users who requested them. This provides a sensible basis for the inevitable trade-offs that will be needed later. They need to be structured hierarchically to detect missing requirements, overlaps and allow them to be viewed at different levels of abstraction. Each user group can have its own viewpoint on the requirement set, by selecting the relevant requirements using the links. Figure 2.3 shows the traceability from the original user groups to the composite set of user requirements.

2.2.   User and system requirements

Separating the sets of user and system requirements is essential because these two elements are so different in their nature and organization. The former defines the results that the system will supply to users, while the latter imposes requirements on an abstract model of the final system. There must be a complete, separate set of information through which users control the system development at any time. Muddling them up with system requirements means that neither set can be checked for completeness. User requirements must be short, non-technical and in a form that users can easily understand and correct. Users are ultimately responsible for the complete set, so they must be able to read and criticize them.

For example, car buyers do not care about functional block diagrams, data flows or state transitions, and so their requirements should not be explained in this terminology. They need to control aspects such as capacity, comfort,

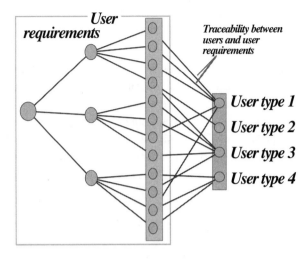

Figure 2.3: User types linked to the user requirements

safety, re-sale value, fuel economy and the type of journeys that the vehicle can make.

Users often initially state their requirements in terms of solutions, and these have to be pushed back to the real requirements. For example a user might start by stating:

'I need to archive the system in a database every week'

A moment's reflection will make you realize that users do not care about archiving, databases or storage of information. They need to avoid loss of work or perhaps to be able to retrieve information. Storage and databases are mechanisms that may potentially help to meet the requirement. By asking the question 'Why?' or 'What is the objective of this?', we can tease out the actual requirement, which might transform the original statement into:

'I don't want to lose more than one week's work by any predictable incident'

The second version of the requirement is very different to the initial statement, and a far better expression of what is wanted. After all, the first requirement could be met by copying the information onto the same hard disk. If that crashes, everything is lost. Recovery software, off-site storage, and procedural instructions will be essential to implement the real underlying need, but these could never have been deduced from the original statement.

System requirements evolve from user requirements, defining what the system must do to meet them. As we shall see later, system requirements for a car could consist of the vehicle architecture, functionality, control structure, material and information flows and dynamic behavior of the vehicle. They are the developers' response to user requirements, and are usually too large and technical for users to understand (and hence control).

Mixing up user and system requirements also deprives users of the strength to influence the development. Neither set of information is likely to be complete or well organized.

Occasionally, users can be too powerful in a development, because they have enough technical knowledge to dominate both the solution and the requirements. For example, space telescope developers and particle physicists are smart, and consider they can build better information management systems than professionals. They will often rapidly build excellent prototypes. The resultant systems may be technically interesting, but can be impractical and unmaintainable.

There are no user requirements for my product

Designers involved in making a sub-system, such as the engine for a car, large telecommunications switches or software to control car engines, often remark:

> *'Users don't understand what I'm building – there are no user requirements for my product'*

Technically this is correct because there are no 'users' of the component, because no-one wants just an engine. The engine is a component supplied to the integrator of the whole vehicle. For commercial reasons, this integrator may want to minimize the flow of information from end users to the parts suppliers. Under these circumstances, designers will often provide functionality which is perhaps not needed by the users. To build the correct component you must however understand the needs of users. Requirements must cascade down from them through the system to the sub-system level. The designer of a digital television system needs to understand new applications such as interactive television, betting, home banking, or viewing photographs on the television. If these end user scenarios are not defined, designers are groping through a fog, and will often resort to adding functionality from their own imagination. Even if it causes problems with the customer, communication must somehow be established between sub-system engineers and end users. Customers and developers must be brought into the same engineering processes.

2.3.   The environment

Every non-trivial system has to interact with other organizations and people within an existing environment . The 'environment' is considered as all those things outside the system that will affect what we want to build (Figure 2.4). The major components influencing the developing system are the:

- *operational environment (cooperating, competitive, and support systems);*
- *development environment.*

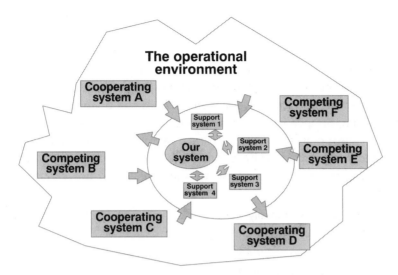

Figure 2.4: The operational environment

For example, the ambulance command and control system will work with external organizations such as the hospitals, ambulances, police, and fire services. The **operational environment** will be influenced by systems such as the road system, traffic density, geography of the area, income of potential purchasers, legal issues, social organization, the attitude and education level of the ambulance staff. The system must eventually operate in the 'predicted', not the current, environment during the whole of its lifetime. For a custom developed product, such as a military aircraft, a different group may prepare various support systems (such as logistics and training). Even a mass-produced consumer item, such as a computer, will always work within a context of power supplies, specified standards for communications, and a fixed temperature range.

Users don't know what they want – a sign that you may be doing the wrong thing!

The competitive environment could be the enemy for a military system, a hacker for an information technology, or a commercial rival for a mass-produced product. The system has to be designed to cope with each of these. If we produce an industrial product, it must compete successfully against other products that will be available at the same time. Producing a good product twelve months after someone else has captured the market is pointless.

The **development environment** is formed by the systems (typically the customer and development organizations) with which the product interacts during development. These will include the software and hardware companies that produce the system. Existing systems, software and test infrastructures will often be re-used across projects. Within the customer environment, there will usually be competition for funding and responsibility within these enterprises.

In some cases, the customer acquires the product, but is not an end user. This is typically the case for an acquisition agency for military equipment. Frequently, the airline is the customer for the plane, financing the whole deal. The customer pays for the development, scopes the boundaries, and decides the relative importance of each user group. Customers are the rulers from a contractual viewpoint, and if the customer tells you to ignore a certain group, then indeed you should usually ignore them. Needs from different groups of users will be prioritized, according to their influence, power, and financial resources.

The environment is initially expressed in user requirements through interactions with external systems e.g.

'The ambulance driver shall be able to communicate directly with the police about criminal activity at the injury scene'

'The ambulance driver shall be provided with information about traffic jams on potential routes'

The environment is not fixed, but will be affected by the system that we construct, by technical opportunities and changes in business objectives. Defining the environment therefore always involves an element of prediction.

2.4.   Business requirements

User requirements work within the context of requirements of the business that has spawned the project. A customer may, for example, specify geographical areas for operations or when operations should be started. Typical examples of business requirements are:

'The product should take 30% of the South American market by 1999'

'The development shall cost less than $10 million'

'The product shall be developed with internal resources'

The first requirement influences the product, and drives the user requirements. The second requirement limits the budget available for the development process. Business requirements are often implied, but rarely stated formally. As a result, projects often stumble around, looking for fixed references. Business requirements are usually oriented more toward schedule and cost rather than the product, and contain decisions as well as requirements (Figure 2.5). Business objectives often need to be teased out, then documented to make sure everyone understands any pre-defined project boundaries. The same business requirements often apply across several projects. Failure to document business requirements can result in them not being known or applied at the project level. On a large ship project, the organizational policy was to design for upgradeability, but this had not been

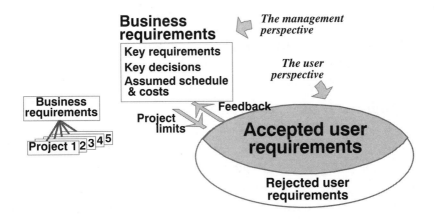

Figure 2.5: Business and user requirements

formally documented anywhere. As a result, the development team was told by their middle-level management to forget upgradeability for this project, and to design for minimum cost of delivery, rather than whole life costs. Primary business objectives and decisions were therefore unknown and unheeded.

Business requirements synthesize the key project issues from an organizational perspective, covering the most important business requirements, major decisions, and important development issues such as cost or schedule. The objectives should also document the commitments from management to the project; for example, the available budget, timescales for decision-making, and delegation of authority. Presenting this synthesis to management invariably generates changes, which then need to be reflected into the full user requirements.

When they are first defined, business objectives are usually over-optimistic, normally with severe contradictions between requirements and the available resources and schedule. Putting the business objectives down on paper allows them to be evaluated, and often exposes any inherent contradictions. Business requirements typically need intensive feedback throughout the development to make them realistic. Logically, business objectives precede the project; in practice they should be defined with the user requirements because of the mutual interactions.

Business objectives should define the interaction between the business and the project management. They represent the delegation of authority that the enterprise makes to the project manager, so defining the project boundaries and objectives. The project manager must be rigorous in allowing the project to be checked only against these objectives, and under conditions specified in the objectives.

Users always know more than you – about what they need from the product

Where systems are built as part of the organization infrastructure, the business itself is a 'user' of the end product. For example, information technology systems for a banking or insurance company are there to satisfy the organizations' needs. In these cases, the business objectives are dominant, and the users are relegated to the role of operators of the system.

2.5.   Sources of user requirements

Figure 2.6 shows a variety of different sources for user requirements. User requirements may be picked up, for example, from interviews, existing documentation, from related products, by prototyping, or workshops.

Interviews with users are the basic method of extracting requirements. Interviewing is too intense for one person to simultaneously ask questions and document the answers. Plan the interviews carefully and have a colleague who understands the requirements process to take notes. The objective is to extract all the relevant information from the user's brain, filter out the irrelevant, get it down on paper, and then improve it by review. The results can be passed to others for correction and improvement. Make users sign for their requirements at the end of each session, to show that they are serious. After all, you are basing the whole system on their information. Interviewing users is a piece of theater, and the process has to be managed to get the information out of them and into an organized form. With experience, requirements can be partially synthesized on the fly, reducing the amount of

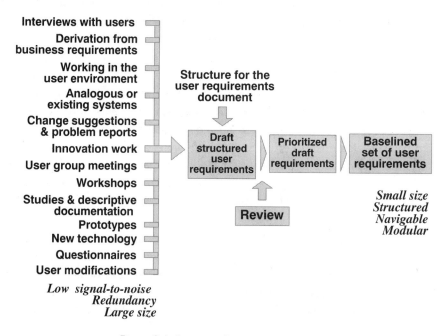

Figure 2.6: Sources of user requirements

information to be analyzed. Recording the information on video or tape recorders is rarely practical because of the time needed for analysis. Effort spent on intense interaction with users, interactive synthesis, and rapid feedback will provide better results.[8]

In dealing with users, start with generalizations and move to more pointed and specific questions. Users will start by giving you solutions, and you must bring them back to the requirement by asking the question 'Why?' or 'What is the purpose of this?'.

Derivation from business requirements typically transforms from the abstract (*'make a test system for cellular phones'*) into more specific form (*'supports on-site testing by maintenance staff'*). This is the mechanism to ensure that organization policy is understood and transferred to the individual project.

Working in the user environment teaches developers what the users are really trying to achieve. Mutual education in this way has a positive effect on the requirements and provides a sound basis for a more synergistic and sympathetic relationship between developers and users throughout the development. Japanese automobile engineers have spent significant time in the homes of typical customers, both in the USA and Japan, before starting the design process. Not surprisingly, the resulting vehicles sold well. Of course, information about the users' needs must be formally captured and communicated to everyone.

Analogous or existing systems may have been developed by someone else for completely different purposes, but contain elements similar to what we want to develop. You can try to find such a similar system, perhaps in a completely different industry. Put users in front of the existing system, and ask them what they like and dislike about it, record their answers, and inject these into the requirements set. Don't be over-sensitive about asking for access to such systems. Many companies will be happy to help you, unless they are competitors or the project is secret.

Change suggestions and problem reports are excellent mechanisms for capturing user requirements. This works only where there is an existing system as in an evolutionary development. These suggestions are often realistic and creative, because they come from real users. For a software development in which two of the authors are involved, about sixty suggestions and complaints are received per month. Most are small-scale and sensible, often repeated by several customers. Some are out-of-scope or impractical, but surprisingly few are mutually inconsistent. Perhaps 5% or so of the suggestions are creative – yet so obvious – that they cause one to gasp with astonishment. Sometimes it is much easier to make specific complaints about an existing system – *'the monitor is not bright enough'*, *'the instruction book is muddled'* – than to write abstract requirements. You must capture the vital information that only users can provide. In many companies, this critical information is never gathered or used.

Innovation work often generates half-formed product ideas that need back-converting into requirements. Some organizations have formal processes for generating new products. The initial idea will be transformed during the innovation process and the requirements form the foundation of systems that move forward to development.

User group meetings are extremely effective at getting good-quality requirements from people who are already using a system intensively. A meeting of 40 users attended by one of the authors supplied 160 prioritized requirements in three hours for the next version of the software product. The quality of suggestions is usually very high. Focus groups may contain a wider range of skills to supply advice on the whole project.

Workshops are an efficient means to extract and even organize user requirements. A few days of intense effort can get the requirements into a reasonable state, sufficient to circulate and improve. An off-site environment – quiet, pleasant and phone-free – helps, but you may need some inducement to encourage users to become involved. For example, a free training course, a beach party or attaching the workshop to an existing conference can make it easier for users to attend. Ask users to present what they want from the system, and stimulate their colleagues to interact intensively. This needs a good facilitator and a secretary experienced in requirements work. Produce a structure for the requirements, and get users to fill it in. Suggestions from users can be rapidly injected, and new versions of the requirements document supplied for correction within hours. Train the users in what you want from them, then get them to provide that information. Organize competitions among sub-groups, each presenting their choices to colleagues. Rapid feedback from users is more important than analyzing the wrong information to death in a closed room. The flow of information that happens in the workshop has to be completely documented. Key factors in organizing workshops are:

Without aggression, there is no interaction

- *plan the workshop down to 15–30 minute intervals and rehearse everyone through their role;*
- *make the users work hard, focussing on requirements, not the underlying process;*
- *bring developers to the workshop, but never let them stop the users speaking;*
- *make sure you have an experienced colleague document the results;*

> '*Over the course of a year and a half, we have had three major airline conferences like this. At the initial conference, we picked up 150 or 170 problems or ideas or suggestions; the second meeting showed up 50 or 60 ideas, and the final review showed ten or fifteen nits they were still picking at.*'
> *– Alan Jankot, (Pratt & Whitney) about workshops with maintenance engineers.*[9]

In presenting what is needed from users, you need to understand the level of process expertise in the audience. If they understand the basics of the process, then they will grasp the underlying concepts fairly quickly. But most types of users will need non-technical explanations of the purpose of the workshop, and their role in capturing requirements.

Studies or descriptive documents are a source of potential user requirements. Business reports may contain valuable information, but usually this is in a disorganized form. Requirements need to be located, marked up, translated into more formal text and then transferred into a structured requirements document. Traceability should be maintained between the formal requirements and the original source material. In one project, one of the authors reduced an unreadable four-foot high stack of documents to less than 100 pages of requirements. These could easily be read in a few hours and this led to the identification of gaps that could never have been found in the original heap of information.

Prototypes can be extremely effective in obtaining requirements. A prototype may be complex and expensive, e.g. a partial implementation of a final product. In other cases, it may be as simple as a role-playing game with a few people, or a computer simulation. However intricate it is, the objective is for users to imagine the final system, and then to supply requirements for it. Prototypes bring users and designers into an environment on which both can comment, reducing the barriers between them. The product of prototypes is knowledge.

New technology will often enable previously impossible requirements to become feasible. These requirements may have always existed, but never been expressed because they were seen as impossible. The practical benefits of new technology have first to be expressed in user terms and confirmed by the users, before being introduced into mainstream products. There is obviously a danger of self-indulgence in injecting unnecessary technology for its own sake. However, a technology opportunity such as the development of Internet, for example, had enormous implications on the banking industry; the business needed to understand what was possible before they could specify novel banking services. Organizations therefore need to scan technology and work out the potential impact on their products.

Questionnaires are often used in the user requirements phase, but they should not be the primary means of capturing user requirements. They can be useful for confirming requirements, but constrain the user to a pre-defined set of questions. They can be effective as a checklist for a structured interview. Our experience is that questionnaires are filled out by the wrong type of user – people with too much time on their hands. On the other hand, complaints about an existing system tend to be generated by those who are using the system intensively, and are usually more specific and of better quality than results from questionnaires.

User modifications of existing systems may be the most significant (and overlooked) source of innovatory modifications of equipment. Even if the design modification is not industrial quality, it can be reverse engineered into requirements to improve the existing product. Von Hippel[10] estimates that in some industries 75% of innovation comes from this source.

2.6. Organizing the requirements

Users 'own' the requirements but they can rarely write them in a structured, organized form. The specialized role of requirements engineer captures the requirements, writes and structures the information in a more suitable form. This demands persistence in questioning users, forcing requirements to be clarified, and pushing back solutions without ever trying to impose personal views. Currently these ego-less skills are absent from most marketing departments.

Requirements are usually captured in a random, disorganized fashion, and they cannot be organized interactively. They must be organized into the right structure and style for designers to use them well. In practice, trying to squeeze requirements into a structure too early can also be counter-productive. The initial interaction is usually intense, and the requirements will need cleaning up and organizing. A word processor or a standard database is fine to capture the initial flow of information, and using the 'outline' mode can help iterate toward a good structure.

As requirements grow and the number of sources increases, traceability and configuration management of the information rapidly become essential. More information – such as source, ownership, priority and verifiability – needs to be attached to the requirements. Different people will need to be able to filter out different views of the requirements. Moving the information into a structured requirements management tool gives greater control from this point onwards.

Operational scenarios, capabilities and constraints

Requirements captured from multiple sources are initially incoherent and duplicated, and the amount of irrelevant material is high. They often emerge as composites that need dissecting into individual requirements (sometimes called 'capabilities'). The individual requirements need to be structured to highlight gaps and remove irrelevant material, duplication and descriptive material. For these reasons, structured information is likely to be much smaller than the heap of descriptive information. Descriptive information must be retained as supplementary material, without being required reading for everyone.

A backbone structure for the user requirements is the 'operational scenario'. This is a 'thought experiment' analyzing the results provided to users as the system is operated, organized by time. This approach allows gaps and overlaps to be detected and corrected. We can 'rehearse' the proposed system by stepping sequentially through time seeing how it reaches our goal. Breaking goals into sub-goals allows the requirements to be viewed at any required level of detail. 'Use cases' in software follow similar principles[11], a rare example of software methods handling user requirements well. The overall set of scenarios defines the overall system concept, and the customer may constrain the system through controlling which scenarios are supported.

User scenarios are best organized hierarchically, so that the major headings represent the key goals. But this is a hierarchy with a difference – it should start from the end goal, i.e. with the net state of the user after using the system (Figure 2.7). Once the final goal is decided, the steps needed to reach that goal can be documented in the scenario. Each major goal can then be broken down into sub-goals that lead to it, gradually defining the scenarios.

Express all your needs, but only insist on what is really necessary

A few examples of end goals:

'The astronauts shall return safely to earth after re-supplying the satellite'

'Patients shall be medically aided within less than eight minutes on average'

'The operator shall be able to detect planes at a range of 200 miles'

'The scientist shall be able to view all reports relevant to his/her project within one hour'

More than one scenario will normally be needed to define the requirements. For the ambulance command and control system, the core scenario might be delivering a single heart attack victim to hospital for treatment. In a secondary scenario, the ambulance staff themselves may provide primary medical care at the scene of the illness. Other scenarios might cover a larger disaster, ambulance breakdown, traffic jams, or the multiple calls that might occur on a busy Saturday night. Defining four to six scenarios is often sufficient to generate the core user requirements.

For some systems, particularly with several different types of users, many more scenarios will be needed. For example, the requirements for a digital television system include scenarios for using the program guide, selecting the show, browsing a gift catalog, ordering on-line, obtaining videos on demand,

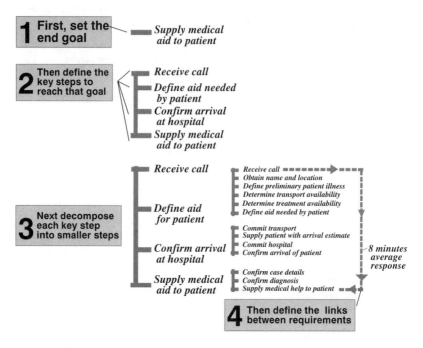

Figure 2.7: Creating the scenario for the ambulance system

viewing digital camera images on the television, interaction with quiz shows and many other types of user actions. Scenarios should be organized to avoid repetition – by picking the key scenarios, and then adding extra scenarios only when they might result in extra needs.

Time-based scenarios act as ideal overviews of the final system because moving through the structure 'step-by-step' rehearses the operational use. Organizing requirements into a good structure inevitably shows up repetitions, overlaps, gaps and inconsistencies of scale.

Relationships between requirements

Relationships will be needed within the user requirements set for a number of different reasons. For example, an average time of eight minutes may be imposed between receiving the call and the patient receiving medical help. This information makes sense only in relationship to both of the requirements, and is therefore best located as a link between the two individual requirements. In this case, the link is itself a performance requirement. Similarly a link can be used to document a potential inconsistency between any two requirements.

2.7. Constraints

Constraints are another major type of user requirement, not adding any extra capability, but affecting the quality of results provided. These are types of requirements which do not fit comfortably within the scenario – they might apply across the whole scenario or parts of it. For example, comfort, noise level, safety and availability are constraints that a user might express for a vehicle – in user terms. Typical constraints might be:

'The system shall be available 24 hours per day, 7 days per week'

'Each passenger shall have 1000 litres of cabin storage'

Constraints are best expressed textually and sit logically in a separate section of the user requirements document. Sometimes a constraint applies to only part of a system, and can be expressed by a link between the constraint and the part to which it refers. For example, a safety-critical constraint might apply to only part of a scenario. We care more about an engine failure while a car is being driven than if it occurs while the vehicle is parked. This approach minimizes the total amount of information, and reduces the need for double updating of information. Sometimes it is better to see a constraint next to the requirement which is actually being constrained. This can be more easily provided if the requirements are held in a tool.

Constraints give us a better quality system, but inevitably and subtly add to the cost. Some of the key constraints involve cost and schedule, and these have to be applied in the management plan, rather than the product definition, as in the example:

'The system shall be available by January 24th 2001

Trade-offs will be needed to keep the costs reasonable. The impact of constraints is much more difficult to visualize than that of capabilities. An over-constrained system may be too expensive and users should always be careful in applying them. Constraints should always be justified and not re-applied unthinkingly from one system to another. In particular, they should be applied only in the areas where they are needed, not across the whole system.

Implementation is not excluded from requirements

While solutions should be minimized, user requirements will always contain some design or implementation aspects. When such pre-defined components are actually needed by users, they must be documented as constraints on any solution. All pre-defined elements need careful exploration to see if there is a deeper, underlying requirement that has not been expressed. Stating design constraints in this way makes them explicit and open to questioning. All too often design constraints are hidden implicitly in capability constraints e.g.

'The user shall be able to detect an aircraft at 240 miles range by radar'

The requirement must be split into two parts, and the second constraint may be unnecessary during the requirements process.

> *'The user shall be able to detect an aircraft at 240 miles range'*
>
> *'The system shall use radar as the means of aircraft detection'*

Explicit constraints from the working environment can be recorded at this time and used in a constraints section of the user requirements document. These may, for example, require the use of existing equipment or operations in a particular geographic area.

2.8. Attributes for user requirements

Attributes are extra information attached to individual requirements, for a variety of purposes such as explanation, selection, filtering, or checking. Individual requirements can be assessed against a checklist and flagged for different characteristics. For example, each requirement must be verifiable, clear and unambiguous. Information to support these characteristics is tagged to each requirement as an 'attribute value' i.e. information linked to the main requirement. Typical attributes that are attached to user requirements are:

- **source** – who asked for the requirement?
- **priority** – how important is the requirement?
- **performance** – how quickly must this requirement be met?
- **urgency** – how soon is the requirement needed?
- **stability** – is the requirement really solid enough to start work on?
- **verifiability** – can the final product be tested or assessed against this requirement?
- **ownership** – who needs this requirement?
- **acceptance criteria** – what is the nature of the test that would satisfy the user that the requirement is met?
- **absolute reference** – an unchanging control tag that identifies the requirement uniquely. The reference is not re-used if the requirement is moved, changed or deleted.

All requirements should be flagged as being stated in verifiable terms, and acceptance criteria attached to the requirement. Acceptance criteria are captured from users themselves by asking the question 'What sort of test would satisfy you that the requirement has been met?' However, the detailed test specification cannot be written until the components to be built are known. As well as forming the basis for testing, this information clarifies the requirements and allows them to be stated more clearly but perhaps in less rigorous terms. For example, consider the nebulous 'requirement':

> *'The system shall be easy to use'*

A test criterion attached to this requirement might be:

'90% of engineers shall be able to transmit an Internet document after 5 minutes of training'

This extra test shows what the user wants much more clearly than the original weak 'requirement'. The information should be attached directly to the requirement, and then used to design the tests.

A requirement may be extremely important, but may not necessarily be needed (or feasible) immediately. Even so, it is well worthwhile stating such requirements, because designers can see how the system is likely to evolve in future releases. Requirements which at first seem infeasible may become implementable and cheaper at a later date.

Potential inconsistencies or mutually exclusive requirements are marked by linking the two offending requirements and putting information about the contradiction on the link. Typical types of inconsistency are between the scope of a system and its performance, i.e. users want a comprehensive system, but they also want it to be impossibly fast. Modular requirements are organized so that the changes most likely to occur can be edited efficiently.

During the attempts to reach a compromise, the term TBD (to be defined) is often assigned as an attribute for the requirement. These TBDs must be cleared before the document becomes formal in any way.

The acceptance criteria are tested, not the requirements

As the requirements near completion, they can be tested as a set rather than just as individual items. The checks to be made include completeness, modularity and consistency. These factors can be documented through attributes, this time at the level of the requirements set, not the individual requirement.

Requirements can be 'verified' by stepping through the various scenarios with the users, to identify missing capabilities. This work can also form the basis of generating test scripts.

Preparing for future trade-offs

In practice, trade-offs become essential as the development confronts the reality of design and limited budgets. When the design starts to form, some requirements will turn out to be impossible to implement, however 'mandatory' they are. Imposing a set of requirements without knowing their cost does not actually work in practice. For example, unwillingness to compromise causes many problems for military projects – reality is the strongest force of all. Organizations often try to impose all requirements, but inevitably some of these turn out to be impossible and the requirements have to be relaxed. Clearly some requirements really are 'mandatory', but experience shows that absolutely mandatory requirements should be no more than about 10% of the requirements. Every other individual requirement is potentially negotiable depending on the cost.

The best approach is to recognize the inevitability of future compromises, and the need to maximize value when those compromises are being met. Attributes and their range of potential values should therefore be chosen to give maximum sensitivity in making those compromises. For example, if 90% of requirements are mandatory, there will never be any scope for cost-benefit analysis, because few requirements can ever be cut. Choices will typically involve cutting requirements in return for saving cost, so the 'priority' attribute on the requirements set should be sensitive in the area where compromises are likely. This might mean partially satisfying or rejecting some individual requirements. Tom Gilb covers the subject well[12].

Sometimes a requirement will be mandatory, but a partial fulfillment will be acceptable. A 'utility curve' that expresses the value versus performance can be attached to the requirement. While these utility curves may be qualitative rather than quantitative, they are still better than no information at all. Utility curves are particularly important for those key requirements that are performance drivers.

Assumptions

If everything is essential, nothing is essential

Unstated assumptions kill many systems, not necessarily because they are wrong, but because everyone assumes different things. Projects often start with incorrect and unnecessary decisions that are never explored, and often never formally expressed. These assumptions are particularly important in terms of responsibility and finance, which are often wildly incompatible with the requirements. For example, it is sometimes crucial to make it clear that some requirements will not be implemented. Document any assumptions you have made which will impact on the system, particularly when you are nervous that others may not be making the same assumptions. These assumptions may need to be revisited throughout the life cycle.

2.9.   The user requirements document

The user requirements document (URD) centers around operational scenarios, with the second major section covering the constraints. The emphasis is on structure and clarifying requirements. Formality is a necessity, but it is not sufficient. Informal communication is essential to reduce ambiguity. Descriptive information in the user requirements document fulfils some of this role, covering elements such as related and external systems, definition of users, critical assumptions and decisions behind the requirements. Casual, discursive conversation is essential, not a waste of time. Problems often arise between users and developers because each has a different 'mental model' of parts of the system. However good the formal documentation, it can never bring all these ambiguities to light. Intense communication – conversations, descriptive material, arguments – exposes and reduces these conflicts to manageable proportions.

Key requirements (typically five to fifteen) and the different user roles can be summarized in the general section of the document. Business requirements will normally be held in a separate document, but traceable to the user requirements or to elements within the management. Management reviews this document. Figure 2.8, derived from the ESA PSS-05-0 standards[1], shows the core contents of a typical user requirements document.

Scoping the user requirements

The overall scope of the system is determined at a user review by the customer. Cutting or changing whole scenarios or parts of scenarios can do this. A user may have perfectly legitimate requirements, but the customer may not have the resources to provide such a system. None of the rejected requirements should be lost – they should be simply marked up as 'not to be implemented', along with the reason why. The customer will often perform this by cutting out complete scenarios.

Notation for user requirements

Because users must 'own' them, user requirements are normally restricted to natural language (including tables and sketches) and the simplest diagrammatic

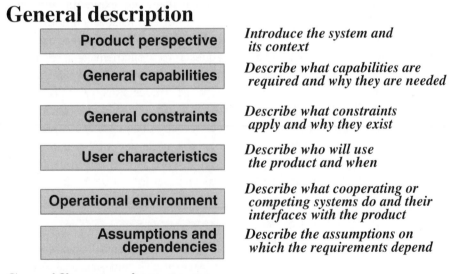

General description

Product perspective	*Introduce the system and its context*
General capabilities	*Describe what capabilities are required and why they are needed*
General constraints	*Describe what constraints apply and why they exist*
User characteristics	*Describe who will use the product and when*
Operational environment	*Describe what cooperating or competing systems do and their interfaces with the product*
Assumptions and dependencies	*Describe the assumptions on which the requirements depend*

Specific requirements

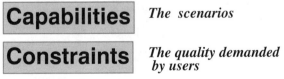

Capabilities   *The scenarios*

Constraints   *The quality demanded by users*

Figure 2.8: Contents of the user requirements document

techniques. Some aspects of requirements can only be expressed textually, and therefore natural language is essential. User requirements ideally should be also viewable textually, but also could be viewable graphically (or even dynamically) as an operational scenario.

2.10. Reviewing the user requirements

The initial user requirements process is closed by a formal review of the user requirements document. Review is a powerful mechanism for making plenty of small enhancements, by focusing brainpower onto the document as a whole. Reviewing requirements is far better than 'management by monthly meetings'. Reviews are expensive, so aim to hold only one formal review, with several less formal reviews leading up to it. The overall process is shown in Figure 2.9.

All user groups should be involved in the review process even if they cannot attend the review. The different user types own their own sections of the requirements. Users should also prioritize the requirements – obviously this cannot be done until the requirements set nears completion or at the review meeting. Anyone can review a document and make suggestions – users, designers, customers, or managers, but users must control any changes.

The review process starts by 'baselining' the user requirements document, and issuing it to the reviewers. They must be notified in advance and allowed sufficient time to read and understand the material (about three to seven days). Reviewers then write change requests to document and locate the problems. These change requests are then sorted by the review secretary against their position in the document. Change requests are typically handled on specific forms, which allows each change to be managed and documented as it flows through the process. Non-specific change requests are rejected and returned immediately – trying to provoke the reviewer into making better, more specific, suggestions. All change requests referring to the same problem are joined together ('stapled') to allow a single decision to be made about the whole group.

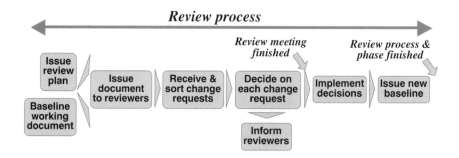

Figure 2.9: The review process

During the review, all the requirements proposed for change and their current status must be available to every reviewer. At the review meeting, a decision is made on each change request, moving through the document. The only allowed decisions are 'accepted', 'rejected' or 'accepted with modification'. A review decision can, however, be put on hold while further exploratory work is performed outside the review. Decisions should be fed back to the reviewers as soon as possible, especially where clarification is required. This often results in rapid re-submission of an improved change request.

When all the decisions have been made, the review meeting is closed, but the review process is not finished. All decisions have still to be implemented in the document and all the background work to make those decisions must be performed. The action list from the review has to be chased down to zero, and only then can the user requirements document be signed off. The user requirements process is then finished.

Changes in user requirements will however continue after this date, but making changes becomes more expensive. Change suggestions need to be collected and handled continually, using a well-defined change control process, particularly for tailored developments.

A review meeting is a decision-making process, and must not be run as a committee or working group. The chairperson therefore has to drive the whole meeting steadily. If the review is run properly, about 30 decisions per hour can be made, passing rapidly through the trivia, and allowing more time for the important decisions. Detailed work cannot be done in review meetings, and so the document must be in good shape before the review process starts. The chairperson for the review meeting directs the decision-making process, and need not be personally involved in the project.

Review is an interesting human process, and it should be an ego-less activity. The author of a document must be completely unemotional about suggestions for change. These are comments on the document, which can improve the end product even if the criticism is negative. In return, reviewers must focus on making suggestions, not arguing about decisions or satisfying their own egos. The end goal is always to improve the document, whatever the source of the suggestions.

Reviewing incremental developments

Where a system is being developed incrementally, the major effort is spent on reviewing the additional requirements. Figure 2.10 is a screen-shot of a requirements tool, with the requirements structured into a hierarchy. Each requirement is classified for priority, using a simple scale (mandatory, very desirable, desirable, luxury). The requirements and their values are controlled from the customer side, while the cost estimates belong to the developers.

ID	Requirements for DOORS Amber release		Costing	Importance	Comment
185	The terminology used in the attribute type definition dialog shall be clarified.			Desirable	
210	It shall be possible to navigate between the entries in a column in a standard view, for the purposes of data entry, with the minimum of key strokes.		5 man days	Desirable	
211	When in-place editing an enumerated attribute value, the option to set no value shall be available to the user.		5 man days	Desirable	
212	The user shall have the option when setting a default value for an attribute type to apply it to all new instances of the attribute or all existing and new instances of the attribute.		10 man days	Desirable	Difficult clear
129	**8.2 Support repeating tasks**		13 man days	Desirable	
105	The user shall be able to record sets of operations that are to be repeated.		3 days	Desirable	Must st range
106	Once a user has recorded a set of operations they may be repeatedly replayed.		10 days	Desirable	
130	**8.3 Information display**			Desirable	
108	The amount of DOORS module content displayed within a specific area of screen real estate shall be increased from that provided by the current version.		3 days	Very desirable	
109	The user shall receive feedback on whether or not a module is being displayed in a filtered form.		3 days	Mandatory	
110	When a module is being displayed in filtered form, the display shall include a definition of the filter being used.		3 days	Luxury	
112	Column titles within module display windows shall line wrap as they did in DOORS 2.1.6.		10 days	Mandatory	
113	The amount of display real estate used by the user interface elements required to control the outline display level shall be reduced.		1 day	Mandatory	
114	The user shall be able to keep specific rows or columns of the standard module display on screen while scrolling through the rest of the document.		30 days	Desirable	

Figure 2.10: Benefits and costs of requirements

The decision on whether to accept a user requirement belongs to the customer, who balances benefits and costs.

Although cost estimation of the complete system at the user requirements stage is impractical, developers can provide an approximate cost estimate for individual requirements. In Figure 2.10, the estimated resource to implement each requirement is scaled as 1 hour, 3 hours, 10 hours, 30 hours etc. On such an exponential scale, developers can often give some idea of the cost of a requirement. While these estimates are not binding, the broad-brush scale can bring a touch of reality into requirements, by indicating which requirements will and will not be implemented and which are still in doubt. This allows trade-offs to be performed even at the requirements stage, for example when the requirement in its original form clearly cannot be implemented.

The 'comments' column on the far right of the figure is valuable in capturing the reactions of the customers and developers during the review. The interactions between these two groups often allow the original requirement to be modified, enabling the customer to get most of what is needed for much lower resources.

2.11. Success factors

The key success factors for user requirements are:

- intense interaction with (and respect for) users;

- *rapid cycling of the requirements documents with the users;*
- *structuring the requirements logically;*
- *a focused, continuous approach to capturing requirements, not a stop and start effort;*
- *keeping documents short and non-technical.*

Somehow it seems to be difficult for engineers to write good user requirements, even when they understand the theory. This section therefore includes a few basic heuristics for checking user requirements. Run through your requirements and check the following:

Do you actually have a set of user requirements separate from other documents?

Have users or their representatives approved this set?

Does each requirement have a user as the beneficiary of the requirement?

Does the requirement avoid proposing solutions?

Does the requirement express a single need?

Can the requirement be pushed back further by asking why?

Are the requirements organized as time-based scenarios, ending in the result provided to the user?

Are the needs of all user types traced into the requirements?

Are all the requirements marked on a simple scale for priority?

Is each requirement marked as being verifiable?

Does each requirement have acceptance criteria attached to it?

Has each requirement been given an approximate cost?

2.12. *Summary of user requirements*

User requirements are the foundation for all system work, but capturing them is not straightforward. Unfortunately, they are often handled in the most feeble way. Even worse, in many cases, there is no understanding of the essential need to have a separate set of user requirements, and they are forgotten or somehow mixed into the system requirements. User requirements should define what users want, in clear, non-technical terms. In the end, users have to own the system. The user requirements also clarify the boundaries of the system for which customer will pay. These requirements form a 'model' of the results wanted by users, providing them with a grip on the later stages. The user requirements are best created fairly rapidly, and the document kept short and clear. The more the operational scenarios can be made to live and breathe, the better the interaction with users.

Some engineers will use every excuse to minimize contact with real users, and will model the wrong information to death behind closed doors. They will point out – correctly – that it is impossible to get the requirements perfectly correct or stable. From this they will draw the wrong conclusion, that it is better not to try to get the requirements at all or (worse) that 'users don't know what they want'. Our advice is to get right in there with the users, produce a draft requirements document as quickly as possible, and then interact even more intensively to improve it. The more you respect the users, the better the end system will be.

The user requirements document (or 'customer brief') will last through the whole project, but even at this early stage it should be clear that the world is moving away from control through paper documentation. The paper document is gradually being replaced by electronic information, itself part of an information set (see chapter 12).

Exercises for User requirements

Answers to these exercises (and comments on those answers) are contained on the Web site (www.complexsystems.com). Any updates to the answers will be put on the Web site. These exercises are based on real system problems which have no perfect answer. They are designed to make the reader think about problems encountered on real systems.

Exercise 1: Are my requirements realistic?

This short exercise allows you to check whether your requirements for a system are realistic, even at an early stage. Give yourself a rating from 0 (bad) to 10 (good) on each of the following questions:

> 1: Will the customer willingly pay for all this to be developed?
>
> 2: Have you successfully built similar systems before?
>
> 3: Are the boundaries of the system well defined?
>
> 4: Do the technical and managerial skills and experience exist to develop the system?
>
> 5: Will a system implementing all these requirements be acceptable and be used by the users?
>
> 6: Do the requirements reflect the need for future enhancements?
>
> 7: How stable are the user requirements?
>
> 8: Are the related elements outside the system you are building defined and manageable?
>
> 9: Are there inherent contradictions between requirements, performance, resources and schedules?

10: Are the requirements organized to provide a logical basis for future compromises?

Surprisingly, these simple questions check in just a few minutes your chance of successfully implementing your project. It is very difficult to argue with the validity of any the questions. Any project that scores 45 or less is in dire trouble. If your project rates 65 or above, you can start to relax. Just look at the low scores and try to improve them. The lowest score we have obtained in using this exercise was 18.

Be warned! When this questionnaire is used in projects, managers invariably give a much higher answer than their engineers.

These questions were adapted from Longworth[13]

Exercise 2: Are these users?

You are at a research center building a radar for a Navy destroyer to detect incoming missiles attacking your ships. State which of these groups can input (and be responsible for) user requirements.

- *radar screen operators on-board the ship;*
- *quality assurance representative for the project;*
- *quality assurance staff on-board the ship;*
- *The information department responsible for developing the radar software;*
- *captain of the ship which will operate the radar;*
- *captains from other ships;*
- *maintenance engineer on the ship which operates the radar;*
- *developers of a competitive radar.*

Name an important end user group missing from this list.

While some of these groups are clearly not users, they will certainly influence the system. How should they do this?

What is the real end-goal for the system?

Exercise 3: Are these good user requirements?

Are these user requirements? Are they stated clearly and verifiably?

Reformulate each of them into a proper user requirement – you may well have to imagine what the underlying requirement really is.

1: The communication system shall break down no more than twice per year

2: All users shall use the same commercial software to handle project management information

3: The maximum delay between transmission and reception of an invoice shall be 2 hours

4: The seat shall be comfortable for 95% of the population of each country in which the vehicle is sold

5: The system shall be easy to use by personnel with minimal training

6: The database shall store 10 years of records

Could you imagine a user asking for any of these requirements? Remember the key question is 'why?' or 'what is the purpose of this requirement?'

Exercise 4: My customer controls the users

You develop sub-systems for a customer who re-supplies that element as part of a larger system delivered to the end users. As a result you have no direct contact with the end users. For example, you are developing a telecommunications switch which is purchased by a telecommunications integrator, and used in building complete telecommunications systems.

The customer refuses to let you talk directly to the end users, claiming that he/she represents all of the interests of those customers. You are nervous that, by accident or design, the customer is not supplying you with good user requirements, particularly as the user requirements are changing fairly rapidly. Define an approach which will help you find these real user needs.

Exercise 5: Developing an operational sequence

Define the top two levels of an operational sequence for your own project in 2–3 paragraphs, rigorously avoiding implementation detail.

This structure should be organized as a time sequence of results that will be available to the users from your system, when it is working.

Start from the end result that users will be able to achieve by using your system, then define the 3–5 intermediate steps which they will need to to get to that goal.

Remember that what you are trying to do is to define the underlying business processes to be supported, in terms of the user. You are not trying to define the system itself.

Now develop an additional exception sequence, defining the conditions under which it will be needed.

Define five constraint requirements which could come from the users.

Exercise 6: Who are the users?

An international organization in telecommunications is spread out across sites in several countries. The project is to upgrade an office automation system at all sites. The current office automation system supplies electronic mail, word processing, file handling, and project management. The first stage is defining the user requirements.

1: *Define a sensible set of user groups, each with a different perspective on the same system.*

2: *Who can state requirements for the schedule of the upgrade?*

3: *Who defines the actual schedule for the upgrade?*

4: *Who should represent the international organization as the customer for the project?*

5: *The organization s information system department says that they should write and manage the requirements. They also want a section of the requirements for themselves. Will you allow them to do this?*

6: *Explain whether a single user should be able to supply answers for an entire group (e.g. a manager for his/her staff).*

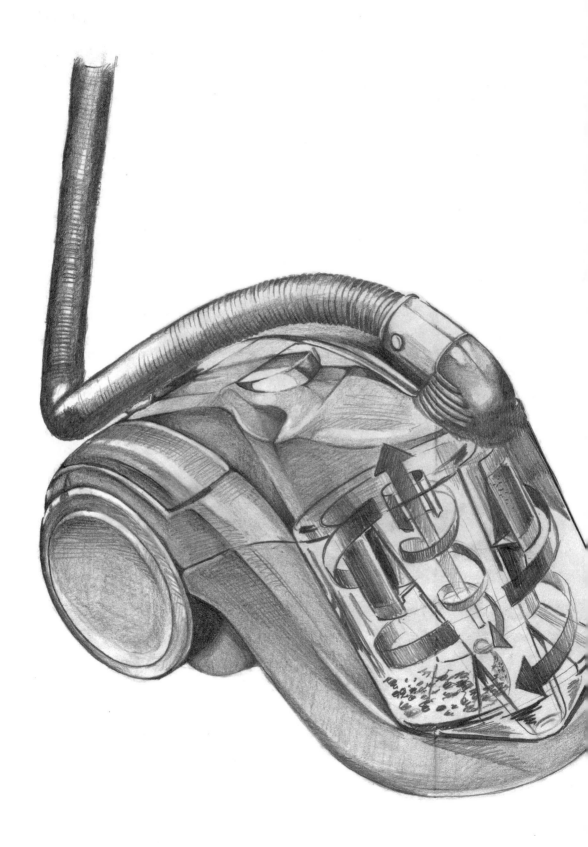

The system requirements process

three

3.1. Defining the solution in abstract

System requirements explore the solution, but ideally avoid commitment to any specific design. Defining them is a highly creative process, aimed at showing **what** the system will do, but not how it will be done. The system requirements form a **model** of the system, acting as the intermediate step between the user requirements and the design (Figure 3.1), often couched in functional terms. A function is usually best expressed as a verb or verb phrase – ('communicate', 'transport' or 'supply power'), not as a noun ('radio', 'database' or 'computer'). This approach means writing requirements that do not unnecessarily constrain the solution, leaving space for designers to work, but giving them a solid foundation. System requirements have to be traceable to both user requirements and design, but they are primarily an artefact needed for the development.

The system requirements say <u>what</u> the system must do, not <u>how it</u> must be done

System requirements contain both formal requirements and descriptive information. They have several distinct uses:

- *giving an abstract view of the system;*
- *allowing trade-offs, exploration and optimization before committing to design;*
- *demonstrating to users that their needs are reflected in the development;*
- *providing a solid foundation for design;*
- *providing a basis for testing the final system;*
- *communicating previous decisions to developers.*

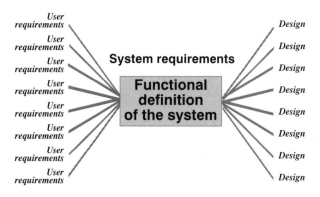

Figure 3.1: Functionality as the core information

The people who use the system requirements document are the designers, test definition engineers, planners and system engineers working on a smaller part. The use of the word 'document' is a historical hangover and does not mean that project information is held in paper form or as a word processed document.

System requirements are detailed enough if they are good enough for the next work that is to be done. System engineers should aim to provide designers and test engineers with what they must know, but leave as much design space as possible for smart designers to explore other options. System requirements must be rigorously linked to user requirements, to ensure that user needs are met, and that the impact of potential changes can be analyzed before commitment.

System engineers, not the end users, 'own' the system requirements, but users should understand them enough to be confident that they meet their requirements. This allows them to check that the user requirements are being met, or at least see which will or will not be met. The extra detail in system requirements allows users to detect those that were not thought through correctly. This can lead to (controlled) change in the user requirements.

Notation for system requirements

System requirements need to be understandable by almost everyone in the project, so they must be short and clear. This also means that the notation for system requirements should be as non-technical as possible, without sacrificing accuracy. A diagram can express structure and relationships more

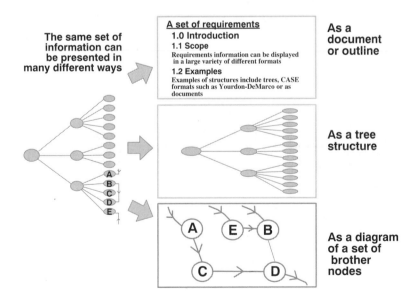

Figure 3.2: Different representations of information

clearly than text, but, however well-structured, is not sufficient to communicate the system engineer's intentions. For precise definition of single concepts, natural language is much better than diagrams. In practice, both textual and graphical notations are essential for a typical mix of users. All of these types of presentations and more can be applied to one set of information (Figure 3.2). Presentation should always be separable from the underlying information being presented.

Specific types of system requirements, such as safety, integrity, security or legal requirements, may need to be expressed formally, and consequently may not easily be understood by users. This is fine as long as the system requirements are traceable back to user requirements, which are more comprehensible to users. Requirements must also be 'atomic' i.e. comprised of individual components that can be tested separately and traced back to their source.

3.2.   The system requirements process

Figure 3.3 shows the overall process for defining system requirements. The first activity defines the major functional elements, typically as functional block diagrams or state diagrams. Non-functional requirements are defined simultaneously and linked to the relevant functions. Transforming functional requirements into textual form can make them more precise and approachable to non-specialists. This is one of the few times in the system life cycle that information duplication is advisable. The review process for system requirements is similar to that for user requirements, but developers control the requirements instead of users.

Requirements should be as small as possible... but no smaller

Brainstorming with your colleagues around a whiteboard is usually the best approach to get started. The results can then be documented in a graphical

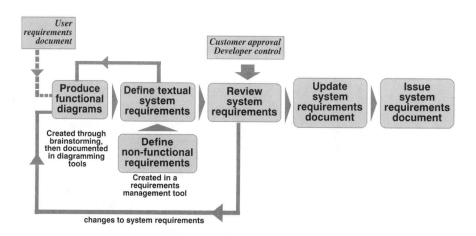

Figure 3.3: Producing system requirements

tool. The typical mistake is to allow a single designer to work intensively using a CASE (computer aided software engineering) tool for box-drawing, and then present the detailed results for review. An incremental, teamworking approach will produce better results. Tools are best used as a mechanism for documenting work, and we must never fool ourselves into thinking that tools or notations are creative in themselves.

Any realistic set of system requirements will need to be organized hierarchically, helping us to view and manage information at different levels of abstraction. Decomposition should be done two or three levels at a time, exploring the levels below before confirming any choice above. At the top level of a system, this may take only a few minutes, and involve intense interaction and arguments between engineers.

No engineering technique is purely top-down – we also need to explore options from a bottom-up and middle-out perspective. Middle-out exploration is ideal where an obvious component for re-use already exists. Top-down presentation is however the clearest way to show a system to other people once it has been defined. Any attempt to define a system at the top level and successively decompose it into pieces will generally fail. Upper-level diagrams summarize the lower levels of functionality and behavior, but we must not neglect the advantage of top-down analysis, particularly in analyzing the interactions between one level and another. A braking requirement is meaningful only in the context of knowing the maximum speed and weight of a vehicle.

As a functional breakdown is made, interfaces between the functions must be decomposed consistently. Any interface between pairs of parent functions must appear between some of their children, with the flows in the same direction(s) and forming continuous chains at the lower level(s).

Functionality is necessary but not sufficient

How big should a requirements document be?

Requirements documents must be clear, complete, yet small enough to be understood as a complete entity. The individual statements must be brief, atomic, and concise. System engineers must hold all the concepts of the requirements document simultaneously to make sensible comments about any part. Experience shows that this limits the documents to about 100 pages, perhaps an absolute maximum of 200 pages. Beyond that, the document becomes impossible to comprehend as a whole, and if a document cannot be read, it cannot be improved. If defining a project really needs more information, then individual engineers must be able to extract small coherent subsets from the total set of information. The document should, however, be big enough for the people who need to use it – principally the designers and test engineers.

Documentation is there to help; if it isn't needed, don't write it. The amount of information does not have to be balanced in size across a system. Focus on the difficult parts of a system and document them well, and minimize the documentation for the more obvious elements.

3.3.   *Different kinds of requirements*

Many different characteristics may need to be defined – functionality is not enough. A product may need to behave differently at different times – a pilot should not be able to raise the undercarriage while a plane is on the ground, for instance. The different possible states of the product, and also what must be possible in different states, must be specified.

System requirements must show how non-functional requirements, such as safety or reliability, are linked to specific functions. These could apply to the whole system, a sub-system, or linked to any system state (e.g. taxi-ing along the runway, flight, or system testing).

Functionality in itself is useless if the function is, for example, unreliable or not fast enough. Any of the following types of requirements may also be necessary (Figure 3.4):

- *performance requirements;*
- *information relationship and history requirements;*
- *temporal and dynamic behavior requirements;*
- *requirements for parallelism or concurrency;*
- *logical behavior (e.g. conformance to a mathematical model);*
- *flow of control;*

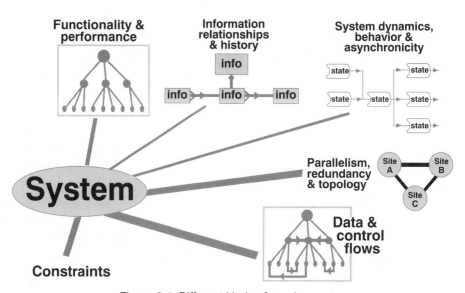

Figure 3.4: Different kinds of requirements

— *flows of data or material;*
— *non-functional requirements (constraints);*
— *interactions with external systems;*
— *end-to-end scenarios.*

The number of different kinds of requirements that need to be expressed depends on the type of system. Only those kinds that are really essential should be employed. For example, in building databases, the emphasis is on data entities and relationships, but real-time aspects may not be so important.

In another example, financial transaction systems with real-time constraints need to consider several key kinds of requirements. Customers may make electronic payments and require instant access to cash and account details. Specifying performance requirements will need some work to analyze end-to-end transactions and temporal behavior. Non-functional requirements like security, protection against data loss, and availability are equally important.

If every one of these types of requirement is needed, a system will be difficult to define and expensive to produce. Development productivity is low in such complex systems, and the difficult, real-time elements need to be clearly separated from the more static components. The latter are far cheaper to develop, providing they are clearly separated from the real-time elements.

Performance requirements

A fool with a tool is still a fool

Performance requirements qualify the functional requirements, for example defining the minimum power, the throughput of an interface or the speed of a function. Performance requirements are best attached as attributes of the functional requirements, or more often links between functions. They impose requirements on both functions, or the interface that links them. For example, in a communication system, the performance requirement should be attached to the channel between the transmitter and antennae, and perhaps also to the transmitter and receiver themselves. Performance requirements are particularly important for defining tests.

Defining practical performance requirements is a difficult area, because performance is often critically dependent on the subtleties of design. An entire architecture can be destroyed by a single performance requirement. Producing a functionally correct, but impractically slow, system is a common problem, and extensive design prototyping may be necessary to define realistic performance requirements.

Interactions between functions

Interface protocols define the nature of the interaction between two functions. This can involve physical flows, as with a supply of fuel, or involve information, such as data about the current engine speed. Specifying a link is not enough on its own, because we may also need to specify, for example, how flows are started and stopped e.g. are they on demand, triggered at regular intervals, or continuous? Protocols are the mechanism for controlling concurrency and synchronization. Figure 3.5 shows some of the different types of interface protocols that are essential to define the nature of interactions.

Control flows

In real-world systems, components inevitably operate concurrently and interactively. Parts need to be switched on and off, processes need to be created, replicated, destroyed, or updated. The system will need to be moved from one state to another. As well as functionality, the flow of control of functions must be specified – how processes are spawned, killed, or whether they are triggered at regular intervals.

Flow of control is often shown as an overlay on the functional breakdown, as linkages between the functions. The work of Hatley and Pirbhai seems to be used extensively within many industries, because it at least attempts to cover the problems of real-time systems[14]. Control flows are normally shown with a different notation to differentiate them from data flows. Messages between functions can equally well pass pure information or control data. In practice, the boundary between data and control is fuzzy. Actions may be triggered either by information or control signals.

Functions can be modeled as pure asynchronous processes, so that the flow

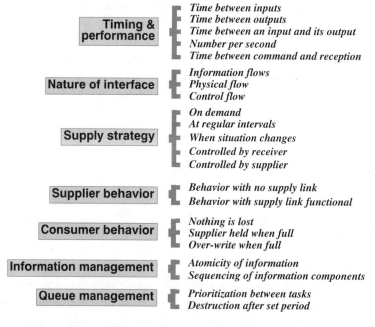

Figure 3.5: Characteristics of interface protocols

of control ensures correct synchronization between them. In contrast, scenarios define natural sequences, organized by the desired results. For example, a medical emergency system allocates an ambulance to collect a patient after the patient's location is known, so the 'allocate function naturally follows the 'obtain address function.

Relationships between classes of information

Relationships between information are often specified in the system requirements. For example, in a car, a single device may read the engine revs and transfer it to several destinations. Hence the requirements need to show different kinds of data, the required relationships between them and the ability to store information. The objective is to build a coherent set of data classes used within the system, to avoid duplication and overlap. Different types of information are structured into coherent and maintainable sets. In a telecommunications system, we may want to see how an individual call is handled and how it relates to the control information as the call is managed. The map of relationships between information is often called an entity-relationship diagram, a 'schema', or a class diagram[15]. The diagram shows key system data and the relationships between them. An example entity-relationship diagram (ERD) for the ambulance system is shown in Figure 3.6. The labels (e.g 1..N) show the cardinality of the relationships (e.g. one-to-one, many-to-one or even whether a relationship is obligatory for an element).

Require only what is really necessary – or you are doing design

Requirements for retention of information

Sometimes we need to specify how information should be created, maintained, changed or destroyed. If an air traffic control system fails, the flight plans of the planes, but not their historical position, should be available

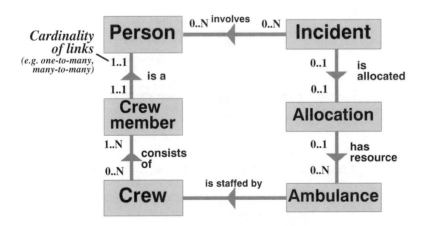

Figure 3.6: Entity-relationship diagram for the ambulance system

when the system recovers. Some kinds of information must therefore be retained across the possible system states, such as that for a computer failure. These requirements about information volatility would normally be tied to the different system states, showing the events affecting information.

Key requirements

Expert engineers can often characterize a system through a few critical parameters, such as power-to-weight, throughput, or fuel economy. These key requirements, perhaps three to fifteen in number even for large complex systems, make the difference between success and failure. They normally summarize other requirements. These key requirements (sometimes called effectiveness measures) should have been flagged in the system requirements document. For any system, they can be derived from the architectural design, and they form the basis for choice between different design options. Even when we do not know them initially, these key requirements often slowly emerge during the development, and then act as the critical determinants for system success.

3.4.   Abstract definition

A functional breakdown is normally organized hierarchically (Figure 3.7), i.e. a top-level function is decomposed into a few subsidiary functions. Each one of these can in turn be broken down into sub-parts. This 'divide and conquer' approach has many advantages. Developers can focus on small parts, view the context of the part being worked on, or view the whole system at different levels of abstraction.

At the system level, we should state only requirements that are system-wide i.e. about the ambulance system, not about database software. If the

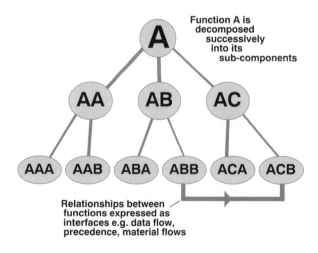

Figure 3.7: Decomposition of functionality

requirements are specific to a sub-system, then they should be left until that sub-system is defined. This allows expertise to be expressed where the domain knowledge actually exists. For example, the requirements for a whole car should not be specific about the engine, but should restrict themselves to the system level (e.g. necessary power). The detail can then be left to the specialist engine designers.

Some elements, such as software, are spread right across each system. In a car, for example, there may be 30–60 separate pieces of software managing the engine, brakes, air-conditioning, caution and warning software, the test system, and even the car radio. They may need common message passing standards, the ability to broadcast certain pieces of information, and share a graphical user interface. These standards then apply to every software package, typifying a system-level approach to handling software.

Abstraction makes it easier to build modular systems, where parts can be separately upgraded. In Figure 3.7, the functional structure is shown as a tree structure. Hierarchy keeps the overall set of requirements small, with all the advantages that brings to viewing and browsing. Interfaces between the functions are also shown as links between the functions. Although it is perhaps the most common, a functional model is not the only possible framework for system requirements; other options are covered later in the chapter.

An alternative two-dimensional representation is shown in Figure 3.8 for the specific example of the ambulance command and control system. This has been broken down into four internal sub-functions:

— *handle callers;*

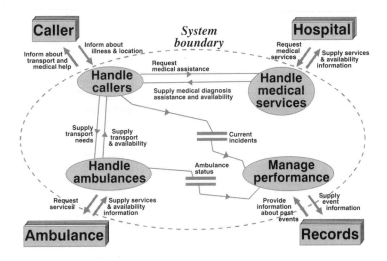

Figure 3.8: Functional and interface breakdown

- *handle medical services;*
- *handle transport;*
- *manage (system) performance.*

The external elements are shown as the callers themselves, the hospitals, the ambulances and the filing system used to store the process records. Interfaces between the system elements are shown as labeled directional lines. The other element shown is the store (two horizontal bars), which illustrates the ability to retain information between two functions. This kind of breakdown forms the basis of many functionally-based tools, with minor variants of notation. Although the entities that can be displayed are extremely simplistic, they are often fine for modeling.

This decomposition can be carried on repetitively, and Figure 3.9 expands the four 'bubbles' of Figure 3.8 into their sub-functions. Trying to show the full details and labels of functions and interfaces makes the diagram rather cluttered. As a result, most tools show only one level on a single diagram.

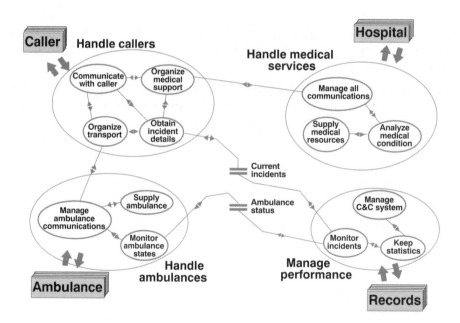

Figure 3.9: Successive decomposition of the functions

3.5.   *External systems*

No real-world system ever operates independently. For example, external systems could provide us with radio links, information, fuel, or electricity. In building a car, we have to consider the existing gas stations, servicing equipment at garages, standards for car radio signals and current systems for tire fitting. The car manufacturer needs to re-use existing engines, brakes, or wheels across multiple projects. These elements are 'external' because they are not directly controlled by the project, yet are essential to make a successful system. The end product may have support systems which are developed quasi-independently (Figure 3.10). For the example, the factory to mass-produce the product or the operational support system may be developed by separate teams. We may require functionality or performance from such external systems, or impose non-functional requirements on it. Alternatively they may impose these requirements upon our system as it develops. The production system imposes requirements which affect the product to ensure that it can actually be manufactured sensibly, e.g.

The tolerance for the dimensions of panels shall be no greater than 0.1 mm

In theory, the partition between core system, support systems and external systems does not occur until the architectural design process. In practice, it is often determined much earlier.

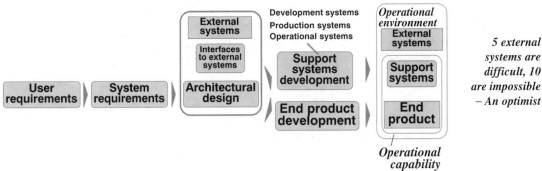

5 external systems are difficult, 10 are impossible – An optimist

Figure 3.10: External and related systems

The interfaces have to be agreed with the party controlling the external system. The interface control document (ICD) defines the interactions between the two systems, i.e. the mutually interlinked areas. Both parties should ideally sign off each ICD, forming a common specification to work toward, and forming part of the system requirements document. An ICD represents a joint agreement between two parties – restricting how it is created and changed. At the system requirements stage, the ICD is defined functionally. No further design work should be done until the ICD is defined in sufficient detail for the interface.

The easiest way to imagine the interactions is to consider the target and the external system as an integrated system (Figure 3.11). When the two systems are torn apart, the ICD represents those parts of the systems that interact with one another. The diagram also illustrates the problems of managing the

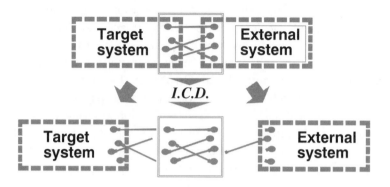

Figure 3.11: Concepts for external systems

interface as a document, because it duplicates information already existing in the two systems. This leads to problems of double-updating of information.

ICDs usually cross a contractual boundary, which may be outside or inside a company. It is often wise to volunteer for the work of defining the interface with the external systems if you can. While it may seem like extra work, it allows you to shape your relationships with the external system.

Get your interface control document (ICD) in first!

The ICD is often the most stable part of the system, because usually it is easier to modify design aspects than to re-work the interface between two systems (and two organizations). Accommodating external systems often causes large delays, especially on bigger systems. The two parties have to formally agree the ICDs, and this can easily lead to conflict. The existence of too many interfaces with external systems can kill a system through administrative delays and the burden of changes. Under these circumstances, you have to standardize interfaces and constrain several external systems to work to a single interface standard. The worst case is when both sides are not fixed, leaving each free to torment the other with continual changes.

ICDs usually involve commercial and even political tensions as well as technical issues. In practice, the relative strength and precedence between the two developments shapes the ICD between them. If the other system is already developed, politically strong, and we need its services, our chances of influencing the external interface are low. If you want the services of an existing data-relay satellite, you will be supplied with a handbook and a price list! There is nothing you can do to change the ICD – they have the power, and you have to organize your new system to be compatible. There may be other interfaces that we cannot control because of commercial standards, e.g. Microsoft products or telecommunications standards. If two systems are being developed in parallel and are of equal strength, they will affect each other intensely as they develop. But at least you have a tangible, stable reference point with which engineers can deal.

The ICD should also contain managerial requirements on how the interface is to be created and changed. For example, you may ask for six months notice before the other party can change an interface, plus any financial costs incurred in updating your side of the interface. The ICD is a contract between the two parties and therefore must cover development as well as the technical issues.

3.6. *Temporal and dynamic behavior*

Many systems need to behave differently in different states. Temporal requirements define the distinct states of the system (or any of its parts) through time. The states and the events that move them from one state to another must be defined as requirements, usually as state transition diagrams (STDs). They also control which functions should operate in different states. For example, a car driver should not be able to engage reverse gear while driving forwards and, for example, we should care far more about an engine failure occurring while a vehicle is being driven than while it is parked. Other requirements can then be tied to those different states. Every system method contains state diagrams in some form.

End-to-end scenarios

Figure 3.12 overlays a scenario path on top of the functions from the initial

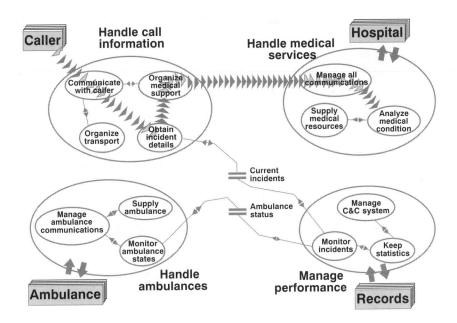

Figure 3.12: Scenario overlay over system functions

phone call to contacting the hospital. Scenarios show how the system behaves dynamically from receiving a stimulus to delivering an output. For example, a scenario might define the end-to-end sequence following the receipt of an emergency call.

The average time and worst allowable cases for scenarios are defined by analysis. Scenarios are a powerful mechanism for system analysis because they involve multiple functions and states, and show the overall behavior to a stimulus. 10–15 scenarios can often define a system's behavior much more clearly than any number of functions or single-state transition diagrams. They show aspects of 'emergent properties' that exist only at the system level.

Figure 3.13 shows the link between functions and scenarios for the ambulance command and control system, from making a call to calling the ambulance and starting to interact with the medical resources. At the bottom of the diagram, the scenario (simplistically) moves from left to right, using the appropriate functions through the scenario. Scenarios also provide good test cases for system acceptance. The scenario flow is clearly similar to the user requirements scenario, allowing the functionality to be checked against the user requirements.

The logic for defining the system is to first look at single, simple threads through the scenarios – the fundamental, but easy, cases. Then examine concurrent, complex scenarios which will require extra functions. Influences

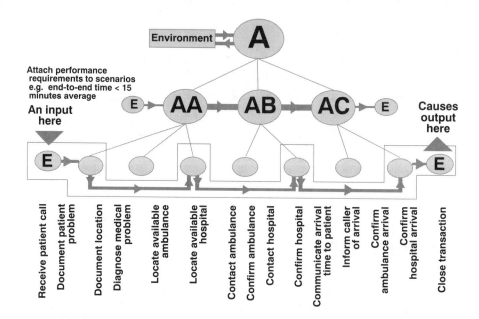

Figure 3.13: Scenario for ambulance command and control

from the environment should be handled before those arising from the architecture.

Animation of requirements

The requirements for a system can be animated even before it is designed. The user requirements can be 'animated' against the system requirements by stepping through the user scenarios and checking that the function exists to meet the user needs. As well as checking the user scenarios, animation can be used for extra safety analysis e.g. by injecting faults into the scenario, and seeing how the system copes. Scenarios can cover both the normal cases defined in the user requirements, and the exceptional cases for fault analysis.

The net product of the work is better system requirements. At its simplest, the task model is a simple sequence, but few real-world systems are so easy. Triggers and resources are added to the user scenarios (the outline of the 'document'). Many tasks involve decisions, where the next step is chosen from the range of branches, for example, to simulate options for treatment, running out of resources or reaching a point in the scenario too late. Other scenarios may need to be performed periodically or concurrently. Some scenarios may interrupt the current task to attend to a more urgent activity. This approach is often used for safety analysis. Extra safety scenarios can be generated to see what happens if for example a component, such as an ambulance, breaks down. These extra scenarios branch off the nominal scenario. Figure 3.14 shows part of a 'sailing scenario' from a software tool which allows task models to be created to produce live animations, scenarios, and indeed acceptance test scripts[16].

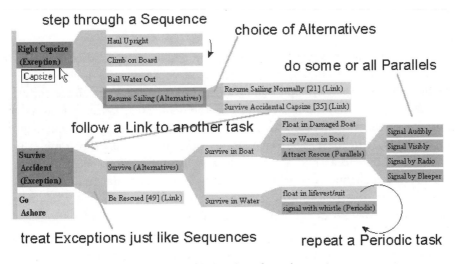

Figure 3.14: Animation of requirements

State diagrams

Figure 3.15 shows the generic components of a state diagram – the state itself, the actions possible within the state, and the event causing the scenario.

We may also need to require other attributes of the state, such as:

- *events that cause the system to change state;*
- *functionality allowed/forbidden in the state;*
- *information flows allowed/forbidden;*
- *constraints that apply while the state exists.*

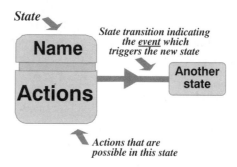

Figure 3.15: State diagram

Figure 3.16 shows the major states for an aircraft. The aircraft behavior, what can be done to the aircraft, and what the aircraft is allowed to do are different in the three states. Even the non-functional requirements are different between the states. To define these concepts in the system requirements, we will need to build a model of the states, and then link the other requirements to them.

Real-time systems

Some systems are triggered into action by events outside their immediate control. These real-time systems typically have to handle multiple events simultaneously. The dynamic and concurrent aspects are frequently so problematic that they dominate the development. Such systems face all the intricacy of states, plus the extra difficulties of concurrency and queuing. In these cases, the best approach is to encapsulate all the time-critical functionality behind a solid and well-defined interface, often referred to as a 'firewall'. Asynchronous aspects are bundled together, decoupled as far as possible from the rest of the system. Defensive strategies at the firewall suppress any rogue process that might compromise the critical functionality.

Large numbers of simultaneous scenarios cause the problems in real-time systems, not any individual scenario. Characteristics such as queues, conflicting priorities, scenario times, or time between scenarios dominate the

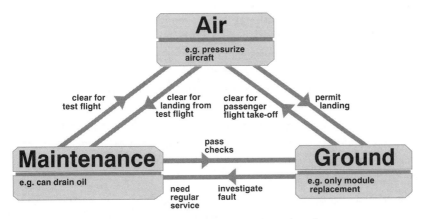

Figure 3.16: Major states of an aircraft

problem. This makes the temporal behavior associated with state diagrams more complex.

The ambulance C&C is clearly real-time. At peak time (Saturday night?), ten scenarios might be happening simultaneously. The worst case might be thirty transactions in an hour, occurring about once a year. However, the system also needs to cope with a major civil disaster such as an air crash. The requirements have to state the typical and worst-case conditions, showing when the performance will start to slow, and how and when the system will collapse. It is much safer when expressing performance requirements to give some service levels, e.g. 70% receiving treatment within 6 minutes, 90% within 10 minutes, and 99% within 12 minutes. These performance requirements clearly relate back to the user requirements without needing to partition the performance to individual functions.

Typical areas that will be part of the requirements for dynamic behavior are:

- *time between inputs – how the system copes with several rapid inputs;*
- *time between outputs – how quickly the system can deliver outputs;*
- *time between an input and an output.*

These requirements will define average needs, and also the worst-case conditions that stretch the system to its limits, perhaps leading to degraded performance. For example, overall savings of 10–30% may be possible if the response time can be allowed to double for 6–12 hours a year. This degrades the performance for short periods, but gives a better year-round performance for any given level of resources.

3.7. Non-functional requirements

A product that performs the required functions is not enough. The product might need to be reliable, safe, legal, comfortable, capable of lasting for 20 years, or surviving extremes of heat and cold. System requirements must therefore define the non-functional requirements (also called constraints) that will apply to the product. Actually the term 'non-functional requirements' is really weak and negative, and calling them 'quality requirements' might be better. They are sometimes called 'the illities' because so many of them, such as portability or reliability, end with that suffix. For example, the product may be required to work within a certain temperature range, with a certain reliability or safety, or conform to government regulations. It may need to be maintainable, safe, or easy to assemble. Non-functional requirements add nothing to what the system can do, but are essential to provide the required quality to these functions.

Non-functional requirements are more important for systems than for software. Software often assumes a 'perfect machine' and ignores factors such as temperature, humidity or logistics. These are assumed to affect only computer hardware, not the software! As software becomes more important within systems, it acquires more of the characteristics of systems. Thus non-functional requirements applying to the software are becoming more prominent (e.g. reliability, or interactions with other hardware).

Example of a non-functional requirement – The mean time to repair a fault shall be less than 30 minutes

To consider the impact of non-functional requirements, think of two different cars such as the Mercedes and the Yugo. In terms of core capability, there is little difference between the vehicles. Both can travel the same roads, at the same legal speed, and carry approximately the same number of passengers. The differences lie in factors such as reliability, safety, cost, comfort, and status. For two systems of equal functionality, the differences are effectively the *quality*, i.e. the non-functional requirements typically add quality but little extra functionality. Note that this definition of quality means 'fitness for purpose' and not necessarily 'best quality'. In some situations, the Yugo may be more suitable, as it might be less likely to be stolen and will cost less to replace!

This increase in quality between the two vehicles comes at a high financial cost. Non-functional requirements can easily and invisibly make the solution much more expensive or even impossible. We may end up paying five times as much for the product for little extra benefit. The cost of non-functional requirements is not easy to visualize, so they tend to be imposed even when they are not worthwhile. Each non-functional requirement looks sensible on its own, but together they may preclude any solution. Only engineering judgement of the requirements set as a complete entity can cope with this situation.

Relating non-functional to functional requirements

Non-functional requirements should not be applied in bulk at the system level. A requirement such as a safety constraint may be limited to a single function

(Figure 3.17). For example, the maximum temperature allowed in the engine compartment might be 110°C, so all equipment in this area must survive this environment. The temperature in the rest of the car never rises this high, so the non-functional does not apply. We therefore need to link the non-functional requirement to the area(s) in which it applies.

Unless non-functional are limited, many functions which do not need them will end up being over-specified. For instance, all the software on a plane would

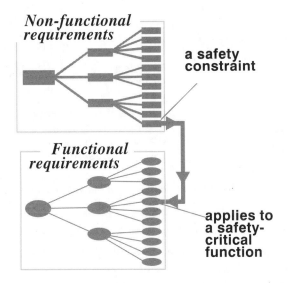

Figure 3.17: Applicability of constraints to functions

become safety-critical, even when it just controls the video programs for the passengers. More subtly, a component potentially becomes safety-critical simply through an interface to another safety-critical component. As an example, if software for a car alarm is mixed with that for an ignition system, an error in the latter could switch off the car engine at 70 mph. Careful analysis can reveal which parts actually need to be especially reliable, and which do not. Safety-critical elements then need to be grouped and kept separate during development.

In a system requirements document, the constraints are typically organized (Figure 3.18) in the following sections:

- *transformation of user requirements;*
- *discipline-specific constraints;*
- *applied and induced environmental constraints.*

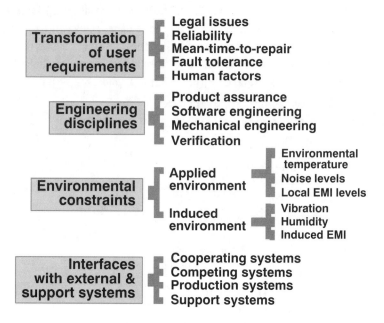

Figure 3.18: Example sources and targets of non-functional requirements

Constraints derived by transforming user requirements

Some user constraints expand fairly transparently into constraints in the system requirements. A single user requirement to have a legal vehicle results in a host of government regulations in the system requirements document. Reliability and mean time between failure are examples of transformations of the original user requirements for availability. The user requirement for system availability may be met with one very reliable system, or two distinct redundant systems which need not each be so reliable.

For example, users (surprisingly) do not care about the reliability of jet engines on a transatlantic crossing. They are, however, extremely concerned about the availability of power during flight. Users should not care if an engine needs to be switched off occasionally in-flight, as long as the plane is manageable with the remaining engines. The availability requirement is therefore translated into a consistent set of system requirements for reliability, recovery, mean time to repair, and redundancy.

Discipline-specific constraints

Capturing problems from previous systems reduces the likelihood of repeating faults in design. The brake systems on 19th century railroads initially relied on cables, which naturally led to disastrous accidents if one of them snapped. The vacuum brake was then developed, making the train 'fail-safe' when the coupling failed. Each engineering discipline builds up domain or corporate knowledge, which can be applied system-wide or perhaps re-applied across multiple developments. These non-functional requirements are the 'rule-base' for the profession, and a good set can easily be tailored for re-use on different projects. For instance, mechanical engineers know the metals and lubricants that can be used in space, and those which should be avoided. Software engineers may impose coding standards or message-passing protocols to ensure software quality.

Constraints imposed by the working environment

Other system requirements specify the **applied environment** in which the system must survive. For example, the range of ambient temperature or vibration levels induced by roads will impact on a vehicle design. Many user requirements translate into constraints on the system functionality. If the user or business requirements demand that a vehicle must work in Brazil, it must survive the extremes of temperature and humidity, and perhaps run on a fuel that contains alcohol. A satellite in space must withstand vacuum, radiation, and a steady battering from small particles. The satellite will therefore have to be tested to ensure that it can survive these conditions. An example of a failure to apply environmental requirements occurred when more than 9,000 motorists were locked out of their cars because their remote locking systems were blocked by radio interference[17].

The **induced environment** is created because the system itself generates heat, electrical interference or vibration. All parts have to survive the combination of induced and applied environments. For example, every box of electronics in a plane has to survive electro-magnetic interference generated by the radar equipment. At the same time, we need to limit the interference that the radar can itself produce. Constraints therefore limit both interference produced by equipment, and the equipment's sensitivity to interference from other parts.

Constraints from external systems

Any aspect of the external environment or any external system may impose non-functional requirements on the system we are developing. For example, a police radio will need to interact with existing equipment, and therefore be constrained in its frequency, power, and communications standards.

Support systems (e.g. training and maintenance) and productions systems will also impose requirements on the product. For example, the car may need a towing hook to be pulled along the production line, or the test system may impose test points on a circuit board. All external systems can potentially impose requirements bi-directionally, and the design may for example impose requirements on the production system.

Summary on non-functional requirements

Non-functional requirements are essential to develop a product of the right quality. The real dangers with non-functional requirements are imposing too many or applying them system-wide unnecessarily. Each non-functional requirement may look harmless and rational individually, but the total set may stop any design being feasible. Non-functional requirements have to be applied carefully to screen out unnecessary requirements, using cost-benefits analysis tied back to the user requirements. Engineering judgement is essential to balance the practicality of the whole set of constraints. Risks have to be accepted in rejecting constraints, and the final set of non-functional requirements is always a compromise.

3.8.   The framework for system requirements

A wide variety of different kinds of requirements is needed for defining a system, and there are complex inter-relationships between them. How do we organize the different types together? The best option is probably to choose one type of requirement as the framework, structure that as a hierarchy and organize the other types of requirements around it. The functional breakdown usually provides such a framework. Performance requirements (which usually apply to more than one function) may be attached as attributes to specific functions or to interfaces between functions. Other non-functional requirements, such as those on verifiability, maintainability, or safety are defined separately and then linked to the functional requirements, to save repetition.

But there are other options for this framework, typically one of the following:

- *a temporal/behavioral model;*
- *an information mode;*
- *the architecture of the proposed system.*

The first two types of framework are covered elsewhere in the chapter, so the next section discusses the 'system architecture' option.

Where the system architecture is stable across a sequence of products, the system requirements tend to be structured around the known sub-systems. For example, the architecture of cars was more or less fixed by the 1920s, and now vehicle requirements are often centered around large physical components such as engines or the vehicle interior. Each sub-system generates its own requirements for the power sub-system, transmission etc. In this case, sections of the document point directly to the departments that will implement these functions. This approach has several advantages. The system requirements, design and the organization all then have a similar structure. This provides modularity, because a change in the system requirements can often be propagated through the design to the implementors, without severe side-effects. The departments can maintain domain knowledge across multiple systems. This traditional approach therefore has many of the characteristics of object-orientation. In many physical systems, such as construction, this is the safest approach, because architectures have evolved for many decades and so reduced the inherent risks.

However, pre-defining the structure of a system requirement document according to a previous architecture is often dangerous, because of the risk that the implied product architecture has become obsolete. The architecture and departmental structure may in fact have become sub-optimal, most probably because of technology changes.

3.9.   Concepts used for representing system requirements

Most 'methods' for handling system requirements employ similar concepts[18]. These tend to be dressed up by using slightly different representations, by capturing the concepts in a different order and, above all, by using different labels for the concepts and the diagrams. Every method uses entity-relationship diagrams, for example, with a different notation in each case. Most have hierarchical decomposition and classification. The net effect is to make it appear that the methods differ quite markedly, but actually they have a tremendous amount in common. Most of these methods have arisen in software, and can describe some aspects of system requirements well.

Three fundamental concepts are functional decomposition, behavior and modeling the information structure (Figure 3.19). These principles for organizing information are basic enough to be re-applied in other parts of the

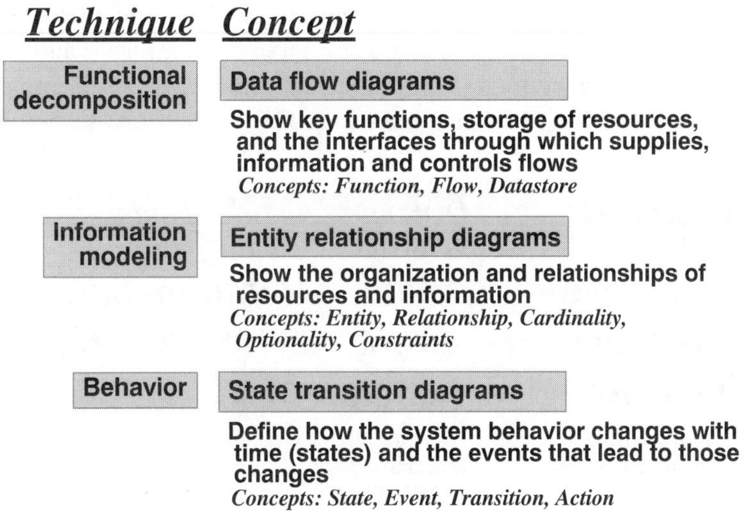

Technique _Concept_

Functional decomposition	**Data flow diagrams**
	Show key functions, storage of resources, and the interfaces through which supplies, information and controls flows _Concepts: Function, Flow, Datastore_

Information modeling	**Entity relationship diagrams**
	Show the organization and relationships of resources and information _Concepts: Entity, Relationship, Cardinality, Optionality, Constraints_

Behavior	**State transition diagrams**
	Define how the system behavior changes with time (states) and the events that lead to those changes _Concepts: State, Event, Transition, Action_

Figure 3.19: Core techniques for specifying system requirements

life cycle (such as for organizing the management plan).

Data flow diagrams (DFDs) show the structure of functions, their decomposition and their inter-relationships. A single function is split into sub-functions. Relationships and flows between the boxes can be expressed. These are often produced as hierarchical box drawings which also decompose interfaces and control flows. DFDs allow complex functions to be decomposed and perform some basic consistency checks, such as whether the interface decomposition is consistent.

State transition diagrams (STDs) model the different operational states of a system (or part of a system), plus the events that trigger the transitions from one state to another.

Entity relationship diagrams (ERDs) model the information structures within the operational system, and the relationships between different types of information. In the system requirements process, the ERD models the information to be stored, not the storage mechanism.

Unfortunately the modeling concepts used within different methods are not independent[19]. For instance, in many systems, the functionality varies with the system state. A flow on a DFD can carry an event that triggers a state change (Figure 3.20). An action on a state transition diagram can be performed by a function on a DFD. The state transition diagram can describe the state of a function or the state of an object. A data store on a DFD can contain one or more entities from an entity-relationship diagram. Non-functional requirements can be linked to any of these elements. Consequently developers normally pick one representation as the framework and tack on the other requirements where they fit best.

Ideally the computer-aided software engineering (CASE) tools used to draw these diagrams would organize these inter-relationships automatically wherever possible, encourage us to express the other relationships, and report inconsistencies and missing elements. Currently tools do not do this,

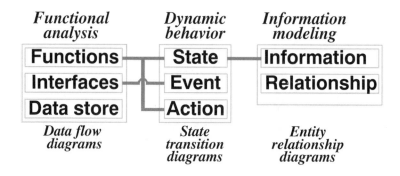

Figure 3.20: Relationships between concepts

and so we have to choose one method as a framework and patch the other concepts to it.

Sequence within methods

Individual methods tend to use a subset of the common representations in a particular sequence. Methods (and most tools) also define cross-checks to ensure that the information captured by the representations is mutually consistent. Some methods identify inconsistencies between concepts used in different diagrams, but require the tool user to make changes so that the overall model is consistent.

Other tools provide more help, by not only making the checks, but making consequential changes in other diagrams when related information is changed. These tools store the underlying information as a coherent model, rather than just as diagrams.

Composition and classification

Composition and classification are distinct types of hierarchical organizations used to represent system requirements. In effect they are relationships which exist between objects and are thus specializations of the entity-relationship diagram (Figure 3.21). Many techniques use special representations to indicate composition and classification. The most widely used notation has been that of Jim Rumbaugh[20], but the optimistically-named UML[15] (unified modeling language) notation is now becoming more common.

In a **composition** hierarchy, the set is decomposed repeatedly, each part being split into its child components. Each level defines the whole set at a different granularity. Composition depicts the design hierarchy e.g. a car consists of a body, wheels, engine, and gearbox as a whole-part hierarchical decomposition.

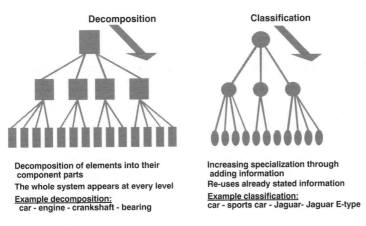

Figure 3.21: Composition and classification hierarchies

In a *classification* hierarchy, the objects at the top are generic, while those lower down are more specialized. For example, if the top object in a classification hierarchy is the class 'vehicles', then the next level down might split up into the classes: 'air vehicles', 'land vehicles' and 'sea vehicles'. These will 'inherit' the properties of the class vehicle and add specific properties associated solely with their specialization. Thus land vehicles may have an attribute 'number of wheels', an aircraft may have an attribute 'wing span', and sea vehicle may have an attribute 'displacement'.

3.10. Object-orientation

Object-orientation methods (OO), have become steadily more popular over the last decade. Many of the principles are much older. The concepts have been developed for software and are being tentatively applied to some system problems.

The goals of object-orientated methods are to describe the world in terms of stable, re-usable components. An object can be envisaged as having a number of properties. Object-orientation is a collection of techniques, such as:

- *encapsulation of behavior (states, events) and information within the same object;*
- *trying to define objects which can be re-used across the requirements and design processes;*
- *creation of new objects by specialization of old objects, rather than producing completely new components;*
- *more detailed definition through increasing the information about the behavior and data of objects.*

These concepts have been expressed by a number of authors and more slowly evolved to become more realistic, and more suitable for systems engineering. Several software gurus have grouped together to produce a composite standard modeling language[21].

OO gives a coherent definition of the product, and also encourages a modular approach. Components should be re-usable because the elements can be incrementally enhanced. They are (like it or not) design components, hopefully linked to their requirements.

In some OO methods, a class can also have operations (or 'methods' as they are frequently known) associated with them and these, too, can be inherited. The inheriting class can then modify the methods and add to them as part of the specialization activity. Classification is important for re-use. Instead of defining an object from scratch, we should be able to add the extra information to an existing object and re-use it. This is much harder in reality than in theory.

A 19th century hardware catalog illustrates many facets of object-orientation. The book is organized hierarchically, and one section covers all of the types of doors on offer. The section on doors is divided into internal and external doors, with some of the exterior doors being insulated. Interfacing elements such as glass panels, hinges, and locks can be used from other parts of the catalog. Any individual door re-uses the characteristics of all doors (size, thickness). The catalog exhibits inheritance, structure, requirements tagged to objects, re-use, price attached to objects, and the ability to add existing components through standard interfaces. Software has not yet reached this level of maturity!

Object-orientation and methods

OO is particularly appropriate where the user requirements have been developed at a system level and been decomposed into a software package, and the design can custom-implement the functions directly. Object-orientation encapsulates the relationships between information using the well-known entity-relationship diagrams (Figure 3.22).

Object behavior is captured in state diagrams. DFDs can indicate how objects pass events to each other, and show how each object uses information from other objects. A flat organization of objects is assumed, because ERDs cannot usually be organized hierarchically.

OO and systems

Object-orientation is clearly successful for some types of software, and many of the concepts of information hiding, re-use, classification, and incremental addition of information have been used for decades. The early OO methods were not hierarchical, which limited them to smallish developments.

A key concept in OO is that the same object can be re-used from

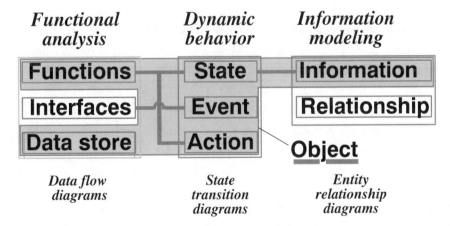

Figure 3.22: Concepts used in object-orientation

requirements to implementation and (hopefully) from system to system. The concept of a linear set of objects that can be carried from user requirements through to design is, however, not practical for most types of systems. The transformation in concepts is simply too large, and the size of the real-world systems demand not just hierarchies, but multiple levels of hierarchies. Consider the system information for a bicycle as an extreme example of transformation of information during development. User requirements will be about the length of journeys, speed, comfort, hill-climbing ability, availability etc. These concepts are completely different to the design components of the cycle, such as gears, tires or pedals. It is impossible to imagine persistent objects bridging this gap. Attempts to define objects across the processes results in leaping directly to solution-type objects (e.g. invoices or traffic lights), where those might not be part of the eventual solution.

Some aspects of the object-orientated approach may be inappropriate for the system level, in which the user requirements, system model and the design structures are necessarily very different. The concept of taking the same objects across processes precludes modeling without committing to design – it is more suitable for systems with predictable architectures, or for design work. In systems there are a whole range of factors which make the requirements structure distinct from the architectural design – non-functional requirements, redundancy, use of commercial components, plus the need to avoid over-early commitment. An obvious extension of object-orientation is to retain the parts that are appropriate for system development – encapsulation, classification, while using hierarchy and multiple models for different stages of the life cycle.

3.11. Heuristics for breaking down functions

Functional decomposition, like creating an architecture, is an art. In terms of organizing information, the principles are similar. These heuristics can therefore act as guidance during the development process.

While these principles are being applied, another process runs concurrently. The sequence is (Figure 3.23):

- *define a model that can meet the user requirements;*
- *cope with faults introduced by the environment;*
- *cope with faults introduced by your choice of model;*
- *cope with deliberate attempts to break the system.*

In essence, these rules mean *do the easy elements first, then cope with successive layers of difficulty*. The rules can be applied repeatedly during the functional breakdown. For example, in the ambulance system, the initial functions cope with an individual patient, assuming an ideal world in which everything runs smoothly. More functions are added to handle, for instance, a phone failure,

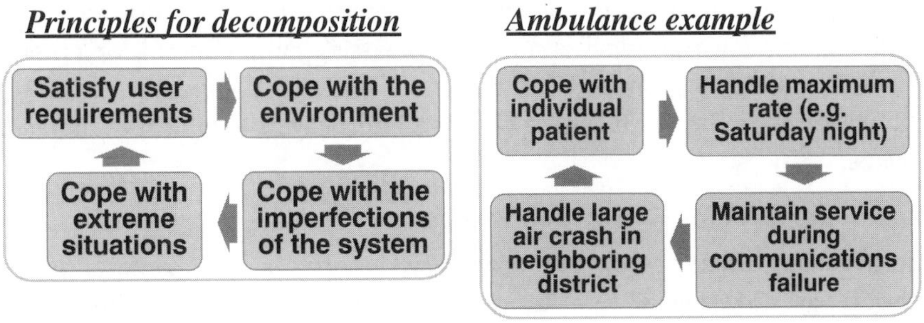

Principles for decomposition   *Ambulance example*

Figure 3.23: Heuristics for breaking down functions

the telephonists not speaking the language of the caller or the ambulance being delayed in a traffic jam. The next step is to ensure the system copes if the computer gives trouble – how to prevent data loss, how to give some degree of service if the computer stays down. Finally, you have to cater for the extreme cases such as a large air crash or a malicious hacker. Each area generates new 'sub-functions' to cope with the problems.

This approach initially shapes the system around a simple functional model, working in a benign environment. This model is adjusted successively to cope with the real world difficulties, with problems that are self-induced, and then with deliberate attempts to destroy the model. The add-on functions are more loosely coupled, and so can be detached if they prove too expensive.

Two other important characteristics in functional decomposition are **cohesion** and **coupling**. Cohesion measures the degree to which elements are related to one another. The more cohesive a component is, the easier it is to understand and to re-use.

Cohesion can be:

> **functional** – *groups of functions that perform similar or related tasks;*
>
> **sequential** – *i.e. the output of one activity becomes the input of the next activity;*
>
> **communicational** – *cohesive functions share the same data;*
>
> **procedural** *i.e. a chain of activities that follow one another in the control structure of the system;*
>
> **temporal** – *activities take place simultaneously. If this is the only cohesive force, it should be avoided;*
>
> **logical** – *functions perform a range of similar activities. Processing is shared, but special effects are controlled by flags.*

Coupling measures the degree of dependence between functions. 'Tightly' coupled functions have too many dependencies to be easily separated. The designer should aim at low coupling, so that elements can be defined and worked on separately, and subsequently upgraded and maintained easily. Coupling can involve physical components, passing data, control, or common information. Coupling should be designed to isolate functions from one another, so that either side can be changed internally as long as it respects the interface.

Methods and tools for system requirements

Despite many claims to the contrary, there is no general-purpose methodology covering all the concepts that have been described. Instead, numerous partial methods, diagrammatic notations and tools must be combined as needed. They are all incomplete, often have small mutual inconsistencies and the inter-relationships between them are unclear. In large systems, engineers have to mix and match techniques creatively to be able to define the system requirements.

Functionality is often defined with data flow diagrams, which simultaneously define the functional structure and the interfaces between them. States are defined through state transition diagrams, and information models are handled by entity-relationship diagrams. All of these notations are supported by a host of tools, each optimistically claiming to support a 'complete system methodology'. Non-functional requirements are usually ignored by many 'methodologies', a typical sign of a software background. Any methodology that does not handle non-functional requirements in detail is irrelevant for systems (and increasingly so for software).

3.12. Success factors

Producing a good system requirements document requires skill and experience. Nevertheless there are some general rules which include:

- question and remove unnecessary design decisions in requirements;
- encapsulate and localize critical interfaces and real-time interfaces – critical can refer to a variety of safety-critical, complexity or cost aspects;
- aim the breakdown toward existing commercial components or other elements that can be re-used;
- keep the system requirements document small and understandable;
- do not imagine that novel methods or software tools can solve your problems; they can succeed only if you have a good underlying process;
- do not allow one engineer to create the whole set of requirements – use group brainstorming techniques.

These principles could be summarized as minimizing risk, making the system requirement information readable, and grouping similar elements together.

Checking the system requirements

The most common errors in system requirements are building solutions into the requirements and going into too much detail. Try to eliminate solutions by looking for noun phrases – center, computer, hardware, database – and replace them with equivalent verbs.

It is still fairly common to see 800–page 'system requirements' documents, an obvious indicator of a poor process. Apart from the fact that they are unreadable, documents this large must inevitably contain large elements of design. A system requirements document should include only things which are essential at the system level, i.e. it should not even impose requirements on specific sub-systems, let alone go into design.

At the end of the process, the system requirements can be checked individually and also as a complete set. A few checks include:

- *are the requirements organized in a clear and modular structure? (functionality or behavior)?*
- *do the requirements state what is wanted without defining the solution?*
- *are all system-level issues covered?*
- *is the required system behavior clear?*
- *is it clear which user requirements will be met or not met?*

The fundamental question that must be answered honestly is:

Would a system that implemented these requirements really be satisfactory?

A few pointers to reducing size are:

- *keep the document well-structured and modular;*
- *take design decisions back to the underlying requirements;*
- *postpone requirements specific to one sub-system for that sub-system group to define (see chapter 8);*
- *structure information to minimize duplication and view it at different levels of abstraction;*
- *separate requirements from descriptive information;*
- *be able to select out relevant subsets:*
- *point to reference material, but do not include it.*

The real needs are to show all requirements, while imposing a low information load on the engineers reading the documents. Requirements management tools can help by filtering out unwanted material, and showing requirements at different levels of abstraction.

A good structure uses one organizational principle as the backbone for the document, and ties the other kinds of requirements around it.

The system requirements review

Review of the system requirements follows the same logic as that for user requirements, but in this case system engineers 'own' the requirements. Designers and users should both attend the system requirements review. Designers are there to ensure that the model embodied in the document can be implemented in practice. The users attend the review to ensure that the model satisfies the user requirements, or at least they can see which user requirements will not be met. They should not complain directly about a system requirement, but they can complain if the system requirements fail to meet their user requirements.

3.13. Outputs from system requirements

The system requirements document

Figure 3.24 shows the components of a system requirements document (SRD), organized around a functional structure. The original information may be stored in several different tools. Performance requirements could be attached as attributes to the particular function or interface. Interface control documents are ideally selectively produced from the same information by the requirements management tool. Sometimes the interface control documents will need to be handled separately because of the joint responsibility for their contents. The relative importance of each section will vary depending on the type of system.

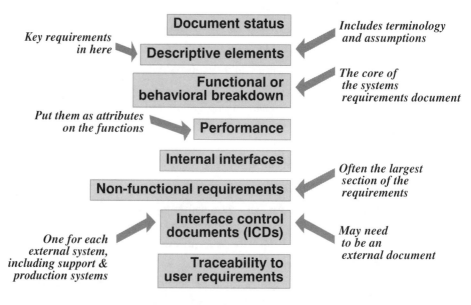

Figure 3.24: Components of the system requirements document

Tracing to the user requirements

System requirements have to be traced to user requirements to show that all the user requirements are met, and that all the system requirements are necessary (Figure 3.25). This task needs engineering judgement, is arduous and error-prone, so a requirements management tool can help document the links and their rationale.

Because the user requirements are organized by time, and the system requirements by function, traceability should be at a level where the concepts are similar. Typically, traceability will be from the lowest level of user requirements to an intermediate level in system requirements. Many user requirements may be traced to one system function. For example, a single communications function may handle different kinds of messages needed by users. The principles of traceability are covered in detail in Chapter 12.

The major outputs from the system requirements process are the system requirements document (SRD), and system test plan. These documents drive the subsequent processes, and define the best that is likely to be achieved from the end product. In the ideal case, the system requirements would satisfy every detail of the user requirements, but in practice, compromises are inevitable, and not all requirements will be met completely. The goal is to produce the best cost-benefit ratio within the available resources. However, users always need to find out which requirements are accepted, rejected or postponed, which is why traceability to the user requirements must be retained.

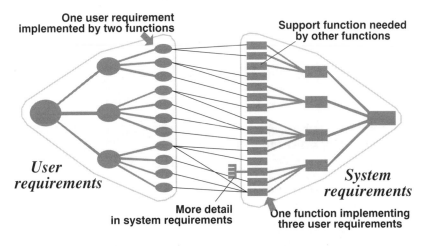

Figure 3.25: Traceability between user and system requirements

3.14. Summary of system requirements

The system requirements define an abstract model that allows us to reason about the end solution before commitment to a specific design. They provide the link between user requirements and the high level design. They will specify system functions, behavior, constraints, and interfaces, and how to trace these back to the user requirements that called them into being. Non-functional requirements are an essential component of the system requirements. A range of different methods is needed to specify requirements; these have to be brought together for the individual system.

Exercises for System requirements

Exercise 7: State diagram

Find the omissions and errors in the state diagram for a civil aircraft below. Label the transitions with the events that cause them.

Hints: Most of the transitions are unlabeled, one transition is forbidden, and there is another more fundamental error.

Divide the states into two logical sets and draw boxes around them.

What is the third high-level operational state that is not covered? Name one set of actions in this third state that would be forbidden in the other two.

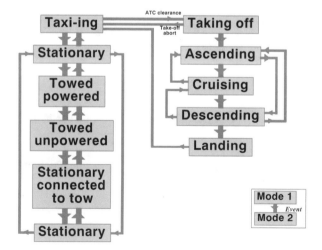

Exercise 8: External systems

Write 4 constraints imposed by a gasoline (petrol) station on the design of a car.

Write 4 constraints imposed by the car on the design of a gasoline (petrol) station.

Write up two developments which have recently changed this interface or will force it to change in future.

Exercise 9: Are these good system requirements?

These requirements are proposed as system requirements (at the vehicle level) for a new car. State whether they are good system requirements. If not, either restate them in a suitable form or say where they should be located.

A maximum of three different sizes of nuts/bolts shall be used in the whole vehicle.

Vehicle testing shall be completed by January 1999.

The powertrain control system shall still function after any single fault where that is a practical option.

All software shall be written in the C language.

The windshield shall survive an impact with any large bird up to a speed of 120 mph.

All software shall be written in conformance to the ESA PSS–05–0 standards.

The communication channel shall have a capacity of more than 10 megabits/second.

The architectural design process

4.1. The objectives

Architectural design defines clearly what is to be built (Figure 4.1). This is potentially the most creative part of the system process, and the point at which the cost of the system is largely fixed. When it is complete, each design component can be seen separately by the group tasked to produce it, and so the design forms the basis for management of the implementation. It transforms system requirements into more concrete form, by allocating functions to hardware, software or people. The architecture should be compact enough to let design options be explored and optimized, before going into the detail of the component design. It should be expressed at a level of abstraction which allows reasoning about the system behavior. When the design is stable, cost and risk can be estimated realistically for the first time. Architectural design optimizes the design characteristics to satisfy the requirements as far as is humanly possible.

The objectives for the architectural design stage are:

- *production of a design that will meet the user and system requirements within the operational environment;*

- *definition of the components to be built, the implementation approach and choice of the core technologies to be used;*

- *definition of how components interact to generate the emergent properties called for in the system requirements;*

- *trade-off between candidate designs to maximize system effectiveness;*

- *generation of an integration test strategy consistent with the design structure;*

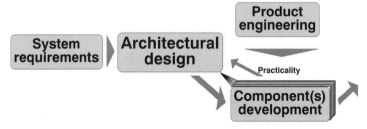

Figure 4.1: Architectural design

- *partition of design components for allocation to different groups of implementors;*
- *definition of the deliverable items (the basis of subsequent management control);*
- *estimation of the most likely cost and risk, plus the contingency needed to cope with the risks;*
- *ensuring that the design work incorporates the results of previous decisions.*

These objectives define the level of detail needed in the architectural design. The over-riding objective must always be to keep it concise and clear.

4.2. Good design practice

A successful design satisfies a known set of requirements, but in practice cannot necessarily meet **every** requirement – no matter how much the customer might insist. A design should strive to be simple, well-structured, elegant, rugged and durable, but above all else, relevant. For the end users, products should be easy to use, as inexpensive as possible, and convenient to upgrade. The benefits of good design are ease of manufacture and integration, good product reliability, compatibility with other systems, maintainability, and potential for re-use. A design must always be evaluated in conjunction with the environment in which it interacts.

The eye is a fine architect – Werner von Braun

Good design methods help ensure downstream properties such as upgradeability, modularity, easy maintenance, openness for change, re-use and low operational costs. For instance, the design should be ***modular*** – a powerful but often ill-defined concept. In a modular system, components can be changed easily, at multiple levels, with minimal unintentional side-effects. This allows the whole system to be steadily improved by upgrading its parts. This in turn requires a strong emphasis on interfaces and behavioral definition.

Interfaces must be ***clear***, ***stable***, and ***decoupled***. In these cases, components cannot distinguish between their test and operational environments (Figure 4.2). This approach hides the internal complexity from those who do not need to know about it. The result may be a platform architecture, i.e. a stable infrastructure on which components can be upgraded (see Chapter 7). Because interfaces are necessarily stable, they must be defined with upgradeability in mind.

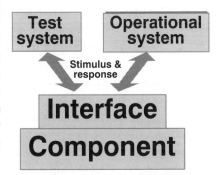

Figure 4.2: Modularity and testability through interface definition

Decoupling is closely related to modularity. For example, the Boeing

747 has evolved over 25 years, through several versions, gradually increasing its capacity. Several different manufacturers produce jet engines for the plane. At the same time, the engines have improved their power-to-weight ratio. The wings have become more complex, yet fold for a smaller surface area during cruising. Hardly a part of the plane is unchanged, but decoupling and modularity have allowed continual upgrade of most of its elements.

Designs should be **upgradeable**. This allows feedback from operations, and injection of new technology. Designing upgradeable systems requires **prediction** of which elements are likely to change. While precise prediction is impossible, many aspects (processing speeds, memory availability, engine power) can be estimated reasonably well using historical trends. Upgradeability needs to be demonstrated at both the design and the initial implementation stages, either by simulation or by demonstration on a prototype. Documentation must be comprehensible, and organized so that upgrading is easy. Accessibility and removeability of elements are desirable, particularly for elements such as cabling, harnesses and connectors, all of which are likely to be upgraded. Software is a powerful mechanism for upgrade during operations (and even during development), providing this strategy is designed into the system at the beginning.

Not to predict is to predict zero change

A design needs sufficient **margins** to cope with the remaining uncertainties, and allow expansion without changing core elements. For instance, these might include building an engine frame to cope with extra engine power, or leaving free memory in a computer system. The need to easily add features also drives standard interfacing methods, plus the tools to help add them. This might, for example, result in a common messaging system, or support tools to ease integration of new elements.

Inevitably some requirements will turn out to be too expensive or impossible to meet. To find a design, the normal approach is to mentally relax the requirements, find a reasonable solution that meets most of the needs, and then work intensively to enhance that solution. **Compromise and trade-off** between design and requirements are therefore integral tasks for designers during architectural design. The architecture design is not produced in one blow or by simple decomposition, but by constant trade-offs as it develops. The designer circles through the design, regularly evaluating it for performance, cost practicality, and schedule (Figure 4.3). The designer focuses on the macro level first, and then checks the micro-levels for practicality. A design is continually tested (mentally or by prototyping) for failure to meet user requirements when operating within the working environment. The designer guides the detail of the system toward known components, and re-evaluates the top levels after finding a design is not practical. The design solidifies top-down, but the work may be done in any order.

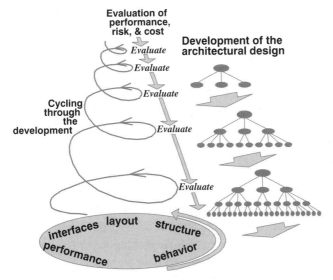

Figure 4.3: Evolution of the architectural design

Even when a design is innovative, it should respect the knowledge gained by **experience**, both of success and failure. As engineers, we stand on the shoulders of those who go before us. Risks are so pervasive that they need to be controlled and kept close to a minimum. Studying the past at least warns us about known dangers, if not about novel threats or changes to the environment. The designer – and the design – must be **neutral** i.e. not preconditioned for or against particular technologies or materials (unless these are part of the requirements). The best designs must not be excluded by prejudice.

4.3.   What is an architectural design?

Having identified the objectives and indicated some properties of a good design, we can ask the question *what is an architectural design?* Architectural design provides a level of abstraction which allows designers to reason about system behavior. Good architecture makes a design intellectually tractable and exposes the issues most crucial to success. Architectural design is the key technical activity which reveals whether a proposed new system will meet its most critical requirements.

Architectural design also serves as the 'conscience' for an evolving system. By documenting crucial design assumptions, it shows which aspects can and cannot be easily changed without compromising system integrity. As with the blueprints for a building, a well-documented architectural design shows the system's 'load-bearing walls', the fixed elements around which everything else has to work. This helps not only during design, but also throughout the rest of the life cycle[23].

To satisfy these multiple roles over time, the architectural design must be simple enough for system-level reasoning and prediction. The architectural design document should be small, ideally less than 10 pages. For complex systems, this may be impossibly concise, and so architectural design descriptions are usually organized hierarchically. The hierarchy consists of different elements and a different structure to requirements, i.e. it is not simply a re-arrangement of the requirements.

Architectural design descriptions must cover the areas of structure, behavior, and layout (Figure 4.4). **System structure** defines what the major components are, how they are organized and decomposed, their functionality, and interfaces and the ties to the system requirements. **System behavior** defines the dynamic response of the system to events, providing a basis for reasoning about the system. **System layout** defines the physical arrangement, packaging and location aspects of design. Packaging addresses how components are allocated to physical resources such as the layout of a vehicle, printed circuit cards, or how software is mapped to hardware. Packaging provides the basis for understanding the non-functional properties of the system such as weight, power consumption and performance. The layout of components addresses installation and environmental issues such as vibration or mutual interference, either within the system or between the system and its environment.

*Arrange the leading lines to convey the idea of strength and stability –
L. B. Alberti (Renaissance architect and engineer)*

The three aspects of structure, behavior, and layout are inter-related and

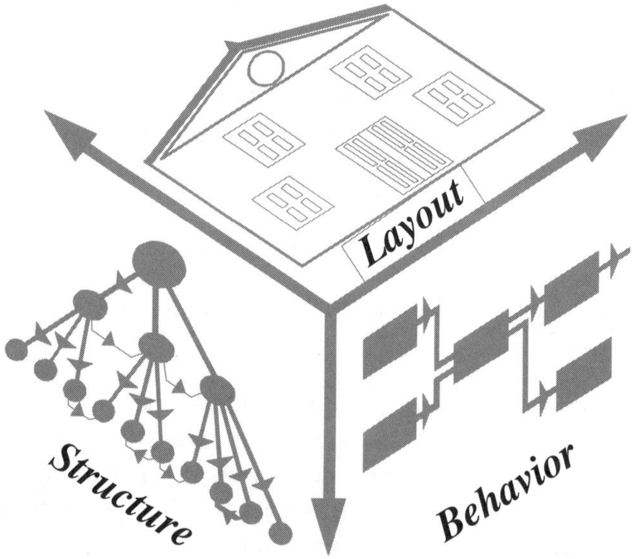

Figure 4.4: Key concepts of architecture

mutually interdependent, especially for issues of feasibility and cost. However, it is more convenient to describe them individually in the next section.

System structure

The structure defines what the major components are, their organization and inter-relationships. The structure shows which components are to be built, links the architecture back to the system functions, and defines how the system is partitioned. It frames the design as a configuration of interacting components. The structure does not define the detailed layout or topology of the system, i.e. how the components are grouped and placed relative to one another. Rather it is a logical definition of what the components are, allowing the design to be laid out in a variety of ways. The structural view also leads directly into a definition of the deliverable items. The structural view – on its own – is essentially static; the simultaneous behavioral view gives a more dynamic picture.

The principles used for creating and structuring design information are similar to those applied in functional definition. Critical interfaces must not be dispersed across the system, because they will infect non-critical elements. The design must minimize coupling between parts, and strive for maximum cohesion of similar elements. The design must always be product aware, to maximize the chances of using off-the-shelf components. Simplicity is essential, because this makes the system easier to understand. A good starting technique is to define a simple structure that meets the key effectiveness measures in the system requirements. More elements can then be added for the exotic functions or constraints, as discussed for system requirements. The cost of these extra elements is then obvious, and they can easily be backed out if they are not cost-effective.

System behavior

A behavioral model enables us to view the dynamics of a system as a 'logical model', without committing too early to the details of component design. Behavioral models are primarily concerned with the following characteristics:

Rich abstractions for interaction Interactions between architectural components – often drawn as connecting lines on diagrams – provide a rich

---

Which designer said this?

First bits and crumbs of the piece come and gradually join together in my mind; then the soul getting warmed to the work, the thing grows more and more, and I spread it out broader and clearer, and at last it gets almost finished in my head, even when it is a long piece and so that I can see the whole of it at a single glance in my mind, as if it were a beautiful painting [24] vocabulary for system designers. Interactions may seem simple (such as requesting a service, or accessing shared data variables), but they often represent more complex forms. Examples include pipes (either for physical or software flows), client-server interactions (with rules about initialization, finalization and exception handling), communication connections and flow of information or documents.

Global properties Architectural designs normally address system-level behavioral issues, such as end-to-end throughput rates, latency, resilience of one part of the system to failure, or system-wide propagation of changes when one part is modified (such as changing the system platform). Similarly the design can be used to impose standards e.g. for digitization or communication across the whole system.

Emergent properties of a system depend on interactions between components (including the environment). Consider a bicycle composed of a frame, two wheels, pedals, a drive chain, saddle, handlebars, brakes etc. The primary emergent property of dynamic balance is produced only by the combination of the rider and the bicycle. Only when human power, control, and intelligence (and a road surface) are added does the bicycle become a means of transport. Take any one away and the system falls apart. Emergent properties therefore cannot be predicted solely by looking at components, such as gears or pedals. This has important consequences for testing, which must be within the operational environment and at the system level to reveal the real system behavior. The system engineer is always trying to enhance positive emergent properties caused by combining components, and suppress negative aspects of interactions. A negative emergent property might for example result from the variation between individual components. Under odd conditions, these variations can add up to cause system failures, perhaps even when every component works within its own tolerance. In mass-produced items, the design has to be adjusted to ensure that manufactured components will work together. Similarly, a circuit board might function correctly on its own, but fail because of electro-magnetic interference from others when connected into a system.

System layout

The layout links the equipment in the structure to its physical placement and grouping (e.g. in boxes). Component packaging defines the physical characteristics and core technology for each part of the architecture. For electronic components, packaging defines the equipment practice in terms of card size, connectors, rack layout and batteries. For software-based systems, component packaging chooses the processors, and organizes the RAM and hard disks. For both electronic and computer-based systems, the inter-connection mechanisms might include microwave links, parallel buses, LANs or WANs. Cost and bandwidth are conflicting, and compromise is essential in choosing between these options. Layout may involve aspects such as the relative positions of transmitters and receivers, to reduce electro-magnetic interference.

In systems in which the physical and structural components are key, such as a satellite or aircraft, layout will be performed with a 3–D modeling tool (e.g CATIA or Computervision). Analysis software allows physical properties such as weight, density, center of gravity and center of pressure to be rapidly checked out for a proposed design. The analysis software can perform a similar task for the interfaces, which in physical systems may end up as harnesses, pipes, or support structures. In such systems, the packaging may be a substantial part of the final system – the boxes, or the exterior structure of a vehicle. In turn, these often provide the frame for the physical interfaces such as connectors. In some systems such as satellites, the electrical harness is a highly significant component making up perhaps 25% of the total weight.

Relationships between structure, behavior and layout

The behavioral model must be mapped to the components, iterating between the two to produce a convenient mapping with realistically available hardware, and then considering installation and location in detail. This often exposes difficulties due to lack of space, inadequate power supplies, lack of cooling etc. Design may need to be constrained to avoid clashing between different parts or between the system and existing equipment. Addressing these difficulties leads to iteration between design and component packaging. Indeed in some cases (batteries in a cellular phone, packaging a satellite into a rocket, or integrated circuit design), locating the components may be a major design driver. Aspects of the behavioral model may need changing to fit with the reality of the equipment.

An 'installation' view of layout may be important for applications where construction costs are high, as in the building industry. The price of a house is highly dependent on how efficiently it is built, as well as the components from which it is made. This view allows the designer to optimize assembly, and to balance the cost of construction, development, and manufacture. Similarly a 'production' and/or a 'maintenance' view may be important for systems where these are critical cost drivers.

Component packaging covers issues such as equipment practice (electronic card sizes, connector types, bus connectors, power supplies etc.), interconnection mechanisms (bus, copper cable, fiber optic cable, microwave, infra red etc.), use of standard component types (engine types, single board processors, connectors). These issues help minimize the number of different components to be managed.

4.4.   Behavior and style

The behavioral model is key to understanding the overall system, and as with any activity, re-use of past experience is essential for better design. In current practice, architectural designs have been re-used by personal experience, word-of-mouth or informal transmission of architectural concepts. For example, a system architecture might be described as a client-server system, a blackboard system, a pipeline system, an interpreter or a layered system. Each of these terms is shorthand for a mixed bag of concepts.

Architectural style

A consistent system-wide design style provides numerous advantages, such as shared structural, semantic or presentation properties. Architectural style typically provides the following elements across families of systems or within individual systems:

Even an electric motor must look like a birthday present – John Thackar (Design magazine, June 1985)

- *a catalog of re-usable design elements, components, and connection types such as engines, doors, hydraulic systems, software packages, or test systems;*

- *design rules or constraints that determine which compositions of those elements are permitted. For example, the rule might specify that a client-server organization must use an n-to-1 relationship, or that an engine needs a specific fuel;*

- *semantic interpretations whereby compositions of design elements, suitably constrained by design rules, have well-defined meanings;*

- *analyses that can be performed on systems built in that style. Examples include mechanisms for analyzing stress in a mechanical design, or schedule analyses for real-time processing;*

- *a presentation metaphor that explains the system coherently. This allows users to construct an internal model rapidly, helping them to interpret and control the system.*

A coherent style makes design re-use much easier. Known solutions with well-understood properties can be reapplied to new problems with confidence, leading to significant component or code re-use. A consistent style eases understanding by users and engineers, supports interoperability, and by constraining design space, permits specialized style-specific analyses. Staff can re-apply that style across different projects.

Design and aesthetics

Form should indeed follow function, but products are (normally) intended for human use and need to satisfy users' aesthetic needs. We neglect style and appearance at our peril, but a consistent style should never mean standardized, boring, products. The Ferrari, Apple Mac, Viking longship,

Japanese sword, and the Concorde airplane are at once consistent and beautiful, without being over-decorated. Design is far more than decoration, but from Stone Age times, designers have always gone beyond mere functionality and shaped their products to be attractive. The concept of pure utilitarian design is recent in human history, limited to dull, invisible areas such as some (but only some) warehouses, drains, boxes and electricity pylons. Even in those areas, designers usually strive for spare, clean designs. With few exceptions, designers and customers usually seem equally averse to ugly, purely functional products. Where this has been forgotten, as in modern architecture, a high price has been paid.

A coherent style may continue for decades within a company, and emerge as a valuable corporate asset. A Boeing airplane, Mercedes car, Mont Blanc pen, or a Hewlett-Packard printer are readily recognizable. The design style has become a logo and a valuable asset, for others to mimic.

An example architecture

Figure 4.5 shows the software architecture for the ambulance command and control system. Each major rectangle contains stored data shown as a rectangular shape, and functions or operations shown as circular shapes. Dependencies between packages are shown by connections with arrows. Each of the main data stores originally defined in the system requirements is handled by a separate package. Each main operator function is supported by a window, highlighting the importance of the user interface in the design. Additional functionality helps operators log on and log off, and facilities needed for the supervisors are organized into a separate package.

By a small part, we may judge the whole –
Cervantes

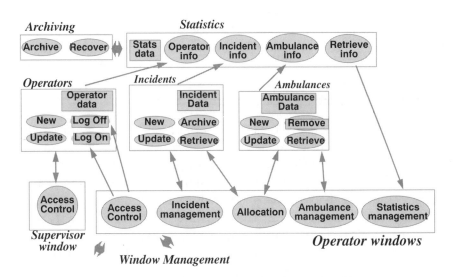

Figure 4.5: The ambulance command and control architecture

4.5.   Architecture requirements

Having discussed what architecture and architectural style mean, the capabilities a good architecture should provide can now be defined.

System-level understanding

Understanding the overall behavior at the level of a system permits key trade-offs. Most development methods provide only a detailed view, while paying attention to low-level details such as the program structures or the details of a signal processing chip.

The crucial system-level issue is how to design components to interact with each other and the environment. Interactions can take many forms, both explicit and implicit, including competition for shared resources. For example, in a car, the engine power is simultaneously used for speed, pollution control and the air conditioning system. In a computer, this could take the form of interaction protocols (e.g. message passing, rendezvous, or reference), the requirements for freshness of data (how stale the data can be before spoiling operational integrity), and whether one part can have access to data before other parts (multiple copies, updates, two-phase commit protocols etc.).

4.6.   Re-use of existing components

Re-use can reduce costs and improve time-to-market compared to custom development. Good architectural designs promote re-use by:

- *re-using existing components;*
- *re-using the same components several times within a system;*
- *producing components that can be re-used in other systems.*

The independence of components is absolutely vital if they are to be re-used. Re-use in hardware is much simpler than for software, because components have well-defined interfaces, which also define their functionality. Because of their obvious physical existence, hardware components tend to be much more self-contained. In hardware design there is both a pressing need to use existing components and the chance to actually do it.

In software, the situation is radically different, and re-use is much more problematic. The cost of developing new software may initially appear to be much lower than for hardware, if only because no actual manufacturing is involved. Developing software is however much more costly than it initially appears, because of the overheads involved in testing, documenting, support and configuration management. The software equivalents of a hardware component catalogs have grown only slowly. They now include generic customizable applications e.g. for the human computer interface, word processing, software for complex algorithms, plus specialized areas of programming (numerics and low-level abstract data types, such as queues and stacks). Successful commercial programs are, by definition, good examples of re-use of the same code by many different groups.

The context-dependency and invasiveness of software interfaces limit the re-use of software components. Failure in a single minor software component may cause a large system to crash. Each module relies on other modules, which in turn rely on still others. Re-use of a single software module may demand specific interface behavior in many other system components, while hardware is much more bounded at its interfaces.

The integrated circuit industry exhibits characteristics of both hardware and software in re-using components. Complex components such as microprocessors, Ethernet controllers, image compressors, or memory cells are designed as re-usable elements and stored in chip libraries. These elements, themselves containing thousands of gates, and can then be combined as part of larger chip designs. These large-scale components are laid out on an integrated circuit through computerized packages which analyze key elements of timing and chip size. The combination of tools and methodologies – called 'system-on-a-chip' in the industry – allows complex chip designs to be assembled rapidly from existing components.

Commercial off-the-shelf (COTS) components

Every building is a prototype

Re-use of components is possible only if an architecture is designed for re-use. In this respect, the architecture determines whether modules can actually be re-used. Re-usability is NOT an attribute of module design, but one of system thinking. Indeed it is highly affected by business policy about producing re-usable objects. Only if the business supports re-use will the effort be made to ensure it happens.

Re-use of existing components is critical for rapid development and reduction of costs and risks. A car designed without re-using many known components would inevitably be expensive and problematic. Designers should therefore guide the design toward known COTS (commercial off-the-shelf) items. Clear interfaces between the system and the COTS components can minimize dependency on a single supplier. In some cases, a design element is pre-defined ('you must use this engine'). The designer must then construct the other components around this pre-defined element.

House-building is a perfect example of re-use of design, components, and also of the development processes themselves. Experience, and skills learned on one job can be re-applied to the next. Standard components and regulations can be rapidly re-applied to make a new design. Builders can acquire components from different manufacturers that connect through standard interfaces (e.g. for electricity or water pipes). Builders use existing components at many levels – large sub-systems such as the central heating system, lower level components such as doors, or bricks. The pipework is 'customized', but composed of existing components such as pipes, joints, flues etc.

The construction industry is ambitiously attempting to make interoperable components by defining standard classes of reusable objects. These include key characteristics such as size, weight, electrical properties, behavior, plus any interfacing requirements. For example, the definition of an electrical switch will include its necessary height above the floor and distance from a door. A 'window' object will contain information allowing it to 'cut' into a wall, creating cavity closures and lintels automatically. The same standards aim to allow cost-estimates and quantities to be derived directly from the (electronic) architectural drawings. The International Alliance for Interoperability, a non-profit making organization, coordinates this work[25].

Part of the re-use problem is psychological. Designers do not trust the work of others, and often prefer to design components themselves, neglecting the intrinsic costs of in-house work. Comparing the real expense of internal construction versus COTS acquisition should flush out many of these problems. The exercise must be performed from a neutral management perspective to be realistic, because internal developers are often blind to the actual cost of their own work and optimistic about its quality. The analysis has to include the loss of key internal staff resources, and lost business opportunity through delay. Staff involved in internal developments have emotional commitment to continuing their work, and therefore should not be involved in choosing between build and buy.

Since the COTS product already exists, its costs, availability, and performance are already known and largely risk-free. Many properties have been confirmed by real experience (e.g. mean time between failures, safety record). This certainly is a strong attraction for the use of COTS components. Nevertheless, COTS acquisition must still be based on requirements. The process is to choose the best, not the perfect solution as efficiently as possible (Figure 4.6) from a range of ready-made options.

COTS elements predominate in the simplest lowest-level components of a system, showing that the added value comes from integrating lower level elements. For example, in a car development, you are much more likely to be able to buy in the nuts and bolts, starter motors, and braking systems than the car interior or a body shell.

Advice on COTS

Use of COTS components is not a panacea for the problems of custom development, and typical complications that occur are:

- *suppliers exaggerate the capability of their products, so paper analysis is never enough;*

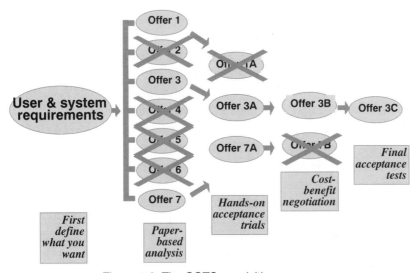

Figure 4.6: The COTS acquisition process

- some requirements are partially met, or are less meaningful because of a different design approach of the COTS component;
- missing functions are always promised for the next release;
- future compatibility and support of the component are uncertain;
- products contain unwanted functionality, which causes unexpected side-effects;
- manufacturers have a take it or leave it attitude, and modifications are expensive;
- some functions may not be available in commercial items;
- interfacing to the COTS component t may be difficult.

Where the customer has enough strength, these kinds of requirements should be reflected in the purchase agreement for the COTS components. All bidders must be aware of the requirements, but the COTS component does not itself have to meet absolutely every requirement. In practice, custom developments are usually far from perfect solutions.

Interoperability problems often happen when new COTS releases are made. A software project in which one of the authors was involved was plagued by version dependencies between a database, operating system and user interface kits. Every time a supplier produced a new version, it made some components compatible, while others became incompatible.

Decoupling

To support re-use, each individual component must be as independent of other components as possible, i.e. it should be 'decoupled'. Its behavior and interface definition must be as unrestrictive as possible to allow component re-use in different environments. The interaction requirements can be defined as a set of interfaces: some help the component utilize the rest of the system; others define facilities which the component can provide to the rest of the system. For example, if we were designing a car engine for re-sale for other applications, we would make connections such as the clutch, fuel supply, the engine control messages, and engine mounting as flexible as possible.

To allow components to interact properly when connected, interfaces must also ensure that interacting components conform to each other's requirements. This insight is gained by defining the properties of the individual components and understanding how components interact. To create this synergy, components must be able to interact, despite the benefits of keeping them as independent as possible. The interface control document between any two components forms a 'contract' agreed by both parties. This interface should be defined as a separate entity, perhaps even by an independent broker. This allows a more abstract definition, provides the potential of sub-setting, and encourages many-to-many interfaces instead of just one-to-one. It allows an interface to be re-used in different contexts and to be decoupled from specific components. Taking the example of the engine, we would define the necessary fuel types, power supply and control signals. The engine imposes a maximum operating temperature on other components.

The component interface also defines the requirements imposed on any component with which it interacts. To connect components correctly, a component must be defined as a provider or a user of the interface. This is rather similar to the need for plugs and sockets in electrical engineering. A physical component is viewed through its connection(s) to the outside world, which allow controls, data or supplies to flow into and out of the connection. The only behavior that needs be defined is the component's response to a stimulus from the outside world. The component will also require an equivalent interface for the components with which it interacts.

As an example, the starter motor interface (Figure 4.7) consists of a static physical connection attaching the motor to the engine block, and a dynamic connection supplying the torque to the engine drive gear. The electrical interface consists of a 12–volt power supply and a control signal to trigger the motor. The behavior of the starter motor is defined by its torque characteristics, response time, and time to disengage when the control is removed. The context of the starter motor includes the behavior of the engine to which it is attached – for example its weight, angular momentum, mechanical gearing, but also non-functional requirements such as temperature and vibrational levels. During high level design, details of the motor, such as the magnet technology, should not be defined. This modular approach makes the equipment easy to develop concurrently, and easy to test. A car

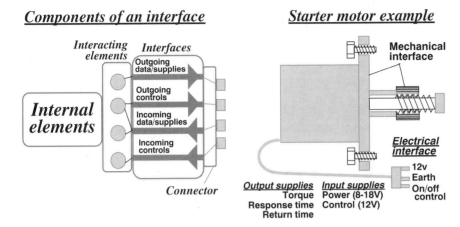

Figure 4.7: Defining components through behavior and interfaces

manufacturer can identify a clear interface and issue it to several potential suppliers. The motor will also inherit other non-functional requirements such as reliability, working temperature, available volume, and accessibility. The system engineer at the level above will have supplied some of these. The starter motor exhibits many properties of a well-designed component.

Interface protocols

In both information and physical systems, concurrent interactions between components are the prime source of emergent properties. For instance, in a servo system, control is achieved by first defining a set point, and then adjusting the regulator settings to keep values close to that set point. The interactions between the function being controlled, feedback loop and target values define how the system performs.

Interactions arise from concurrent actions in different components sending and receiving material or information. In a physical system, such as an oil refinery, the flows may be involve fluids or gases. In software, the interfaces carry only information. When timing and concurrency are involved in the transmission of material or information, the following questions are relevant:

- *is the information pushed or pulled?*
- *is the sender held up if the receiver is not ready to receive?*
- *is the sender held up if there is no space to place the material or information being sent?*
- *if there is no space to deliver the material information, does the sender remove old material and replace it by the more up-to-date material?*

When a concurrent function wishes to receive information does it:

- *take the latest information which has been delivered?*

- *take the oldest information which has been delivered (first-in-first-out)?*
- *wait until a new delivery of information is made?*

In software, key questions in any sender-receiver situation are how up-to-date should the information be, and what should be done with information that has passed the receiver's freshness criteria.

Multiple instances

In distributed systems, the same functionality is often needed in several places or concurrently in time. The same component must therefore be replicated, perhaps with minor variations. Component re-use within a single system has enormous advantages, because fewer elements need to be designed and tested, and the manufacturing and maintenance become much simpler. The design information for wheels on cars, telephone switching circuits, fighter aircraft, and radar systems is re-used. A plane may consist of *four million parts flying in formation*, but the vast majority of them are rivets and fasteners! When the design is upgraded, all instances are affected by the changes, and the design must have been organized to assist this.

Identical hardware components need to be physically manufactured, but in software they can be 'cloned' trivially. Replicating a piece of software is essentially free, and each copy is totally identical. A software car would have only one wheel, but would swap it around every millisecond! In hardware engineering, the re-use of the same component actually means not only re-using the same design, but a completely different (manufactured) instance of it. Therefore architectural requirements must include the notion of 'component type', and identify each individual instance of the type to avoid confusion.

System construction or composition

Architectural design shows how a system will operate before it has been constructed. The construction mechanism defines how the components are connected, satisfying the needs of the components and also obeying the interconnection rules. The construction features must therefore be able to:

- *create instances of component types;*
- *place multiple instances in the system;*
- *satisfy the interfacing requirements of the component instances.*

In hardware engineering, these factors emerge naturally from the need to manufacture and assemble individual components. In software engineering, these requirements can be satisfied in a variety of ways. At one extreme they could all be handled off-line, leading to the generation of executable images. At the other extreme, they could all be done on-line so that a system could be built up dynamically, and modified during execution. Dynamic on-line composition opens up many possibilities (and dangers) for system evolution, such as support for fault tolerance, graceful degradation and even reconfiguration to cope with unforeseen situations. Changing the software in an operational satellite – as happened with the Voyager satellite to the outer planets – is an example of such an evolutionary system.

Designs that use strongly decoupled components are in principle easier to test, since the behavior of a component is independent of its local interfaces (Figure 4.8). As far as the component is concerned, the test and operational environments are the same.

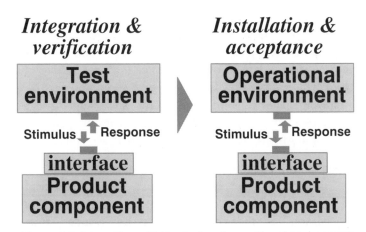

Figure 4.8: Interacting with the test and operational environment

Summary of requirements for architecture

A good architecture provides a sound understanding of how the system will work. The design should be modular so that interfaces can be defined independently from the components that use them. Components can then interact with more than one interface as provider, supplier or both. Modularity helps interconnect components across the system, according to their connectivity rules.

In summary, an architecture defines a set of generic component types together with:

- *a description of the properties of each type;*
- *the rules governing the way each component type may interact with each other type;*
- *the style of interactions allowed between components;*
- *the rules governing how a system (or sub-system) may be composed from instances of the generic components.*[26]

A 'good' architecture provides the facilities defined in the previous section, and must also:

- *allow freedom and flexibility in how the components may be associated;*
- *support the specification of design-specific but context-independent (re-usable) component types;*
- *support the composition of systems (and sub-systems) from instances of these design-specific components.*

Classification hierarchy for architectural design information

Information about the design can be organized through a classification hierarchy (Figure 4.9). Generic information is written once, and re-applied many times wherever it is applicable. Generic information at the top applies to every system, while the larger, more specific, and prescriptive information is at the bottom. The top two levels of this figure should be part of the business standard, applying generically to all systems and reducing the volume of documentation needed in any individual system. The top two levels help us to understand all systems that conform to a particular architecture.

The third level is only documented once, irrespective of how many times the component is used. It conveys the most detailed description of the component in isolation. The crucial information added at the bottom level is the specific reason for the component to be included and defines the emergent properties created by component interaction. This saves effort and

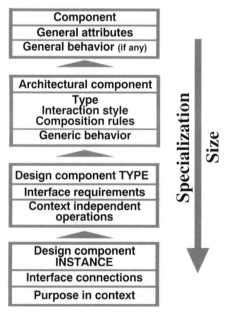

Figure 4.9: Classification hierarchy for architectural components

helps understanding.

Without an inheritance-based approach, all the documentation must be provided at the bottom level. This makes it difficult to find anything, requires every system to document everything and will mean the same information is written many times, usually incompatibly! Instead of managing a single design element, multiple different versions will evolve. This creates enormous configuration control problems, because documentation becomes more difficult to write, read and understand. Lack of structure also makes such systems difficult to maintain, and causes deterioration as they are updated.

4.7.   How to do architectural design

Architectural design has to work in the real world where things fail, components are constrained by the laws of physics, and resources are limited. The link between requirements and design is thus not one-way, because requirements must be influenced by design practicality. The design team must deduce the emergent properties, define an appropriate set of components and predict the properties of the set. Good designers can easily achieve this, but poor designers rarely can!

Design as directed evolution

For most types of system, past experience is the biggest design driver. An advanced jet plane or a luxury car are designed using the experience of generations of engineers, and could never have been produced in a single step. At every system level, designers build up enormous skills in what to do, and perhaps even more importantly what to avoid. The availability of existing designs, components, training, and connectors inevitably drives us toward solutions that are similar to current systems. While we have to be careful to avoid being excessively conservative, novelty is intrinsically dangerous. Many important design practices have been discovered by analyzing past failures[8]. Buildings collapse if they are poorly designed, planes crash when structures fail, and software systems fail when the parts do not interact correctly. Knowledge is captured as constraints in the system requirements, e.g. which materials to avoid and which to use, best architectures etc. In many cases these 'best practices' are not explicitly understood or documented, but are locked into individual experience and expertise.

Design can therefore be considered as a form of intelligently directed evolution – less blind than natural evolution, because we can analyze and choose which direction to go. In practice, we are always restricted by the past, and must often retain compatibility with existing equipment and standards. Of course, the past can also be a prison. In most countries, the rails for trains are four foot eight and one-half inches apart, too small to make trains really comfortable, and inconvenient for countries using the metric

Progress depends on retentiveness. Those who forget the past are condemned to repeat it – George Santayana (The life of reason)

system. When British engineers started to build trains in the early 19th century, they re-used components and tooling that already existed for farm equipment and stagecoaches. In turn, these had been standardized to fit the existing ruts on 19th century roads. Evolution from Roman times had produced a natural, self-reinforcing standard. Brunel's 19th century attempt to impose a seven foot rail gauge on the London to Bristol line ended because it needed to link up to other commercial rail systems (interfaces again!).

Failure mode analysis

Good design draws on experience and we should consider the failure modes of previous systems in detail. The impact of failures must be determined, and the design adjusted to stop the failure or avoid the consequences. This starts by looking at the results of 'single-point failures' and making the design more resilient or reducing the impact of failure. As an example, the braking systems in cars are duplicated to avoid single-point failure of the hydraulics.

Disasters are not usually caused by catastrophic events such as wings falling off or sudden collapses of buildings. In practice, 'normal accidents' are caused by multiple failures among loosely coupled elements[27]. Strings of small, unrelated errors propagate into a total system collapse, aided by mistakes by operators who cannot interpret what is happening. Deviations from specifications add up in unexpected ways. Lack of clarity in a display may result in a pilot shutting down an engine that is functioning correctly, rather than the faulty engine. Disasters are commonly blamed on operator error, even though the operators have been confronted by mysterious and inexplicable interactions. After the event, these disasters are easy to explain. Keeping the user interfaces clear and simple can reduce the likelihood of such failures.

Searching through design space

A large, possibly infinite, number of designs are possible, each with advantages and disadvantages. A typical design approach is to focus on a sub-optimal, but reasonable solution, then work intensively to improve it by multiple, small changes. The designer focuses on the key requirements, and reducing failures to meet such key requirements. To avoid being stuck on a local optimum, designers must first scan the totality of 'design space' to make sure every potential winner is covered. Prototyping may be needed to learn about the range of different design options and eliminate the non-runners. 'Genetic programming' software can search design space to ensure that unexpected design solutions are not overlooked. Design competitions by different teams increase the chance of a successful solution.

This approach can be seen in slow motion in research or through design competition in the marketplace. When a designer makes a breakthrough, others can often improve it very quickly. For example, when two IBM researchers, Muller and Bednorz, produced a high-temperature superconductor in 1986, it was replicated at the University of Houston within a week, and by AT&T within two weeks. Another researcher then produced equipment to examine 20,000 different materials simultaneously. In a rapid series of incremental developments, the superconducting temperature was raised from 13°K to 90°K. All of these design options had been available before, but the initial discovery had shown which design space to search[5]. This is a typical example of a breakthrough, followed by an exploration of local design space for optimization. Thomas Edison was a master at this approach, and in a matter of months during 1879 built prototypes that raised the design life of an electric light from 13 to 600 hours.

A similar story can be seen in competition between designs for a market niche. A new design concept may overwhelm the previous market leader, and then several different design options battle for supremacy using that breakthrough. Continual improvements follow until the intrinsic qualities of the best design win out, and it crushes the opposition. Older designs are first relegated to specialist niches, then evolved out of the system. The winning design then changes slowly, becoming a commodity until another discontinuous technology jump occurs, destroying the old leader. Computer printers show the process almost perfectly, with the low-end market captured successively by golf ball printers (1970s), daisy-wheels (1980–1985), dot-matrix (1982–1988), laser printers (1985–1993) and currently held by ink-jet printers.

The ruthless process of design evolution can be seen in the history of agriculture, weaponry, cars, aircraft or even between artists, competing societies or political creeds. The designer goes through a similar, but more rapid, approach on a single system design.

The approach can be carried through levels of architectural designs. At each level, the designer finds the best design space, but leaves local optimization for sub-system designers. Designers must balance a comprehensive search of design space with detailed local optimization.

4.8. Creating a behavioral model

Multiple concurrent processes

Concurrency is vital in most systems, because the real world is composed of cooperating and competing systems, not a sequence of individual actions occurring one at a time. The concept of 'sequence' has been encouraged by the influence of programming in software engineering. Sequence is a powerful agent for simplification and decomposition, but fails to model many critical aspects such as system loading. For example, breaking down a telephone call into a single sequence is valuable in illustrating everything necessary to service a single call. Each call must obey the same sequential logic, but running concurrently and asynchronously. However, the most difficult problem in a telephone exchange are handling thousands of calls simultaneously or handling worst-case scenarios, such as call overload. The architectural design must therefore address concurrency and define equipment to cope with failure or handle excessive loads without total collapse.

Contention or implicit coupling may be introduced by design decisions. The worst problems of contention usually occur when several components demand resources simultaneously. These cases are often difficult to simulate to any degree of accuracy, particularly when the architecture is intricate. Even if the overall system could cope, the system may slow down enough to cause a component to fail (or vice-versa). Examples of possible implicit couplings include running several processes on the same processor, contention for power, or contention for landing facilities after delays to aircraft.

Different technologies exhibit different problems of contention. In hydraulics systems, several hydraulic 'functions' normally operate one or two at a time, but if they are operated simultaneously, the hydraulic pressure could collapse. This worst-case situation could cause an impossible load for the compressor supplying the driving force. Within electronic systems, bus contention is often a problem. The available power supply may also be an issue, as high power may be required simultaneously in several systems. In communications systems, bandwidth is often limited, and information may take longer than expected to traverse a physical path. Where several logical communication routes share a single physical path, contention may potentially cause more delays.

External systems in the design phase

The principles for handling ICDs are similar to those used for system requirements, but now need repeating in design terms. Relationships with external systems form an important part of the behavioral model during the design phase. The protocols for interactions must be agreed within an interface control document (ICD) showing the commitments and obligations of both parties.

Figure 4.10 shows how an interface to supply power is transformed between the stages of system requirements and design. For example, communication will be defined functionally during the system requirements process. In the design phases, this ICD will be transformed into cables, amps and voltages. Unfortunately, most projects start to define ICDs much too late, performing the initial work with a physical ICD during the design process. By then, any changes made to the interface have a severe impact on the cost and schedule of the project.

As the element is further defined, greater detail about types of connectors, cable and layout will be provided. Figure 4.10 shows a simple one-to-one

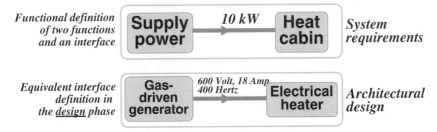

Figure 4.10: Evolution of external systems

mapping between system requirements and design but normally the designer will adjust the functional structure with, for example, extra power supplies to cope with failure. This change in structure leads to more complex traceability between the system requirements and design. This difference between the structures wrecks any object-oriented approach based on re-use of objects across phases.

The process of formalizing ICDs can be lengthy in large systems. For each system, a single individual should be assigned responsibility for managing the negotiations on the ICD with the other party.

Timing

The time taken to perform a task is important for behavioral definition. A detailed understanding of timing can only be gained once the design components start to emerge. Good engineers usually have an intuitive 'feel' for design feasibility, based on experience of similar situations. A protocol defines the interaction frequency and whether the sender and receiver work with a consistent interaction strategy. For instance, a rendezvous happens only when the sender, receiver and communication channel can all take their part in the transfer. If the sender works at 10 times the frequency of the receiver, the receiver will constrain the sender to work much more slowly.

Throughput

A system could perform all the tasks correctly, but simply be too slow to be usable. Throughput is a key system parameter and a prime example of an emergent property. Throughput is a dynamic characteristic, specified in the behavioral aspect of the design. Performance modeling is very desirable, but typically performance can be predicted only approximately before the design is well-understood. Performance depends on multiple interactions between system components, and can often be improved by minor compromises and 'tweaks' to the design. Designers then have to balance the advantages of better performance versus the damage done to the design integrity.

4.9.   Layout

Layout addresses where the equipment is to be installed and/or assembled, and the physical placement of the components. On a physical system this will include aspects such as weight, heat generation, center of gravity, access, center of mass, density of materials, potential for clashing of moving parts, fitting cables and pipes in a confined space, and their removal for maintenance. In the construction industry, installation aspects are a huge cost driver and an installation view is essential during design. This involves modeling the on-site installation of equipment, seeing the critical time-dependencies and even altering the design to make installation more effective.

Physical properties include whether the equipment fits into the available space, whether there is sufficient power, and whether the equipment generates more heat than can be vented away. Again design changes may be needed to components or their implementation to prevent clashing between moving components. Environmental requirements may demand ventilation, cooling, or better insulation for one or more components to reduce the impact of heat or vibration. Once these aspects have been considered, feasibility and cost can be revisited.

The design needs to be analyzed to see whether the parts fit together, if the system can operate, if the parts can actually be assembled, and if parts can be changed during maintenance. Dangers here include the introduction of 'common mode' or 'single-point' failures for example, by using a single power supply for several pieces of equipment. A short-circuit in a non-critical component may destroy power to critical functions. This is an example of implicit coupling being introduced by a design decision. For instance, an aircraft hydraulics system should be as well protected as possible against single-point failure. An Airbus plane survived a hand-grenade explosion that cut two of its three hydraulics systems, because the lines were well separated. Coupling is not necessarily bad, but it should not be ignored.

Other examples of coupling include mutual interference such as:

- *spillover between a transmitter and the receiver antennae;*
- *electromagnetic coupling caused by cable runs inducing erroneous signals into sensitive detectors or amplifiers;*
- *mechanical coupling such as vibration, resonance, or extreme acceleration affecting a detector or even shaking a system to pieces (as with rockets during launch).*

4.10. Creating an equipment design model

The design must determine how concurrent functions and interaction protocols will be implemented. The key decision is whether the implementation technology can be defined at this point or delayed until later. The options that can be chosen for design are:

- *hardware;*
- *software;*
- *people;*
- *any combination of the above.*

Figure 4.11 shows two options for the design of operating consoles for part of the ambulance command and control system. In one case, a generic console has been designed for several different roles, and is tailored for the specific task. In the second case, consoles are specialized for different roles. The former approach allows easier maintenance, but each individual console is probably more complicated and expensive as a result. Essentially there is a trade-off between development and operational costs.

After identifying the implementation technology, the next task is determining how functions will actually be 'motivated', i.e. what force causes the function to be provided? The processor for software components must be chosen. For hardware functions, the decision might be to use electronic, hydraulic or mechanical hardware. Each technology has specific characteristics that must be taken into consideration.

Humans as part of the operational system

Where humans form any part of the final system, their characteristics must be taken into account. Architectural design defines the functions to be performed by humans, trading off the benefits of fulfilling the same functions in hardware or software. In choosing between humans and machines, the obvious factors are the size and weight of the intended users, and typical human traits such as intelligence, flexibility, low boredom threshold and potentially high error rate.

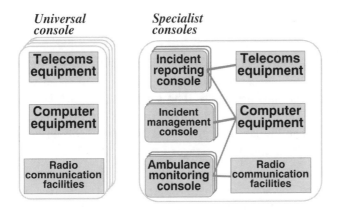

Figure 4.11: Options for architecture

The choice between humans and automatic control is done during design, based on analysis and requirements from the system requirements phase.

The tasks performed by human operators are chosen through the nature of a function, scheduling, the control interactions required, and the nature of the human-system interface. Design may need to minimize the effects of non-deterministic behavior from human operators. In other cases, human beings may need to over-ride automatic control. For example, aircraft have survived over-stressing beyond the design limit, yet landed safely. An automatic control could possibly have prevented this over-stress, but in doing so may restrict the pilot's actions, causing the plane to stall and crash. An added dimension is introduced if there are multiple operators, for example to control a power station or a plane. The design must specify the structure of the team, their individual and group responsibilities, and the way in which they interact.

Since we are dealing with humans and not automata, their workload and behavior may interact in complex ways. As tasks vary over time, operators may for example:

- *increase or decrease their effort to maintain a consistent level of performance;*
- *maintain a constant level of effort and so change the system performance;*
- *defer or shed less important tasks when demands become too high, to maintain performance on more critical tasks; or*
- *complete some tasks ahead of schedule during low workload periods, to conserve effort for high-workload periods in the future.*

The unpredictable behavior of humans demands modeling at the architectural stage by workflow analysis, dynamic computer modeling, prototyping or mock-ups. Iteration may be required before arriving at a satisfactory task allocation. Safety-critical functions require special attention. Analyses of failures in large control centers have repeatedly shown that errors are linked with poor control layout and misleading cues[28]. Controllers are confused when they do not understand the functioning of the basic system and its controls.

When humans operate a system, they create an internal model of how the system works. When errors occur, this model is analyzed to determine the cause, and corrections are made. The simpler and more faithful a model, the less the likelihood of disaster through misinterpretation during operations or development. The human computer interface (HCI) should be an integral part of the requirements and design stages (see chapter 10).

Task analysis also defines the human skill or training requirements, which in turn contribute toward the whole system cost. There may be requirements for dedicated training equipment, such as simulators, embedded help facilities and manuals. Operating procedures have to be captured, specified, and revisited throughout the systems engineering life cycle.

Human needs in maintenance are easily overlooked. Components must be easily reached or replaced, and the clearances allowed for tools and test-gear. Anyone who has ever repaired a car is aware of the discrepancies between the manual and the uncomfortable reality of performing the repair. Maintenance has a major bearing on the quality and cost of the final solution to the eventual user or the maintenance organization, and simulation technology is increasingly being used for modeling the maintenance process as an integral part of design.

4.11. Design trade-offs

At all times, the designer is circling around quality, performance, cost, schedule and risk, reducing the inevitable contradictions. For example, compromises in functionality may well be acceptable where time-to-market is crucial. Candidate designs are assessed against key requirements to choose the best compromise (Figure 4.12). The triangle of user requirements, system requirements, and architectural design is traversed as many times as necessary to obtain a consistent, practical, satisfactory design.

You can be certain that the uncertainty is not zero

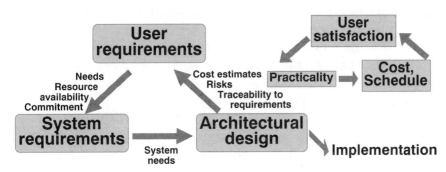

Figure 4.12: Trade-offs between design and requirements

Cost-benefit analysis

Cost-benefit analysis analyzes requirements against costs. The chosen design can be optimized through cost-benefit against the requirements (Figure 4.13) by:

- attaching an estimate of price to each design element that could be detached;
- attaching an estimated value to each requirement;
- defining the maximum cost for the complete system.

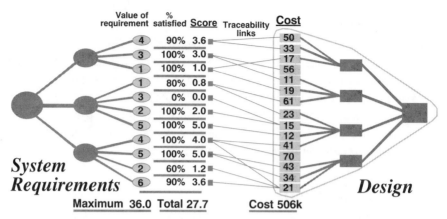

Figure 4.13: Optimizing an individual system through cost-benefit

The decision on which elements to include is then semi-automatic on the basis of cost-benefit. We can maximize the value delivered to users for the available resources. The more modular the system, the easier it is to add, change, or cut pieces without knock-on effects[29].

Architectural design is the ideal time for this value engineering, because the components are visible at a high level, but still abstract enough to be easily altered. Relatively painless design compromises may increase the value for money significantly. With care, some parts can be eliminated, or less expensive materials can be substituted. The design can be organized for ease of manufacture, for production by outside specialist contractors, or for re-use of existing parts. The dangers in these compromises are obvious, but the results can considerably improve the system cost-benefit.

The better the traceability between design and requirements, the more sensible these compromises can be. This is particularly important at this stage, because the emergence of the design makes the implementation costs more obvious. The horse-trading and interaction that lead to consensus can produce all-round enhancements with only minor losses. Compromise depends on organizing both the requirements and design with an eye toward adjusting both.

Trade-off analysis can be applied to the smallest components. Petroski[30] shows how, for example, even apparently simple components such as paper clips and soft drink cans have been improved through multiple incremental steps. These improvements reduce costs by cutting the amount of material, or make them easier to use. The end result is invariably a compromise that balances cost, attractiveness, and functionality.

Any successful design must simultaneously meet the requirements, satisfy business and financial goals, yet be practical to build. Any satisfactory solution must reach minimum values in each of these dimensions (Figure 4.14). Any potential design is therefore a point in multi-dimensional space that may or may not lie within the target space. Uncertainties in our knowledge expand this point into a spheroid, i.e. the design lies somewhere in the spheroid in the diagram.

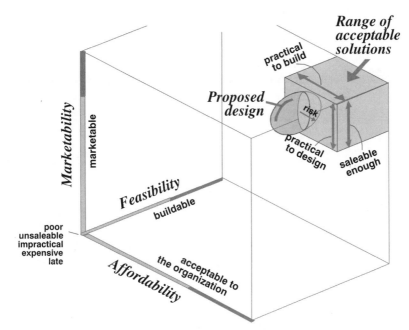

Figure 4.14: Quality, affordability, feasibility and risk

Quality function deployment

Quality function deployment (QFD) is a well known technique used in industry, particularly in Japan, for relating end user needs to design[31]. A matrix is formed by the customer needs and the design, on the left and top respectively. Figure 4.15 shows QFD built as an application running above a requirements management system, i.e. using the real project information[32]. At the top of the diagram, the roof of the 'house of quality' is formed by an n^2 matrix which shows inter-relationships between design elements. Multi-phase QFDs add extra matrices to extend the approach to show the relationships between derived requirements and design. QFD can therefore be considered as part of the systems engineering processes, dealing with the traceability between user requirements and design elements.

Change control

Inevitably some design changes will be needed for:

- *features that prove impossible;*

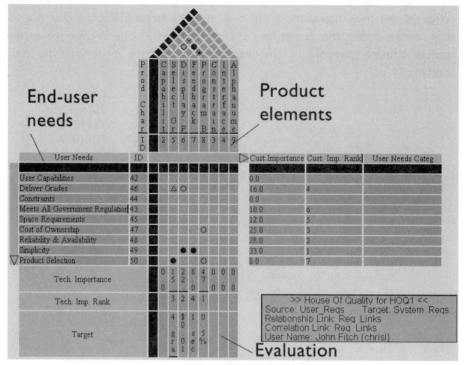

Figure 4.15: Quality function deployment (QFD)

- new features that become possible;
- changes in requirements;
- cutting back on expensive features.

The development team track potential changes back upstream to the point of furthest impact. If a change affects the user requirements, then the impact has to be balanced against cost and time saved.

Design margins

During the design process, many uncertainties confront the designer:

- the behavior of the design itself may be difficult to predict;
- there may be a variation in the manufactured units;
- testing can never be exact or complete;
- the operational environment and the external systems may not be entirely understood.

As a result, designers must always add sufficient margins to ensure requirements are met under all likely operational conditions — not just when the equipment is new and being tested in a perfect environment. Designing to meet the requirement exactly under test will guarantee failure of units under severe conditions. The more exactly you understand the design, test requirements and manufacturing process, the lower the margins may be. In large aerospace systems, margins may be as high as 50% at the unit level, gradually diminishing to 5–10% at the system level. In extreme cases, such as buildings designed for a 50–year life, the safety margin for a load-bearing part may be 6 times the underlying requirement[33]. This reflects the long lifetimes, and the variable quality of build and maintenance.

Margins are normally centered around key requirements such as weight, drag or power consumption. Experienced design architects will often start with a contingency of 10–20% up their sleeve. On the Boeing 777, the initial design was 17,000 pounds overweight. Hard redesign work brought that down to only 4,000 pounds over the target, and below the weight Boeing had promised the airlines.

Margins gradually diminish as the development proceeds and the uncertainties shrink. But some uncertainties will not have disappeared at the time of test, and therefore tests include a contingency above the original requirements (see chapter 3). Engineers are initially reluctant to consider testing above the value of requirements, but margins are never zero, so you have to budget for them.

Methods and tools for design

In the requirements phases, the same methods can be used for widely different systems. As we move into design, the design methods start to become distinct for different types of component. Design method(s) should be appropriate for the nature of the system, e.g. physical systems, 3–D systems, 2–D drawing systems, electronic or electrical circuit design. For many types of systems, we may need to understand the physical layout, and for example, the basis of a car design may be a solid modeling tool. This 3–D model provides a clear design framework to which all other aspects can be tied, allowing the specification of materials, center of gravity, weight and amount of space available for different components. The project management information is handled by software tools such as those for configuration management, project scheduling, and budgeting are used to support the managerial aspects of development.

4.12. Concurrent engineering in design

At the design stage, the system has to be split into major components, some of which will be developed separately. Instead of finishing the design of a product then starting to design the manufacturing system to produce it, concurrent engineering largely performs the tasks in parallel (Figure 4.16). The same applies to the test system and the operational support system. The end product is the lead for these derived systems, but they in turn influence the end product to make it testable and operable. The production system

Architectural design

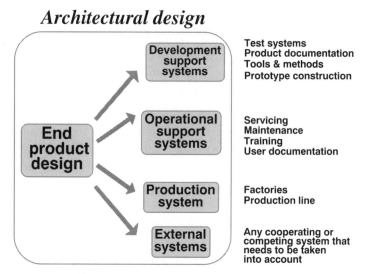

Figure 4.16: End product and derived systems

Example verification requirement – The complete test process shall add no more than fifteen calendar days to the development schedule

must be able to manufacture the end product, but will itself constrain the product by, for example, limiting the tolerances on dimensions and temperatures.

Large gains of productivity have come from increasing concurrency between designing the product and designing the support systems. Concurrent engineering effectively treats them as an integrated architectural design, rather than as a sequential definition process.

4.13. Verification work before testing

Verification work is needed before the testing actually starts. During the system requirements process, each requirement should be marked with the method of verification and the level at which the requirement should be tested.

The **verification level** tells us whether a specific requirement will be checked by testing the whole system, a large sub-system or a smaller unit (or any combination). System-level testing has a number of drawbacks; it is expensive, ties up the whole system, and produces faults which are difficult to locate and diagnose. System testing cannot stress small parts as much as we might like. System-level testing therefore needs to be limited to those elements for which it is unavoidable.

The **verification type** defines whether the requirement will be checked by testing, by inspection, by analysis or some other method. Testing is usually the most satisfactory method but it is not always the most effective, and sometimes not even possible. Figure 4.17 shows examples of requirements, marked with both the level(s) and the type(s) of verification. The process and

Object	Verification levels	Ver level	Ver type
17	**4.1.3 Obtain incident details**	Sub-system Unit	Test Inspection
25	Incident management shall obtain and document background information about the medical emergency.	Unit	Test Audit
26	Incident management shall obtain details about about the patient including name, likely medical condition, medical history and name of doctor.	Unit	Test Audit
27	Incident management shall obtain and document the location of the patient.	Unit	Test Audit
33	Incident management shall communicate the likely arrival time of the ambulance to the caller, and update this value if it changes by more than 5 minutes.	Unit	
18	**4.1.4 Organize transport**	Sub-system Unit	Test Inspection
28	Transport organization shall allocate an ambulance to the patient on the basis of the seriousness of the diagnosis and the availability of ambulances.	Unit	Test Audit
29	Transport organization shall inform the operator of the likely time before arrival of the ambulance, and supply an update for this value if it changes.	Unit	Test Audit
30	If the likely time to arrival of the ambulance exceeds the guide values, transport organization shall alert the shift manager.	Unit	Test Audit
12	**4.2 Handle medical services**	Sub-system	Test

Figure 4.17: Verification levels and types attached to requirements (right-hand columns)

principles of integration and verification are covered in detail in chapters 5 and 6 respectively.

Verification requirements

System requirements also need to document two related, but distinct, types of requirements that relate to verification.

Requirements imposed on the way that verification must be done (e.g. time allowed for verification, limitation on the need to repeat tests, independence of the verification team). These requirements are created and owned by the system engineers, and imposed on the verification team.

Requirements imposed on the product to ensure it can be verified (e.g. test points, modular separation and visibility of faults). These requirements are owned by the verification group and imposed on the product, but have to be approved by the project manager.

Unless a complex system is designed for test, it will not be testable. A modular design enables a test environment to simulate the interface environment on the other side of the component. Individual sections will be easy to check 'on-the-bench', and then plug into the system. The design may incorporate self-checking, providing some confidence that the part is working. Requirements to ensure testability should be written by the verification staff in the system requirements, and tested at the design process.

Verification requirements define the overall approach to testing. They cover aspects such as common policy, test tools, calendar time allowed for test, inspection time versus the time for test, and the amount of risk allowed by testing. Verification requirements are defined in detail in the system requirements document, in a section controlled by the verification and validation discipline.

Verification requirements are crucial for making the right compromise between resources for testing, the time for testing, and the risks to the quality of the product. Good verification requirements will encourage immediate up-front, low-level testing. Low-level, early testing locates faults quickly, and ties them to individuals while the work is still fresh in the mind. The source of the problem can usually be detected quickly, and the fault eliminated. Even more important, the message will be drawn *my work will be checked, therefore I will ensure that it is high quality* . A key aspect of integration and verification is the psychological impact that it has on the developers' attitudes to their own work.

Characteristics of testing

Verification involves an intricate mixture of characteristics, such as the:

- *level of the system at which testing occurs;*
- *verification method(s);*
- *the different objectives of verification at different stages.*

Verification of the product is a bottom-up process that compares:

- *component and sub-system tests versus detailed design specification;*
- *integration test versus architectural design;*
- *system test versus system requirements;*
- *acceptance test versus user requirements.*

Identifying the levels of testing

During the system requirements process, each requirement is tagged with an attribute indicating at which level(s) verification is to be performed and the type(s) of verification to be used. Typically testing occurs at three or four levels – materials, component, integration, and system. The tests can be performed on small components, medium-sized assemblies, a complete system, or any combination of these elements.

Low level testing is far more effective than detecting faults when the system is completely assembled, because:

- *faults (and the cause of faults) are easy to locate;*
- *there is time to correct problems and adjust other components to cope with the deficiencies detected;*
- *tests can be far more severe;*
- *tests can be performed more quickly;*

> — *tests can be performed in parallel without waiting your turn to work on the system;*
> — *component testing encourages clear interfaces, modularity and re-use.*

For instance, a starter motor for a car could be tested on its own, connected to the engine, or as a part of the complete vehicle. But because a starter motor is small and fairly self-contained, it can easily be subjected to extreme temperature, vibration or voltages. As the starter motor is integrated into the car, tests become less severe, more realistic, but slower to perform. The test on the starter motor connected to the engine actually tests the engine as well. If the car fails to start, locating the source of the problem is more difficult – engine problems, a low battery voltage or a poor mechanical connection might cause it. Testing the starter motor in the whole car is the only test that matters to the end user. However it takes too long, ties up the car and causes many problems in locating faults.

In principle we should be able to bolt all the pieces together and know that the car will work without further testing, i.e. without any emergent properties caused by component interactions. Finding a fault at this stage is better than not finding it, but represents a systems engineering failure because of the potential cost of re-engineering.

Example requirement on verification margins – All unit tests shall include a 40% margin above the system requirement

Built-in test (BIT) is particularly useful for locating faults in smaller components. Units often contain software and some hardware that allows the component to partially check itself on start-up or when stimulated by the test engineer. BIT has to be designed into the system. This kind of test is not usually comprehensive, but it can be an inexpensive way of performing basic checks, and supplying some confidence in parts. For example, most computers check their memory, processor, and some components and give a confirmatory message to the user.

Modeling and simulation are slowly growing in importance, but engineers still seem to prefer test to computer simulation. When vehicle engineers were asked which types of modeling had the largest effect on the final development, they still considered that engineering models were more significant than analytical models[34].

Test margins

Testing serves to check that the equipment meets the requirements, plus the margins to cope with the remaining uncertainties. There is always uncertainty about manufacturing tolerance, the operational environment, or the completeness of the test – even at the moment of test. Margins have to be added to tests to ensure that requirements will be met, even with this level of uncertainty. The size of margin is a policy issue for the project. The lower the level of the test, the higher the margin required on the test. The margins ensure that the system works even with variations in the individual parts and their interfaces. This ensures that the system will work when the elements are bolted together to form a system. Tests against the engineering models will typically include an extra margin of 10% to 50% above the original requirements. These margins must be sufficient to ensure that production components will still meet the requirements, with the range of quality that manufacturing produces. The first operational model(s) then requires testing only with sufficient margin to cope with manufacturing and operational tolerances.

Test values are based on the original requirements with margins added to cope with:

design uncertainty *– when we sit down to design a product, we lack knowledge about the performance of components and their interfaces. This particular uncertainty reduces significantly by the time that full systems are tested;*

manufacturing uncertainty *– when a product is mass-produced, there will be manufacturing variations. We normally want to ensure that all units will pass the tests, as long as the manufacturing is done properly;*

operational uncertainty *– however hard we try, we never know the exact conditions of use of the product. We have to be sure that it meets the user requirements several years down the line, when it is worn, operating under severe weather conditions, or in unforeseen operational conditions;*

test uncertainty *– tests can never be comprehensive, and so we have to provide margins to cope with missing areas or unsuspected weaknesses. We are relying on overstressing the system to indirectly flush out faults.*

Verification is more than test, although engineers perceive test as the most satisfactory verification method (Figure 4.18). Sometimes it is not always possible or even desirable to verify by test. For example, it may not be possible to test elements under zero gravity, for 30–year lifetime, or completely test a floating-point multiplier. Testing may be possible only with

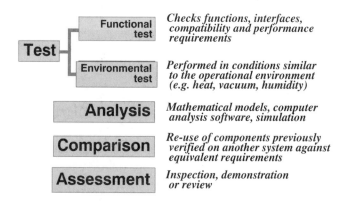

Figure 4.18: Different methods of verification

destructive results, preventing the component being used in an operational system, e.g.

All containers shall leak before bursting explosively, when over-pressurized

The container to be used operationally clearly cannot be tested against this requirement! Verification therefore consists of a mixture of tests, analysis, comparison and inspection. A single requirement may be verified by combining several methods. Although modeling is slowly becoming more important, it is naive to imagine it will ever replace test. For example, the weight of the Boeing 777 was analyzed by software throughout the development, but as soon as it was possible the plane was physically weighed to reassure everyone.

Verification by test can be used for design verification or acceptance of the complete system or part of it. Tests are normally divided into functional tests and environmental tests. **Functional tests** check compatibility, interfaces and performance requirements. **Environmental tests** check for example that the equipment will work under the most severe operational conditions, such as extreme heat, or intensive electrical interference (e.g. as it passes a radio transmitter). The environmental test simulates conditions similar to those found in the intended operational environment. When the environmental test is finished, the equipment is then checked with another functional test to make sure it still works.

Verification by analysis may be performed using mathematical models, simulation, or computer software specific to the type of system. Verification by analysis can replace or minimize test, where this is uneconomical, impossible or unrealistic. Verification by analysis is almost always used in conjunction with tests. As computer models improve and computers become more powerful, modeling and analysis programs are steadily reducing the number of physical rigs needed to test systems.

Verification by comparison can be used where equipment has been verified on another system, and it may be possible to re-use equipment directly. Previous verification information is inspected to ensure that the old equipment covers the requirements of the new system in the new environment. Verification by comparison is suitable for all levels up to sub-systems.

Verification by assessment may involve inspection, demonstration or review by the project. Review may cover the whole system, but other methods are normally suitable for verification at equipment-level or down to the actually materials-level (e.g. the type of metal used in a component).

Model philosophy

The model philosophy defines the relative effort which will be put into test systems at different phases and different system levels. Models can vary from

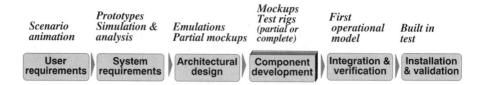

Figure 4.19: Model philosophy for verification

computer analysis software to complex test rigs (Figure 4.19) which might test the data management system or expose the equipment to extremes of temperature. They can cover the whole system or just a component. The model philosophy also defines the extra margins required for the different types of verification. For example, the Boeing 777 wing structure was tested at 50% above the maximum requirement, before being destroyed to see how it failed and at what level.

Verification models become closer to the final product as the development proceeds. Engineering models construct a complete physical prototype, an extremely expensive and time-consuming activity when building a car or a plane. The number and representativeness of verification models depend on the acceptable risk, actual risk, cost and schedule of the project. The model philosophy should be defined and frozen in the system requirements process. This work is performed in support of system engineers and will lead to separate sub-projects to create the models.

4.14. Outputs from architecture

Figure 4.20 shows the major components of the architectural design document (ADD), centered around the components to be developed, and organized in a hierarchy. The behavior of each component, its layout, and interfaces can then be defined. At the system level, this covers the behavior of the whole system and the way it interacts with its environment. The document typically starts with configuration information about the document status, followed by a description of the key components, interaction with the environment, plus a definition of the decomposition method.

Traceability to requirements

The design must be kept traceable back to the system and user requirements. Where necessary both of those types of requirements must be changed, and kept traceable to the design, so that users can see what they are to get. This way users do not need to become involved in the complexities of the system design, but can be informed when compromises in requirements may be needed.

This allows users and system engineers to see what will and what will not be met. Designers can be sure that components are really necessary to meet

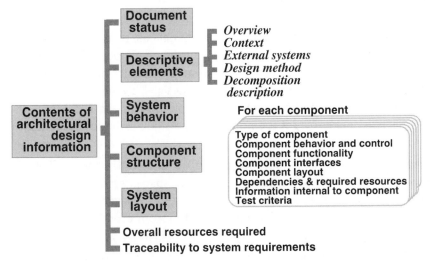

Figure 4.20: Contents of the architectural design document

requirements. Inevitably, compromises will be forced upon the team. Cost-benefit analysis is feasible because the architectural design can, to some extent, be costed, and this allows trade-offs with the requirements.

In practice, the flow of information between requirements and design is a spiral of gradual commitment. As costs and schedules become realistic rather than dreams, decisions are made to delay or drop requirements. In practice there is never a single sequential process from requirements into design, but always a flow back from design that alters the committed requirements. Commitment from the customer is gradual as the price, schedule and quality of the system become firmer and more consistent.

4.15. Summary of architectural design

At the architectural design stage, systems turn from the abstract to the concrete, and the likely costs of implementing the requirements become more evident. Architectural design defines the set of components that must be acquired or produced. More importantly, the architectural design defines the behavior of those components and the interactions between them. It therefore defines how the components must be integrated to form the complete system. The architectural design enables the deliverables to be defined for the first time, and so sensible cost estimates can be made. Improving the value of a product becomes much more straightforward if this preparatory work is done well.

Increasingly the role of design is to create new systems out of existing components. Design components can be bought 'off-the-shelf', acquired from specialized outside companies, or built in-house. More information on how these decisions are taken can be found in chapter 8, which covers the reality of complex systems.

Design is a mysterious art, and notoriously difficult to teach. Success factors include simplicity, clarity, decoupling, good definition of behavior and interfaces, and the ability to compromise on requirements in the face of reality and limited resources. Good design always involves creative breakthroughs, followed by extensive optimization of the breakthrough. The designer must never forget the non-functional and aesthetic aspects that make a product successful.

Some of the strategies that designers use are understood. They include brainstorming, local optimization of design space, systematic searching of overall design space, researching of existing designs, restructuring the problem, and collecting small inventions (often from users)[35].

Having said all this, design is usually an individual activity and laying down a generic design process is not feasible except for limited, well-understood areas. Externalizing design methods beyond generalities may never be possible. Committees are notoriously poor at design, except for camels. A single mind seems to be necessary to produce coherence, efficiency and elegance. The best we can do is to provide guidance on how to evaluate designs. The key principle is the clear definition of the behavior of system components through their interfaces. In all but the smallest systems, a hierarchical design structure that allows a gradual commitment is essential.

Exercises for Architectural design

Exercise 10: Architecture for the ambulance system

The diagram shows the components of the top level architecture proposed for the ambulance command and control system. It does not show the behavior or interfaces.

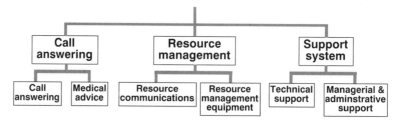

Figure 4.21: Architectural design for the ambulance C&C system

Propose another architecture and decompose it down one level.
Add two example physical interfaces, and one control link.

Exercise 11: Upgrading the system

You have a requirement that a system be designed for a mid-life upgrade of
both the software and the electronic hardware (e.g. for a car or airplane).
Define reasonable and measurable requirements for mid-life upgradeability.
Show how you would verify this requirement on delivery on the product.
Show how you would verify this requirement at the design phase.

Exercise 12: Design, style, and decoration

Define the functions performed by the 'designer' of a car.
Define the differences between style and decoration.
The car body for a new vehicle is to be styled by an Italian design studio. They
will be responsible for the body shape, styling, and interior of the vehicle.
Show where this task fits within the life cycle and indicate the interactions
with the vehicle designer at each stage.

Exercise 13: Architectural specification

Pick one of the following components.

>   1: Vacuum cleaner;

>   2: Satellite launch rocket;

>   3: Video recorder.

Once you have chosen one, define 1–2 paragraphs for the key requirements
for the system:

>   1. Internal behavior;

>   2. Interface(s);

>   3. Major constraints on the component or by the component.

From integration to operations

five

5.1. Introduction

Previous chapters have indicated how to capture user requirements, define a set of system requirements and then produce an architectural design. This results in a specification for a set of realizable components, to be built by different, specialist groups. Construction of the components is outside the scope of this book, although there is a technical management role during component development (see chapters 8 & 9). The assumption is that each specialist discipline knows how to produce components against a specification. Indeed the detailed design of those components will be performed within that discipline. But systems engineering must continually check this by watching interactions, overlaps or inconsistencies between the groups.

In this chapter, we pick up the story at the point when the components are delivered ready for assembly, integration and installation. Figure 5.1 shows integration and verification integrating the system in a test environment, followed by installation and validation in the operational environment. The starting point for integration and verification is acceptance of components from the component supplier. Configuration and quality checks are needed to ensure the right parts have been supplied, and check that no damage has

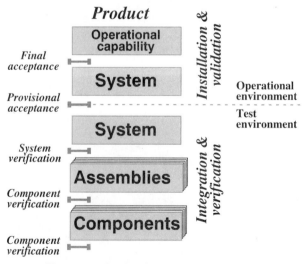

Figure 5.1: Integration to operations

happened during shipping. The parts may go into a bonded integration store, accessible only to integration and verification staff. Individual components are tested, before being integrated to produce higher level sub-systems or assemblies. These are in turn individually tested before being integrated with others to produce yet larger assemblies, until the complete tested system has been produced.

The system is ultimately installed into an operational environment, validated against user requirements, and handed over to the operational staff. This involves integrating the end product to the support systems, such as the operational and maintenance systems, which may have been created separately. An extended period may be required when staff need training to become part of the operational capability. It may therefore be a multi-stage process.

The acceptance process varies with the nature of the product. In one-off systems, the operational staff may be involved in the final testing, but when you buy a mass-produced item like a car, you perform the equivalent of 'initial acceptance' through a user manual and five minutes of instruction on the garage forecourt.

Integration and verification can sometimes be a frustrating process, made more difficult by being well separated from the requirements and design stages. For this reason, integration and verification staff should ideally be involved during the initial requirements stages.

Example verification requirement – All units shall provide a self-check of core functionality on start-up

Integration and verification is always a compromise, balancing the rigor of testing against the resources and calendar time needed to perform it. Testing everything would take too long and be too expensive. Tests therefore have to be designed for effective fault detection. They must ensure that the product does what it should, does it only the way it should and does not do what it should not do.

Figure 5.2 illustrates the complete flow from verification requirements to the test result of either 'pass' or 'fail'. The inputs to the process are the test plans, themselves derived from test requirements in the system requirements document. The verification system has itself to be created as an associate

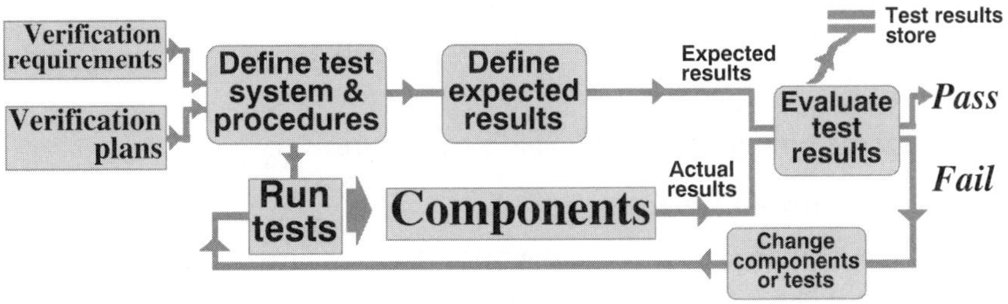

Figure 5.2: The verification process

system of the product system. After running the procedure, the test results are checked to see if they are in the range of the expected results. Any 'out-of-tolerance' result causes the component to fail the test.

Verification is always comparative, checking a product against its specification, i.e. requirements or design (Figure 5.3). But verification is not only about testing against the values set in the requirements. Requirements must be checked against the full range of operational conditions, not just in new equipment in a perfect test environment. The most important tests are the acceptance tests, but faults found then are expensive and time-consuming to correct.

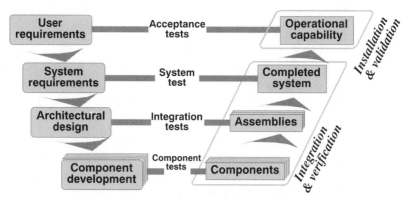

Figure 5.3: Verifying a single system

The golden rules of verification are:

- *verify at as low a level as possible;*
- *verify as early as possible;*
- *only use good people for verification and give them the strength to resist developers;*
- *balance verification by analysis with testing of the real product;*
- *reduce the need for test by suppressing problems before they have any impact (e.g. by inspection);*
- *ensure the design is testable by imposing design requirements on it;*
- *verify the test and simulation tools with the same rigor as the deliverable items;*
- *verify the procedure that will handle test failures.*

Design and production verification

In producing a complex product, integration and verification may be repeated several times (Figure 5.4). Firstly, the process certifies that the design is satisfactory by testing the development models, giving clearance to

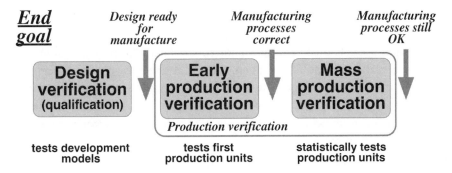

Figure 5.4: Design verification to production verification

manufacture operational units (**design verification**). When the production units are built, a similar process tests them to certify that the manufacturing process is working satisfactorily (**production verification**). Verification occurs after this to check mass-production units, and even during repair and upgrade. Testing costs are optimized across all the development and production units. In a mass-produced system, this means intense design verification to reduce the cost of testing each mass-production unit. Because software manufacture is a trivial process, each unit is exactly the same and hence design and production verification are amalgamated.

Design verification certifies that the design meets the requirements and that the product will work correctly if it is manufactured properly. During system integration, tests are performed against all levels of design, and may require construction of mock-ups and rigs for high-risk design areas.

For example, on a satellite development, separate test rigs will verify the data management system, shake the satellite model to simulate the launch conditions, and test against the vacuum and temperatures of outer space. Prototype equipment on the rig may be stress-tested, sometimes even to destruction to show what fails first and how it fails. The net product of this work is design verification, that is clearance to produce flight models according to the current design.

Usually about three satellites are then built – an engineering model, a qualification model and the system which actually goes into space. The engineering model is used as a test-bed while the qualification model is essentially identical to the flight model. Testing of the qualification model is only to the expected operational margins, whereas the engineering model may be stress-tested. The flight model is tested only to check the quality of the manufacturing process. Any 'dangerous' tests are therefore performed on the engineering model, not the flight model. No risk of over-stressing the flight model can be taken. The qualification model acts as a back-up to be raided for sub-systems, or to be brought up to flight quality if the first launch fails. For a mass-produced product, like a car, there may be dozens of each type of model.

Qualification models must be equivalent to the final system. For instance, the seats for a plane may not have been chosen at the design verification stage. To verify the aircraft design, the seat fittings, physical connectors, and the loadings on the aircraft must, however, be completely representative of the final system. Verification of the seat design can then come after the system – level verification of the aircraft.

Production verification checks that the system has been manufactured correctly (Figure 5.5) – at this stage the design no longer needs to be tested. In the early stage of production, units may be heavily tested, while in mass-production individual units will be much more lightly tested, or tested only by random sampling. For software products, testing is primarily a matter of design verification; some 'production' testing will be needed to ensure that manuals and disks have been replicated correctly.

Verification is about facts, not opinions

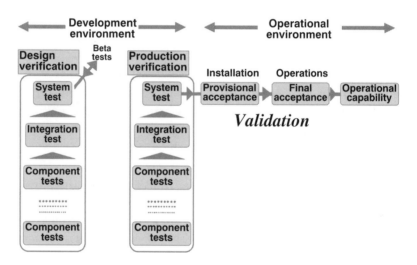

Figure 5.5: Multi-level verification for design and production

5.2.   Integration and verification

Multiple levels of verification

In the test process, the procedures are run against the components, checking the results against what was expected. A single requirement may need to be verified by multiple tests at several levels. For example, an integrated circuit in a video recorder will be tested as a chip, tested again as part of a circuit board, and again as part of the complete video recorder. The chip may be tested functionally at a range of temperatures or may be shaken to test the build quality. Figure 5.6 shows how a single requirement is related to many tests. The overall status of a requirement changes with respect to its tests as the tests are defined and the results emerge from the tests. For example, the status of a requirement might step between 'tests not defined', 'not yet started', 'not yet finished', 'pass', and 'fail'. Links between the requirements and the tests that

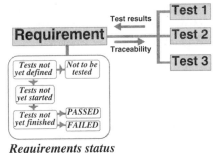

Requirements status against test

Figure 5.6: Requirement status and tests

check them are now used to flow back information used to calculate the test status of the requirement. Requirements are verified by analysis or comparison in combination, as well as by testing the physical components. Figure 5.7 summarizes the characteristics of different levels of testing.

Component-level verification checks a component against the design specification. In a complex system, components will exist at multiple levels and so therefore will component-level testing. The more modular the design, the more comprehensive the component-level testing can be.

Integration-level verification checks the interfaces and control mechanisms of the system against the architectural design. Integration tests should test all internal and external interfaces, data flows and control structures, and the interactions with external systems.

System-level verification checks the finished product against tests based on the system requirements. Some aspects can be tested only at the system level, particularly those involving end-to-end scenarios or overall system behavior. For instance on a car, the most difficult aspects to test are the overall aesthetics and 'feel' of the vehicle. These requirements can be confirmed only

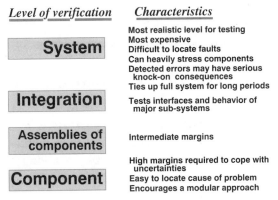

Figure 5.7: Characteristics of different verification levels

with full-scale, realistic vehicles. Undesirable emergent properties caused by interactions between system components need to be detected and eradicated. System-level testing is expensive, but very desirable to provide confidence.

Handling test failures

Inevitably some elements will fail their tests, and a formal management procedure is needed to manage the consequences. Failures are documented on non-conformance reports (NCRs), and the consequences tracked back to the highest system level affected by the failure. Requirements traceability also helps test engineers understand the strategy behind the tests, and comprehend the consequences of the test failures. Where changes are needed, an engineering change request (ECR) is made, estimating the costs and merit of the changes, followed by a technical proposal for the work. At component-level, correction of faults is relatively cheap and rapid. Faults detected at system level will usually have serious side-effects. For example, if an engine turns out to be too powerful for its drive shaft, large-scale changes may be necessary to both components, even though both parts had apparently passed their individual tests. The same may be true for the brakes, engine mountings, and clutch.

The test plan must cover what happens if the test fails

In a perfect world, a failure would cause the test process to stop until the problem is repaired, and tests would then resume. In practice, fixes are normally made rapidly, testing continues, and these fixes are documented in a non-conformance report. 'Regression testing' attempts to provide thorough coverage with a minimum of repeated testing when corrections are made after a test failure.

Provisional acceptance

The acceptance data package for the provisional acceptance therefore consists of:

- *the installed and tested system;*
- *the configuration status;*
- *the outputs of all previous processes;*
- *a statement of provisional acceptance (i.e. readiness of the system for operational use);*
- *transfer document (including a summary of acceptance test results);*
- *verified test tools.*

The process formally closes when the review process is finished for these documents, i.e. all agreed changes have been implemented. In planning integration and verification, contingency should be set aside to cope with the expected level of test failures (it will not be zero!).

5.3.   Building the verification system

Verification aims to detect non-conformance between the product and its specification as efficiently as possible. The test system therefore forms an associated system which has to be built. The verification system has its own life cycle driven by requirements to efficiently test the system and its components.

Figure 5.8 shows the development of a verification system for a relatively complex product. Development of the test system is constrained by the life cycle of the system itself. In some cases, it may take as much effort as developing the product. The requirements for the verification system are derived directly from acceptance criteria attached to each user requirement, the verification requirements from the system requirements and the integration test requirements from the architectural design. Starting from these requirements, a logical model of the test system is produced, followed by design and implementation of the test equipment and software. In some cases, expensive test facilities may be re-used across developments.

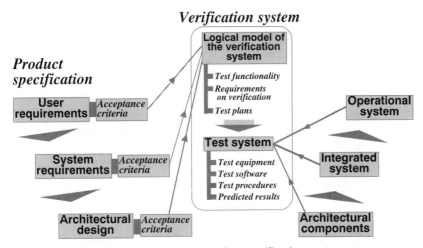

Figure 5.8: Development of the verification system

You cannot design tests in any sort of detail until you know WHAT end products you have to test – i.e. until the configuration items for the main system product are defined. Although verification work starts in the user requirements process with the capture of acceptance criteria, detailed test cases can be devised only after the architectural design is firm, for example while the components are being developed (Figure 5.9).

The verification system consists of the test equipment, special test harnesses, software, documentation, test scenarios and test staff. Normally the same

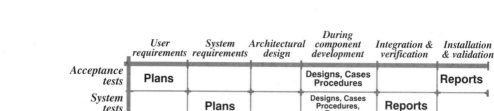

	User requirements	System requirements	Architectural design	During component development	Integration & verification	Installation & validation
Acceptance tests	Plans			Designs, Cases Procedures		Reports
System tests		Plans		Designs, Cases Procedures, Reports	Reports	
Integration tests			Plans	Designs, Cases Procedures, Reports		
Component tests				Designs, Cases Procedures, Reports		

Time

Figure 5.9: Developing the verification system

verification system is designed as a complete entity for use by all system levels.

The test environment effectively simulates the operational environment as faithfully as possible. If equipment is modular, and can be checked through its interface, then the equipment can be tested as though it were in its operational environment (Figure 5.10).

Most problems of integration are due to poor design, revealed late

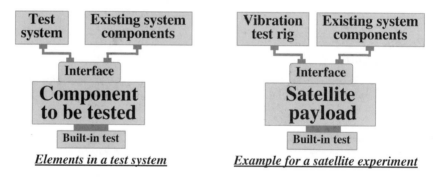

Elements in a test system   *Example for a satellite experiment*

Figure 5.10: Verification system elements

Integration path

Verification might take the components, integrate them together and test the assembly, i.e. the assembly order could be the inverse of the design decomposition. In practice, integration is rarely this straightforward; for example, components will often be tested against a specific test rig. With a plane, the electrical harness will be installed, and then tested itself using a test set. The harness can then be used to test other pieces of equipment as they are introduced into the plane. A single component such as the landing gear contains parts of the much larger hydraulic, electrical, and data management systems. This component has to be tested as an entity, but these elements have to be tested as part of their sub-systems. Some components can be best tested with parts of the system already working, or need specific test rigs to enable them to be checked. For example, a test rig for a satellite will shake the whole system to check it can survive launch. The integration plan defines the order in which the equipment is integrated and tested. The integration approach is planned while the components are being constructed.

Often one component will be needed to test another, and while the test happens, both parts are being tested. Such implicit testing is almost 'free', and should be maximized. The only problem is the likelihood of mis-diagnosing the source of any fault. Parts of the test system may be built into the product, to allow self-checking during operations. These built-in test (BIT) components need to be tested themselves, and also can be useful during the testing of the product.

5.4. *Installation and validation*

Once the completed product has satisfactorily completed all its tests in the factory, it can then be installed in the operational environment ready for validation. Validation, or acceptance as it is often called, ensures that the operational capability meets the user requirements. Although validation is performed in a largely operational environment, for reasons of economy some parts of the external environment may still be simulated. For instance in a large air traffic control or air defense system, the early stages of acceptance testing may use either simulated radar data or even recordings of previous live data.

Installation and validation may be involved and difficult. Sometimes (e.g. for a house or a telecommunications system) the system is assembled in situ in the operational environment, even when every system is 'different'. A mix of standard components may be integrated on site with 'glue' components. In cases, as for a plane, the first version of a product is completed in a factory and gradually introduced into a real operational environment in stages. Each large-scale telecommunication system is a different design made from standard components. Deployment and test of a telecommunications system across a city will need full-scale tests of the equipment, people and billing systems in the real environment. Interaction between the installation team and the real users always causes surprises, and some hard-bitten engineers believe that operational testing is the only worthwhile test.

Building a house provides another example of an installation strategy for a complex individually-designed product. Intricate components, such as the central heating boiler, will have been tested at the factory. The central heating system cannot even be constructed until the frame of the house is ready, and the water and the electricity supplies are working. The electrical supply is the 'harness' and many components cannot be tested until it is ready.

For a satellite, operational checkout takes place after the satellite has been launched. Although it is too late to change the satellite hardware, both the ground station and the on-board software can still be (carefully) adjusted if minor problems are found. For commercial products, installation procedures are needed to help users through the options. Installation and manuals should therefore be tested before use. Requirements for manuals are primarily derived from the definition of user types in the user requirements. On-line or telephone help should be provided for installation wherever possible.

Installation and validation is, in general, a three-step process. The first step entails installing a fully tested system into its operational environment. This must be a 'clean' environment not polluted by previous installations, particularly for software. The next two steps are validation activities. The initial validation step involves running the acceptance tests in a stage-managed situation with well-defined scripts for each operator. When all these tests have been run successfully, the system can be certified for initial operational use. At this point the system can be used operationally, but there are likely to be some user requirements which can only be validated after a period of operational use (e.g. availability). Therefore the system is limited in its operational use until these aspects can be certified, using part of the test system and most of the operational support systems. The system then achieves full acceptance and enters full operational use. The steps are summarized in Figure 5.11, which also show the progressive integration with the support systems to provide the operational capability.

You may be forgiven for delivering late, but not for delivering a poor product

Provisional acceptance certifies that the completed product meets its system and user requirements in the real environment under test conditions. Provisional acceptance tests are performed against a system representative of the production units. Passing this test gives clearance for provisional operations of the complete system. During provisional operations, the development team is on stand-by to correct small problems, but the system is now under the control of the operations staff. Provisional acceptance may still

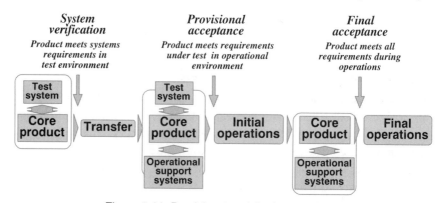

Figure 5.11: Provisional and final acceptance

happen even with small non-critical faults, which are then cleared as soon as practical.

Final acceptance certifies that the customer agrees that the system meets its user requirements during actual operational use, i.e. in the working environment. The system has been integrated with all the operational support systems. The development role is finished, unless a product upgrade is required immediately.

For a mass-produced product, the provisional operations stage is replaced by the guarantee period. If a fault occurs, the onus is still on the producer to repair the system.

5.5.   *Alpha and beta-tests*

However intensely testing is done, it can never flush out all the faults in a system. The operational environment and the actions taken by end users are so unpredictable that they can never be covered completely by testing. But you do not want to release an imperfect product to all of the user community. Alpha- and beta-testing (sometimes called field testing) can reduce the pain caused by faults by several orders of magnitude. Alpha-testing is testing by members of the customer-side organization. Beta-testing is testing by friendly, but real, end-users.

You cannot avoid field testing – the only question is whether it is planned or unplanned. If you do not plan to have beta-tests, the first end users will be the unwilling guinea pigs for a system that has never been tested in a wide range of operational conditions. Failures are likely to be embarrassing and expensive.

Policy for alpha- and beta-testing

Beta-testing has to be a managed process, with the objective of reducing the overall risk and costs of system problems – where cost includes costs of repair, loss of reputation with customer. These costs have to be balanced against the business losses caused by time and effort taken for alpha and beta-testing.

It is easy to spend effort on beta-testing without generating useful results – i.e. detecting problems. You should choose and encourage users who will really detect faults, through intensive use of the system. The product has to be exposed to as many dimensions of use as is feasible – different kinds of users, varying kinds of use, different countries, different language support or computer equipment, and different weather conditions. PC software released by one of the authors had problems on a specific brand of computer caused by a fault on its serial port. Nevertheless, users (correctly) blamed the problem on failure to perform the tests on that specific equipment.

Users have to understand that beta-systems are not production quality equipment. Beta-testers need to be painstaking and pedantic, but positive as well. ISO 9001 insists on a contractual arrangement between the supplier and the beta-test user. The overall fault detection rate should be monitored, from individual sites, and those sites that are not detecting faults should be culled. The major objective of beta-testing is detection of the faults in the equipment – operational confidence is a useful, but expensive, by-product. Beta-testing should therefore be optimized to trigger any key problems.

The underlying concept is that beta-testing is excellent for revealing multiple, small-scale faults. Beta-testing is unsuitable for managing severe, structural problems, because they take too long to correct. Therefore, do not use beta-testing as a prime mechanism for finding faults – it is too expensive and too late.

You do not have to be pleasant to do verification – in fact it might help if you are not

The problems that are flushed out initially by beta-testing will tend to be immediate, obvious, easy to locate, severe, and generic to most operational environments. These early faults can usually be cured quickly, and a new release rapidly re-cycled into the beta-test. Later problems will affect a smaller proportion of users, be more difficult to tease out, more subtle, specific to the environment, harder to locate and (generally) less catastrophic in their impact. In the initial stages, beta-testing is limited by the ability to correct faults. In the second part, it is constrained by the ability to find faults. Resources are therefore switched from curing problems to finding them. Early beta-tests therefore need short cycle times and only a few test sites, which should be local to the developers.

A problem detected and eliminated when there are five users is far less expensive to cure than if there are 1,000 users. Moreover, you have avoided inflicting the pain of this problem on 995 of the users. Figure 5.12 shows the

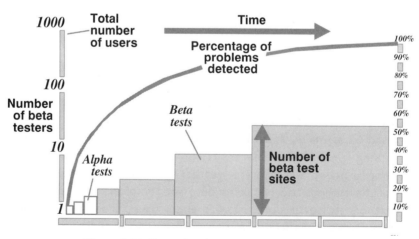

Figure 5.12: Detecting faults through beta-testing

release cycle for beta-testing, with the number of users increasing exponentially, and time spent per release growing steadily. Early beta (or alpha) iterations should therefore be short, intense, local, and heavily supported. Later beta-tests will be the converse – longer, larger, more variable, and with many more users.

The largest investment made in beta-testing involves the costs due to the calendar time needed – the 'delay' in introducing the product. Installing a product for beta-testers, training users, getting news about the problems, correcting the faults, then releasing a new version takes weeks even for a software product. Consequently beta-testing should usually be organized to minimize calendar time, even at the cost of extra resources. Compressing the early beta release cycles, and using a more parallel approach than shown in the figure can cut calendar time. Design verification and production verification should overlap, and beta-testing therefore has to be handled concurrently rather than sequentially. But the product has to be good enough for release, because the cost of offending users is even higher.

5.6.   Project history

If a business does not learn from the experience of projects, it cannot hope to improve its overall effectiveness. The **project history** is one of the main mechanisms for this learning process (Figure 5.13). This information compares what actually happened with the original plans – the overall performance, size,

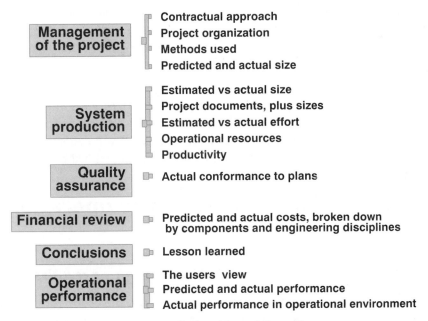

Figure 5.13: Project history information

schedule and cost of the system compared to what was planned. The document should be written before the end of the installation and validation process. shows a suitable structure.

Unfortunately, project history information is rarely documented well, and typically this is the only document handled worse than the user requirements. Development staff from the 'completed' project are always dragged on to new projects, and the last thing anyone wants is to document what went wrong on their previous project. Valuable information is thus lost. The organization has to demand project histories, and use the results to improve the process if it wants staff to actually produce the information.

5.7. Summary

Success in integration, verification, installation and validation is highly dependent on work that should have happened before these processes start. If the early systems engineering work has been mis-handled, problems will appear as this process gets underway. A clear set of requirements and a modular design with strongly defined interfaces are pre-requisites for success.

Quality can never be tested into a product – it must be required from the start, designed in, then implemented. Nevertheless verification and validation should catch as many of the remaining problems as possible.

Verification and validation needs skills in analysis, attention to detail, and a nose for digging out inconsistencies. The objective is to detect problems at as low a cost as early as possible. The attitude to verification and validation is critical. If it is obvious that you will not let any low quality item through, then everyone will have a different attitude to the product. Verification and validation is a continuous task and a state of mind from the beginning of the project. Verification should be done at as low a level as possible, and as early as possible, preferably before the error has even been made.

Full operational capability is achieved only when the system is integrated with the other supporting systems in the operational environment. The quality of the final system, and the effort needed for integration will depend strongly on how well the supporting systems and their interaction with the core product were initially defined.

Exercises for integration to operations

Exercise 14: Do we test against design or requirements?

Consider the following arbitrary requirement, where the user basically wants as high a value as possible. Ignore the cost aspects for this exercise.
The requirement from the user was for 'at least 120 per second under all

circumstances' (whatever the requirement is). The user will not pay for more than 120 per second, but will be happy if the value is higher. The design (with margin) was for 160 per second. The test at the factory of the first pre-production model revealed 140 per second.
One thousand of these systems will be produced over the next year.

> *State what, if anything, needs to be done.*

> *State the reasons that the design was higher than the user requirements.*

> *What key value is missing from this question?*

Exercise 15: Accepting the completed system

You have a new task to verify (and decide whether to accept) a complex computerized command and control system for your business. This has been under construction for five years. The chances of failure are high, with embarrassing repercussions all round. The contractor seems to be working very hard and claims to be losing money on the contract.
Remember you are responsible for the test.
Write your approach to acceptance when:

> *1: There is a good set of requirements for the system;*

> *2: There is no longer a relevant set of requirements.*

In case b) the original requirements were a muddle of requirements and design, went out of date quickly and were not updated, and the project was then controlled through the design, including managing design changes.

Exercise 16: Defining test requirements

Write three requirements that might be imposed on the verification system by the product that is being developed. Define which document in which these requirements should appear. State who is responsible for these requirements.
Write three requirements that the verification system might impose on the product being developed. Explain if these are likely to alter the final product in a positive or negative way.
State who is responsible for defining these requirements.
When should these requirements be written, and where should they be stored?
Is the project manager free to reject these requirements?

Exercise 17: Defining test policy

You are a manager with responsibility for several large software projects at a software company such as Microsoft. Write 5 requirements that you might like to impose on the development process for all major products. Describe the likely reaction from the project managers. How would you verify that the requirements are being applied in practice?

Exercise 18: Alpha and beta-test policy

You are the customer for a PC communication system (both hardware & software) for use by about 1,000 people across many different countries. The complete communication system is just finishing its systems tests in the development environment of the contractor who is implementing the system for you.

The system is a communication package (hardware and software) for a group of aerospace scientists to exchange information internationally.

You are sure that the system will have some bugs, but it is critical that the impact of faults on users is minimal.

Define a multi-stage process for eliminating these problems and:

state the number of beta sites for each stage;

state the time needed for each stage;

define the tasks needed to resource each stage;

Exercise 19: Estimating the remaining faults

Two testers independently check out your system. Tester A finds 40 faults, and tester B finds 30 faults. Ten of the faults that they find are common. Estimate how many faults remain in the system, and generate a general formula for this case.

State the assumptions that are behind that formula.

Exercise 20: Humans in the final system

You are involved in a large fixed-price contract for a system which involves a high degree of operator interaction. You are negotiating the final acceptance tests and the contractor refuses to accept any responsibility for the outcome of tests which depend on the skill of the operators.

Who is in the right?

Could this have been avoided, if so how?

Exercise 21: System integration problems

'The problems of system integration are caused by design'.
Discuss this proposition, and define a set of likely causes of problems that will be encountered during integration, and classify them in terms of likely impact and likelihood.

Project management and systems engineering

six

6.1. Introduction

This chapter covers the links between systems engineering and project management. It is not a treatise on project management, because there already are hundreds of books on that subject. But project management in the absence of systems engineering is meaningless, and the ties between the two disciplines have not been well documented. Moreover, in the sorts of multi-level projects discussed in later chapters, systems engineering will actually shape management across a complete project. The two disciplines are primarily linked through the project deliverables, whether end products or documentation (Figure 6.1).

Time to market – but with the right product

Project management and systems engineering are highly inter-dependent, because every technical decision has a management consequence and vice-versa. Systems engineering defines the deliverables; these are the objects handled by project management and which come together to satisfy the requirements and integrate to form a complete system. Systems engineering bonds the requirements and the design to the deliverables, against which progress can then be assessed. The project management information involves costs, schedule and quality and work, all are attached to the same deliverable structure.

Figure 6.1: Quality, cost and schedule

Perhaps the core difference between the two disciplines lies in the fact that the systems engineering role is responsible for creating, defining and improving the product. This involves definition of requirements and architecture of the system, so that cost estimation and risk management can be handled by project management. The project management role is more concerned with the delivery of that system on time and to schedule.

In fact, a number of management disciplines are needed. These are project management, configuration management, verification and validation and quality assurance. Systems engineering generates the information which allows the product to be organized into deliverables by configuration management. Project management then controls the development through those deliverables, while verification and validation uses the deliverables as the elements that are tested. Quality assurance monitors that the project plans and enterprise process standards are being followed within the project. All of these key roles must be single-point responsibilities – i.e. one (and only one) person is in charge of each role, although one person can have more than one role. The end result is that each deliverable is linked to cost, schedule and its requirements.

What is a project?

This book is constructed around the concept of a 'project', a temporary creation brought into being to implement specific goals. At the end of the project, the team dissolves back into the business that spawned it. The concept of working within projects may seem self-evident, but we often come across industrial developments where it is absent. In some cases, responsibility for success is spread across several departments, each with control of their component parts, their finance and staff. Needless to say, this approach rarely works effectively.

The advantage of not managing projects is that failure comes as a complete surprise, not preceded by months of worry
– Sir John Harvey Jones

The control mechanism for a project is the management plan, completed before the end of each stage and controlling the next. This plan documents the deliverables, schedule, tasks, responsibilities, applicable standards, cost estimates and resources. Figure 6.2 illustrates the information that must be covered in a management plan. An overall plan can be produced at the start of the project, but must be updated and reviewed periodically at major stages, and more often if necessary. Management plans must be centered around the deliverables to be produced, with the schedule, responsibilities, and necessary work to create those deliverables. Risks to project success are identified and the mechanisms for monitoring progress are defined in the plan.

Each project needs a single project manager with responsibility for its success, to ensure everything gets done, but not necessarily do it personally. This involves leading the project, delegating authority where necessary, producing realistic plans, ensuring they are implemented, monitoring the development

Configuration item structure — **What** items are to be developed and integrated

Schedule — **When** they will be delivered

Organizational breakdown structure — **Who** will produce them

Work breakdown structure — **What work** is needed to make, manage & test them

Cost breakdown structure — **How much** they will cost

Process standards — **What standards** apply to the work

Process choice — **What lifecycle** will the development follow?

Figure 6.2: Contents of the management plan

and keeping it on track. The project manager handles 'external' elements, such as the customer, the enterprise, and related projects.

The core difference between systems engineering and project management lies in this role. The system engineer is the technical authority responsible for defining the product – capturing and organizing the requirements, creating and improving the architectural design, ensuring consistency and balance between all parts. The project manager is responsible for ensuring this work is done, but not for doing it.

Whoever controls the budget is the project manager

6.2.   Project management tasks

The project manager has the responsibility for planning and controlling the following tasks:

Leading the project and creating a good working atmosphere is the essence of good management. Good people, working together as a team, can make a success of anything, as long as the manager points them in the right direction. The manager has to keep the staff enthusiastic, especially when things look really tough for the project. Even if a development appears impossible, high quality staff can transform its nature and then make it a success. Making painful decisions is part and parcel of management, and it requires good information, leadership, communication skills, and good timing. The manager must be able to take actions that are painful for an individual, but essential for the project.

Plans are useless, planning is vital

Planning the project is a core management task. Plans are based upon deliverables and milestones – delivering the item on the right day, at the right cost and meeting all the requirements for that deliverable. ***Process definition*** defines the life cycle and its deliverables (see Chapter 7).

Projects succeed through advance ***preparation***. Nothing should come as a surprise to the well-prepared project manager. Every project management task involves risk management, prediction of what is likely to happen, and preparatory effort.

The project manager therefore needs to **monitor progress** and re-align the project and its plans, whenever the two drift apart. Metrics need to be defined and collected, to predict the likely course of the project.

The project manager **chooses the methods and tools** to be used for project management, getting the tools and training the staff so that they are ready for action when needed.

The project manager is in charge of **spending, budgeting and cost estimation**, transforming the initial targets into more solid estimates based on the components when these are known. The project manager is responsible for what is spent, but the costs are obviously affected by the results of systems engineering work. For many systems, the cost of operations and disposal may dwarf the development costs. There may be a tendency to cut development costs without awareness of the impact on operations and close-down costs. The business requirements must lay down a clear organizational policy to be followed.

Most developments are high risk, and hence **risk management** pervades all project management work. Hazards have to be identified and evaluated, and risk mitigation performed.

The project manager **allocates roles and responsibilities** to individuals, particularly the responsibilities for development, configuration management, verification and validation, and quality assurance. The plan defines the tasks and allocates the staff responsibility for performing them.

Staff capability is perhaps the critical element in success, and so the project manager is responsible for ensuring that **staff training, and choice of staff** are satisfactory for the system. The manager should identify the skill set needed to successfully complete the system, compare that with the current staff and organize to meet the differences.

Managing all the elements outside the project, including negotiating with suppliers, and managing contracts, is a major component of management work. You have to keep your customer on your side. Strong interaction with the enterprise helps generate support for the project within the development organization. This task combines reporting and marketing, and absorbs a substantial proportion of a project manager's time.

Change is inevitable during the course of a project, and so **change management** needs to be handled coherently. This needs to be a formal process, examining the costs and benefits of making a change before committing to it. Weak change management leads to continual 'requirements creep' and eventually destroys the whole system. Managing change is a classic example of needing to consider the system as a whole. Every individual change

The Commanding General is well aware that the forecasts are no good. However, he needs them for planning purposes[36]

If the plan is not realistic, it is a dream, not a plan

may seem sensible, but in total they may be impossible, and an individually sensible change has to be sacrificed for the common good.

Project management and project control

Project management is sometimes naively considered in terms of software planning packages for 'project management', but this misses the essence of the role. Project management is not about drawing Gantt charts, but leading and preparing the project, negotiating practical agreements, pointing it in the right direction, yet delegating as much as possible. Project control is important, but there is little benefit in managing cost and delivery dates if the deliverables do not do what the customer wants.

'Management of projects' is a broader term which covers every issue, including systems engineering (Figure 6.3). Project management starts before the boundaries of the system are fully defined. It shapes the system, manages the risk, chooses the staff, manages the budget, plans and monitors the project, and reorganizes it if it goes off track. Current project management tools are of little help in shaping the system until the deliverables and their requirements are known, and yet these deliverables are not defined until the architectural design process is over – probably more than half way through the project. By the time that architectural design is firm, the decisions with the highest impact have already been taken.

Milestones = deliverables + schedule

Figure 6.3: Management of projects

6.3. Configuration management

Configuration management is the foundation for project management and the tie back to systems engineering. It helps co-ordinate the work and ensure reproducibility of any system state. The discipline defines and controls the configuration items (CIs), and the intermediate products produced during development. CIs are also referred to less formally as deliverables or outputs. The name configuration item arises as these are the items that are actually worked on during development – the pieces that fit together to form the system.

Configuration management is critical for work efficiency on any but the smallest systems[37] and, unless it is done properly, effort is wasted for reasons such as:

- *two people simultaneously working on the same element;*
- *large amounts of repetitive information stored just in case ;*
- *outright loss of components or information;*

- *inability to reproduce a design, a version or a set of tests;*
- *difficulty of accessing an item or information to work on it;*
- *changes to components that should have been locked ;*
- *work on obsolete versions;*
- *inability to find out what happened or who made a change;*
- *inconsistent versions of requirements, design and products.*

The configuration items actually built may differ subtly from the design structure, because of changes needed for build and assembly strategy. Consider an aircraft with similar components such as electrical motors scattered across the design. A single aircraft might have 50 motors of several different types. These motors are not ordered or delivered separately, but as a complete set of 50 for each aircraft. The plane manufacturer accepts a single CI from the supplier with the 50 motors, rather than controlling production at a lower level of detail.

The configuration item structure defines what is actually to be built and it therefore occupies a central role. It ties together the product definition, the development system, the production system that replicates the product, the verification system, and the operational support systems (Figure 6.4). However, the definition of each of these systems must influence the definition of the rest.

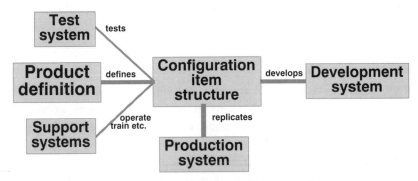

Figure 6.4: Configuration item structure links to other systems

CIs are the components that are tested, and successful completion of that test represents a milestone. The CIs are then assembled into larger CIs, making the CI structure the basis of integration. Figure 6.5 shows how the planned schedule is tied to the deliverables. The configuration item structure is logically identical to the Gantt chart, assuming that every task in the Gantt chart produces one or more deliverables. The big advantage of being able to transfer information between a Gantt chart and a CI structure is that the deliverables can now be linked to requirements.

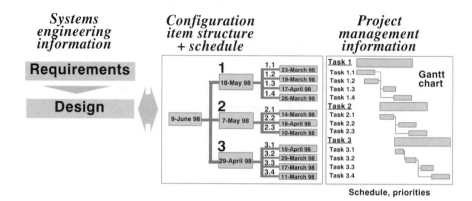

Figure 6.5: Linking the product to project management

Managing change

Every part of the development is subject to change, and the project management team must have a policy on how to cope. Each proposed change should be documented in a change proposal, and put under configuration management control. At intervals, decisions should be made about the collection of changes. These decisions should be taken by a 'change control board' appointed by the project manager. On small systems this 'board' may just be the project manager, while on larger systems many disciplines are involved in deciding whether a change is sensible or not. Drip-feeding changes into a system causes maximum confusion, and so normally changes are evaluated in batches.

Baselines

Another core concept is the use of a communal **baseline**, the product on which everyone works. The baseline is usually a complete version of the system, but can also represent sub-trees being worked on communally. Developers working on part of the system need to exercise it against a stable version of the rest of the system.

The process of configuration management is much easier if the interfaces of configuration items are handled independently from their internal aspects. Other developers can then work to a stable interface even if the internal elements of other components change.

The overall system baseline always lags behind the most recent versions (Figure 6.6) of individual components. Access to the latest baseline may cure some faults plaguing an individual developer but introduce others. Changing the baseline is therefore a compromise between **stability** and **currency**. **Consistency** across a baseline provides everyone with a stable platform

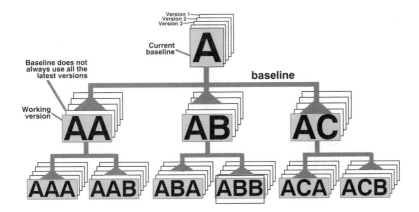

Figure 6.6: Baselines and configuration items

against which to check their own work. On the other hand, we need a system which is as up-to-date as possible.

Work can be wasted on testing old versions of design, if for example, a program compiles outdated code or an engineer builds to the wrong design. Modern software tools can compile automatically on charge-in, avoiding inconsistencies, but this option is not open to hardware systems. Consistency can take many forms, such as:

— *design and production items;*

— *requirements and architectural design traceability;*

— *test plans and results;*

— *documentation and software.*

Summary on configuration management

Configuration management is sometimes thought of in mechanistic terms, but the benefits are so high it should be handled carefully. The discipline ties systems engineering to project management. Configuration management enables work to be efficiently partitioned to different individuals and organizations.

6.4. Verification and validation

The discipline of verification and validation determines whether the system meets its original specifications. Verification involves checking products against their specifications (Figure 6.7). This is true of end products, but system information needs to be checked for consistency. For example, the design must meet the system requirements. Validation is end-to-end verification i.e. meeting the user requirements in the operational environment.

Tasks of verification and validation include:

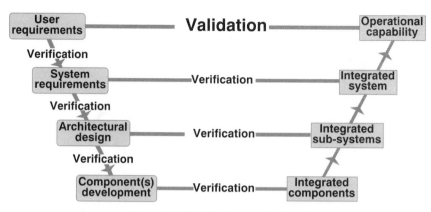

Figure 6.7: Verification and validation

defining the verification requirements – defines the principles on how the system will be tested. For example, the verification requirements define the emphasis on inspection or test, on component test or system test, and what risks the business will tolerate.

planning the verification – this involves all of the planning and preparation for the verification.

Verify as early as possible at as low a level as possible

capturing the verification criteria – verification criteria need to be captured when requirements are defined.

test methods and tools are planned and provided by the V&V function at the system level.

review management – the planning and running of reviews are typically handled by V&V for the project manager, because reviews verify the output product, either against standards or the product under review.

implementing and performing the tests and managing the results. V&V manages the tests.

traceability allows us to answer questions about why something is being done, to check that the right things are actually being done. Traceability needs to be maintained back to the requirements, to ensure that the final system will meet the requirements of the customer.

auditing is needed to check the reality of what is happening against the documentation. Systems engineering is primarily based on delegation and trust, but auditing is the check to make sure that we are not too trusting. Every project needs to analyze future likely problems, and check what is really happening against what is being reported.

Different kinds of reviews

Review is a verification activity – it checks outputs to ensure they are consistent with inputs. Three levels of review are:

- *technical review (chapter 2);*
- *walkthroughs;*
- *inspections.*

Technical reviews cover the whole system as an entity. The complete output of the current process is reviewed for compatibility with all previous documentation. Other smaller, reviews are essential and can improve the system enormously for relatively little effort.

Intermediate reviews examine the structure of documents or design before the formal review. Any problems picked up at this stage can be eliminated at low cost, compared with finding them at the process review. These structural reviews need not be formal, nor take long.

Inspections and walkthroughs

Walkthroughs are pre-review efforts aiming to detect and then suppress detailed problems by stepping though the documentation and testing it for problems. The working atmosphere must be moderated and blame-free – the aim is to find problems before the requirements or design are fixed. This is much less expensive than finding errors in the end product[12]. Subsidiary aims include education of the engineers involved in the process, for example by suppressing errors of style.

Inspection is a formal process, and suitable for handling ANY documentation (requirements, design, source code for software). The theory was initially documented by Michael Fagan at IBM (1974) and is covered well by Gilb[38]. Inspection is performed by a team of developers checking the documentation. The manager of the team is in charge of the process. Inspections must be comparative, i.e. documents are always evaluated against some pre-defined qualities, rules or a checklist (Figure 6.8).

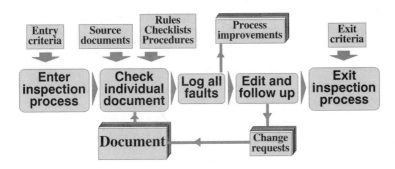

Figure 6.8: The inspection process for project documents

Inspection must be a measured process – this means logging all defects and their severity, and the effectiveness of the overall process. Inspection is not started until the document reaches pre-defined entry criteria. Similarly the document must be good enough for release, i.e. it meets pre-defined exit criteria. After the inspection, brainstorming techniques can find the root cause of problems – and stop them re-occurring. Training for inspections has been shown to produce improved documentation. Inspection can easily degenerate into wasted effort on trivial faults (grammar, spelling) and it is often poor at detecting omissions, because these are only weakly implied by surrounding material. Other types of review such as brainstorming or simulating system behavior may be better at flushing out these kinds of faults.

Inspection is exhausting and so short, controlled meetings are all that are practical – two hours is about the maximum time that developers can retain concentration. The severity of each defect should be classified. Inspection is slow, painstaking and expensive, but practitioners such as Gilb claim that:

- *inspection is extremely cost-effective (5–10 times cheaper than testing at finding faults);*
- *quality is higher (fewer defects);*
- *maintenance cost is lower.*

As with many aspects of verification, the real message is in the sub-text, not the text. Knowing that your colleagues will inspect your work concentrates the mind wonderfully, and many faults will be removed by developers themselves in advance of the inspection. Inspection is also an excellent mechanism for educating engineers in good style.

6.5. Quality assurance

As the name implies, quality assurance delivers confidence that an acceptable quality product will be produced. This is the most misunderstood management role. The task is essentially a monitoring role, done in support of the project manager. Quality assurance checks that the project can demonstrate it has done what it promised to do. In small systems, the role may be performed by the project manager. Quality can never be successfully imposed by an external organization or by testing.

However, quality assurance also has an enterprise perspective, i.e. ensuring that the enterprise is not exposed to excessive risks. Quality assurance must ensure that business standards are really applied in practice. This can lead to divergence of interests between project and enterprise, and therefore requires some tact. Sometimes the rules are not sensible in the context of the project. Quality assurance then becomes the link to obtain project-specific waivers for the project from the business.

The formal tasks of quality assurance include:

- *monitoring that business standards are applied;*
- *monitoring the implementation of the project s own plans;*
- *controlling the acceptance of deliverable items.*

The quality assurance role often acts as a reference center for methodology and process issues, for example the widely used ISO 9001 standards. By helping projects choose good processes, methods and tools, a good QA manager can often act to prevent problems much later. This role of preventing problems can be the most valuable aspect of quality assurance to the enterprise.

Auditing

Auditing is a specialized form of test, the objective of which is to check that the project is really doing what it says. Auditing is tough, so plan it out in detail, and leave enough margin to cover any problems. Auditing is a public event, and making a mistake in front of the group being audited destroys the aura of perfection for which auditors must strive. The key rule is that if something is not documented, it never happened. You might only have recorded it in your laboratory notebook, but if the standard says that notebooks are good enough, then it passes the audit.

Attempts to hide from an audit team are futile. Management may try to disguise the facts, but it takes only a short time for a competent audit team to find out the reality in a project. Audits should be done to pre-empt faulty procedures, not to find out why parts of faulty. Auditors need to think carefully about the goals for the audit before starting.

If it is not documented, it never happened – The Auditor

Both the project and the business are the beneficiaries of a successful audit. Good external auditors provide a clear view of the project status. Although the picture is always known subconsciously, auditors crystallize and document the situation in a way that makes it difficult to ignore. The objective is to detect problems and track them to their source. For instance, consider the situation where poor quality components are detected by a test procedure. An audit might track the reason to poor specifications, and then further back to a lack of training for the engineers who did the drawings. Detecting the problem after the parts are made causes severe project delays, expenditure on testing, expense of re-making the components, and the cost and delays in re-training the staff involved.

This would classically be logged as a component fault, but the underlying problem may be staff capability i.e. lack of training – a business failure in recruitment or training. Auditing the skills before the process started would be much better, together with training the staff in advance. Even better, the project manager should choose staff who already have the experience. Choosing untrained staff because they are cheaper is a classic mistake.

6.6.   *Decisions and risks*

This section covers decision-making and risk management within a systems engineering context. These two tasks are the foundation of systems engineering and pervade most management work.

Decision-making

The success or failure of a large system often turns around the outcome of five to ten key decisions. Ideally these critical choices should be identified, made rationally, at the right time, and communicated to those who need to know. Important decisions within projects are often made sub-consciously, individually, illogically, in the wrong order, or by the wrong people. Decisions are needed throughout the whole development process – on what life cycle to use, what design architecture to have, whether to develop internally or buy in equipment. Decisions might, for example, involve choosing between designs, commitment to a set of requirements, or accepting a plan to accept a set of risks. Decisions are commitments to future actions, i.e. plans are based on decisions, either implicitly or explicitly. A disciplined, documented process (such as the well-known Kepner-Tregoe[39] method) should be followed for identifying, then making the most important decisions.

Nothing is more difficult and precious than being able to decide – Napoleon

Decision-making is intimately involved with system information – decisions are made on the basis of requirements, and new requirements are 'derived' as a result. Every decision should be made by evaluating different solutions against a set of criteria. The criteria are themselves requirements – typically a summary of several individual requirements. For example, in evaluating the best way to get to work, we might consider comfort, cost, safety and reliability as the vital criteria. A decision to use a motorbike will lead to 'derived' requirements such as storage, training and clothing.

For example, in the ambulance system, a key decision might be:

Do we supply first-line medical help through ambulance staff or start to treat all cases only at the hospital? (Figure 6.9)

The criteria for making the decision might be effectiveness of treatment, costs, legal implications, staff availability etc. The decision might be to provide medical assistance in the ambulance, based on the rationale that early medical intervention is essential to saving lives. This will lead to requirements on the ambulance staff, the need to know about the available skills, need for training etc. The decision to perform the medical work solely at the hospital will lead to more stringent requirements on the time to transport patients. Decision-making occurs in different forms throughout the life cycle at different levels.

For instance, an organization might decide whether or not to proceed with a particular system. The **decision criterion** might be whether sufficient budget is available to proceed. The **decision options** could be to proceed with the

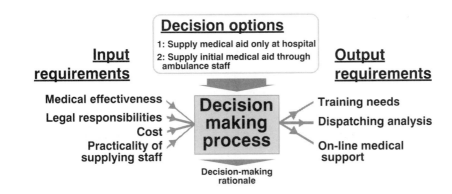

Figure 6.9: An example of decision-making and requirements

current system, cut its scope or cancel the project. At every stage of decomposing or adding new requirements, decisions are made between one option and another. The decision-making process chooses between different available **options (or alternatives)**, using information generated specifically for that purpose. The **criteria** are the basis upon which the decision is made, and the **rationale** is the set of reasons for choosing the winning options.

Risk management

Figure 6.10 illustrates risk management, a generic process across the whole development arena. Risk management is not necessarily tied to the project processes, but any problem or any decision that needs to be made can trigger it. However, risks also need to be checked at each stage boundary, generating a risk management plan for the next stage. Risk management is an integral part of the requirements and design stages, as engineers try to define what might go wrong and shape the system to reduce risk to acceptable levels.

Key concepts of risk management

In taking a risk, we are betting on an uncertain outcome. Opportunity is the opposite side of the coin to risk, and if the reward is high enough, a high risk approach may be the best policy. The essence of risk management lies in maximizing the areas of partial control, and minimization of areas where we have absolutely no control[40]. Risk management utilizes a range of concepts which need early definition. A **hazard** is the undesirable event that will affect the system quality, cost or schedule. The **risk** is the chance of that hazard occurring. The **associated cost** is the cost if the hazard actually does occur. **Risk exposure** is therefore the average likely impact of the hazard (= risk x associated cost), i.e. it indicates the overall size of the risk which is being

The key management skill is guessing the right answers with insufficient information

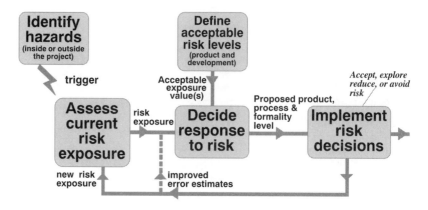

Figure 6.10: The risk management process

faced. **Contingency (or margin)** represents the total likely sum of all the exposures added together. The **estimated cost** is the predicted cost of the system without hazards. The most likely cost of the project is called the **expected cost** and is defined as **estimated cost + contingency**. The **associated value** is the benefit to be derived from taking the specific risk. These definitions are couched in financial terms, which is how they are often evaluated. Risks may however be evaluated in any unit appropriate for the problem, e.g. the number of days on the critical path, or the chance of an operational failure etc.

Put your resources into eliminating risks rather than trying to measure them exactly

A two-phase approach is often used to handle risk. Initially, a simple, comparative process is used repeatedly and informally to get close to the lowest risk, at which point a more quantitative risk management approach takes over.

Everyone should be continually scanning their domain to detect actual and potential hazards. Risk analysis has to be repeated through the development to mitigate risks as they emerge. Once a hazard is identified, it must be quantified and, if it is serious enough, dealt with.

Although it is logical and essential, risk management is not an exact science, but a means for applying intelligence. Each estimate of exposure should always be accompanied by an indication about the expected tolerance in that value. In practice, risk management is often recursive, dynamic, and concurrent. Resources in risk management should be spent on elimination or reduction of key risks first, not on trying to assess the risks too precisely.

Outline of the risk management process

Risk identification must never stop, and once a hazard is identified, the steps of the risk management process are:

- assessment of the current risk exposure;
- definition of an acceptable level of risk;
- decision-making on the response to the risk;
- implementing the decision (outside the scope of risk management).

During the initial **risk assessment** stage, potential hazards that can hurt the project should be identified and recorded, their chance of happening estimated, and the impact assessed. From this information, the total 'risk exposure' can be calculated, defining the level of risk faced by a system. Typically, this starts by generating a checklist of potential hazards (Figure 6.11). Risk involves the probability of loss or not receiving what we expect. When different kinds of risks need to be compared or prioritized, the risks need to be measured in consistent units – a process that inevitably leads to even greater tolerance in risk estimation.

Each project must **identify the acceptable level of risk.** This will be based on the policy for both the system and the business.

Deciding how to handle risk compares the actual risk with the acceptable risk, and decides whether to proceed with the current system and process definition, prototype, modify the system, or cancel it. These correspond to risk acceptance, risk exploration, risk mitigation and risk avoidance respectively. Risk can be avoided or eliminated, or the rewards from risk may

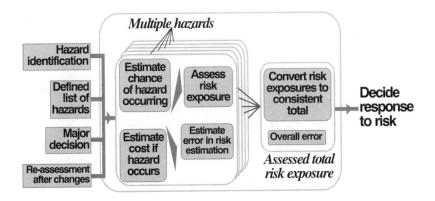

Figure 6.11: Assessing the risk exposure

make it worthwhile to take.

The *implementation* of a decision on handling risk is done within the project, but is outside the scope of risk management. The action may happen immediately or may be delayed until a hazard actually arises, in which case a pre-determined set of actions decided at the planning stage is activated. In some cases, the error in our knowledge of risk exposure may be high. *Prototyping or feasibility studies* can clarify those risks. In practice, these mitigation strategies will also tend to produce decisions and actions that reduce risk.

In other cases, the risk may not be acceptable currently, but by de-scoping the product or altering the life cycle, it may be possible to reduce the risk. *Modifying the product or process* is followed by a re-assessment of the risk. Process tailoring is covered in detail in chapter 7. The extreme case is to *cancel* the project, when the risk cannot be reduced to an acceptable level.

The outputs from risk management are **decisions** on what should happen to the project – proceed, modify, or cancel.

Summary of risk management

The best engineers and managers perform risk management continually and almost invisibly in all their work. Although the goal is reduction of risk, risk management can also generate useful system information. The end objective of risk management is to generate information for the main project to make decisions.

Risk management is highly formative in shaping the system. Before full commitment, risk management may re-shape the boundaries of the system, or cause a different bundle of requirements to be taken as the basis for the system.

6.7. Summary

Project management is core to system success or failure, and can be more important than any technical issue. Poor management can wreck any system, however good the engineering effort. Project management is meaningless unless it is tightly coupled to systems engineering. Successful project managers and system engineers repeatedly apply commonsense risk and decision management throughout the life of the project. Key technical decisions always have a managerial impact and vice-versa, and the two disciplines cannot therefore be handled separately.

Exercises for Project management and systems engineering

Exercise 22: Are they really separable?

Define a project that you know in a few paragraphs.
List the functions needed to perform project management and systems engineering.
Write 3 paragraphs defining the boundaries between systems engineering and project management.
Define an organizational structure. Allocate the functions within your project to the organizational structure.

Exercise 23: A better configuration management process?

A talented developer refuses to follow the standard configuration management procedures, saying they reduce productivity, and his own configuration management procedures are better and faster. Unfortunately he is right on all counts. His work is needed urgently within a month. In two paragraphs, explain to this developer why he should follow the standard configuration management procedures. Then in one paragraph, explain how you should have avoided this situation.

Exercise 24: What can go wrong with my backup?

You take a backup of the computer system every week and store the tape nearby.
The objective is to avoid more than two days work being lost under any reasonable circumstance.
Define five things that could go wrong with such a simple procedure. Write requirements that should preclude these problems if implemented.

Exercise 25: Promotion time

You have been offered an appointment as project manager of an existing area which has several large, operational computerized systems. The systems are undocumented, but seem to work reasonably well. All the systems need further development.

The following changes are needed in the three different systems:

a: A large number of new features are required;

b: An existing system must be used at a different site with 2,000 users instead of 100;

c: The operating system on which the system runs is scheduled to change dramatically in 4 months time.

You are directly responsible for the operations of all of these systems after they have been implemented. Prepare one page on different approaches to handling the future development of these systems as individual projects and as a set.

Exercise 26: Defining milestones

For a project that you are involved with, choose and name the next 3–5 milestones over the next 6–15 months (starting from the end goal of the project).

For each milestone state:

The key deliverable;

A paragraph defining the key characteristics of the deliverables which would allow you to finally accept it as satisfactory;

The target date for the milestone/deliverable.

State if these milestones have been defined for your project, and if all the team members understand them.

If not, state why not.

Is any work being done which is not attached to a milestone. If so, expalin its purpose.

State if you know the cost of reaching these milestones.

State if an individual is defined as responsible for producing them.

Exercise 27: Divided loyalties

You are the quality assurance manager on a large system project. Normally you work for the quality assurance department, but you have been appointed to the project for its duration. The project wants to do something which seems sensible and logical from the project's viewpoint, but it contradicts the business policy on quality assurance. The project demands loyalty from all those involved in it. The project manager asks you to approve the policy that is being proposed for the project.

Write down what you will do under these circumstances.

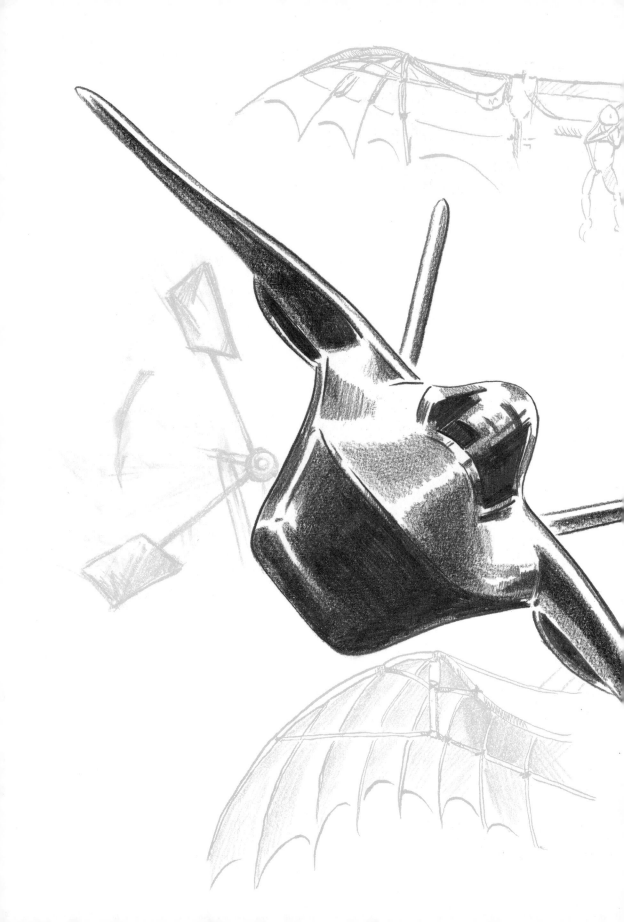

Tailoring the simple life cycle

7.1. The reasons for tailoring the process

The life cycle has been discussed in terms of a simple, sequential development process so far. In this approach, the product steadily develops through a single sequence of systems engineering processes. This life cycle is sometimes referred to as the waterfall approach, implying a continuous movement in one direction, with clear transitions from one process to the next. This model is attractive because it implies (falsely) that the future can be predicted with confidence.

In practice, when we start to think about design or manufacture, new requirements always emerge and the projected cost of implementation changes. Changes in the working and competitive environment may force alterations in the design. Nothing worthwhile can be developed without the assumption of change, handled by feedback into a newer development. Even if we developed a marvellous system, users would always demand enhancements. In practice, knowledge gained during a development inevitably questions the validity of previous work and decisions (Figure 7.1). Sometimes this feedback will cause changes, but in other cases it may simply arrive too late to be incorporated, and it may need to be stored for a later version. Feedback helps to ensure that this simple life cycle generates an end product

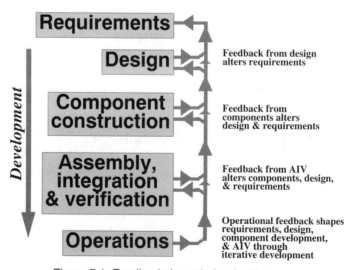

Figure 7.1: Feedback through the development

that meets the requirements and the design.

Every successful system, by definition, has changed or will change. Even something as apparently fixed as a building will be slowly altered by its inhabitants, to make it more pleasant or practical. The development approach needs to be tailored to make change and upgrade more straightforward. Making systems upgradeable costs extra initially, but it is often worth the effort. Some 1960s buildings that could not be upgraded (e.g. to add new cabling and air-conditioning) have already had to be destroyed.

Having said all of this, some kinds of systems cannot be developed iteratively. A Channel Tunnel, a large bridge, or an aircraft have to work right first time. One-off, large, physical systems have to be developed using a single-shot development approach, at least at their system level. To cope with the intrinsic risks, such systems are developed in a low-risk way, using known components, existing designs, extensive analysis and modeling work, and using iterative development for their lower level components. Thus large tunnelling projects will generally use known methods, machines and modify existing rail equipment. There is always enough risk that cannot be avoided without choosing to take on more by unnecessary novelty.

The simple approach must therefore be tailored, by re-structuring the individual steps of the sequential approach, using the elements of a more intricate life cycle, i.e. a temporal reorganization of the sequential processes. In an evolutionary or incremental approach, the solution is optimized step-by-step. This approach delivers some functionality earlier to users, and produces rapid feedback about requirements or the practicality of design. However, tailoring should not be used as an excuse for loss of discipline in the development approach. Falling back to an ill-disciplined 'build-then-try' development approach has to be avoided at all costs. We still need the momentum of the sequential life cycle, without its impracticalities.

A variety of different development approaches are possible. The result could be an evolutionary or incremental approach (or any mixture of the two), and this could be altered as the project becomes more firm. Designing a life cycle for the specific needs of the project should be an early task, to be re-visited throughout the whole life cycle.

Information modeling

In choosing the life cycle, we are simultaneously defining a model of the product information. The model might show the business, user and system requirements and the order in which they should be completed. Figure 7.2 illustrates an information model for a simple product definition, which forms a type of entity-relationship diagram (ERD). The model shows the traceability and precedence between the different sets of the information.

Figure 7.2: Information model = life cycle definition

The structure of an information model is best defined in a brainstorming environment, documented on a whiteboard, then finalized later. The key factors driving the choice are initial system process, risk, commitment and the need to deliver some functionality as early as possible, and so the life cycle should be chosen to optimize these needs. The chosen development approach should be documented in the management plan for the project. As with management plans, a draft version of the information model needs to be produced early on, and updated at later stages. For instance, a project may define the user and system requirements before choosing the development approach.

A more real-world example of an information model is shown in Figure 7.3 for a telecommunications system that is strongly affected by both government and State legislation. This huge system splits up into multiple sub-systems which actually install the equipment in each State. Each local installation is effectively a variation of a standard design. Modeling is considered in more detail in chapter 12.

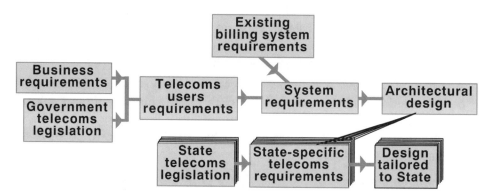

Figure 7.3: Information model for a telecommunications system

7.2. The sequential life cycle

Before casually discarding the sequential approach, we should look at its advantages, particularly when compared to a complete lack of process. It embodies an underlying discipline which should not be lightly discarded.

Breaking down the project into a series of life cycle processes each with deliverables enables us to:

- *evaluate progress against milestones, before the product is finished or even designed;*
- *evaluate process against checklists;*
- *analyze and minimize risks;*
- *progressively estimate life cycle costs;*
- *control changes;*
- *check for consistency between information such as requirements, design and tests.*

In the unlikely case of zero risks, the sequential life cycle would be the best approach. In practice, this baseline life cycle is therefore suitable only for low-risk, smallish systems. The underlying premise is that the end product can be developed in a single shot, and that it will not need updating after it has been delivered. This is rarely realistic, but can be attractive to management because the early plans give the reassuring illusion that the future is predictable.

7.3.   Different kinds of tailored development

The number of potential development approaches is without limit. Within a single large system, the sub-systems may follow different development approaches. Some typical approaches include:

- *sequential (waterfall-like);*
- *incremental;*
- *evolution by risk, cost-benefit, infrastructure;*
- *rapid application development;*
- *competitive piloting;*
- *framework architecture;*
- *re-engineering existing systems.*

Complex systems will evolve more quickly when there are stable, intermediate forms –
H. A. Simon[41]

Risk is the overall force in shaping the life cycle. This can be driven by factors such as the size of the target system, the nature of risks (e.g. in requirements or design), volatility in the technology, the predictability of the operational scenarios, or the degree of novelty in the solution. Another driver may be priority, that is the need for getting functionality quickly to the users. These development approaches meet a different package of requirements at a different cost.

7.4.   Incremental development

In an *incremental life cycle*, the sequential approach is followed to make a complete architectural design, but then that design is implemented in parts (Figure 7.4). Normally the most cost-effective parts are implemented first.

The system can be extended by adding extra features, or by enlarging the number of units that are being operated.

The incremental life cycle could be chosen when:

- *full finance is not immediately available;*
- *time to market is important;*
- *there is a smaller initial demand.*

Good – and bad – incremental development

Schipol Airport in Amsterdam is an example of well-planned incremental development. The design has been mapped out for the future as a single integrated airport. When more capacity is needed, it is built in the same style and logic as the existing airport. Each new terminal is compatible with the old, looks similar and is easy for passengers to understand. The passenger, for example, can walk through the terminal without climbing up and down stairs or passing through extra security checks. Because the design was thought out in advance, the connecting parts such as tunnels, bridges and passage-ways fit together logically. Even more important, new components can be constructed without too much disruption of the working airport.

The future will always surprise us – so plan for surprises

By way of contrast, Heathrow Airport in London indicates what happens without early systems engineering. Although individual facilities are now often excellent, there was no (visible) long-term planning of the airport. As a result, the pieces of the airport fit together uncomfortably. Successive terminals have each been added as if they would be the last to be built. The airport is now a

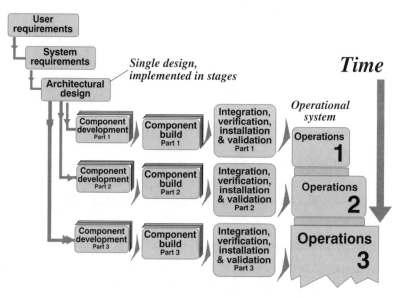

Figure 7.4: Incremental development

tangle of arbitrary connections – 'spaghetti code' written in concrete. Any passenger traveling between the terminals at Heathrow suffers from this disorganization, walking through multiple tunnels, stairs, security checks and travelators to get from one place to another. Car parking is scattered for miles around the airport, in different areas for different terminals. Adding any extra elements to Heathrow has always been painful, and for example, connecting to the main railroad line a few hundred yards away took fifty years.

Even a supposedly single-shot facility is often implemented incrementally. The overall capability for a bridge, tunnel, or a theme park will be made available step-by-step. The incremental approach is a useful theoretical concept, but is rarely encountered in a pure form. Whenever a system is used operationally, new requirements will be generated, demanding adjustments to the supposedly stable design.

7.5. Evolutionary life cycle

What we discover immediately on first using a system is what we forgot to ask for

In evolutionary development, the basic life cycle is repeated to deliver successive versions of the product with a period of operational use to gain feedback. Figure 7.5 illustrates this spiral of development, cycling through the different processes of the life cycle[42]. Figure 7.6 shows how information is organized, and how it flows back from operations to the next version of the product. The first versions are small, and get the product into action quickly. This approach reduces the risk involved in taking a long time to supply a product, which then may turn out not to be what the users want.

The advantages of the evolutionary life cycle are:

- *earlier delivery of partial functionality;*
- *earlier and more realistic customer feedback;*
- *faults are found more quickly and repaired at lower cost;*
- *opportunity to include updated technology;*
- *encouragement to the practical team members and rooting out of the dreamers;*
- *and hopefully, earlier delivery of full functionality.*

I don t need requirements – I m doing evolutionary acquisition – Anon

The evolutionary approach requires care. At some point, the architecture may need to be re-worked to cope with requirements changes. Also the planning horizon is limited, because customer response can re-direct the development at short notice. Reasonably enough, management and developers would like to plan and budget far ahead and do not take kindly to the thought that the future is inherently unpredictable. These apparently negative factors illustrate that evolutionary development reflects reality, rather than the fictions that underpin the waterfall life cycle.

Evolutionary development is particularly beneficial when a system is the first of a kind, has complex interfaces to external systems, or is destined for a

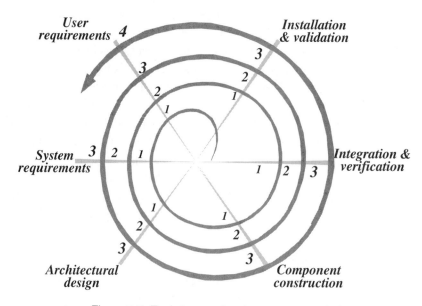

Figure 7.5: Evolutionary development as a spiral

*Don t build
the paths
until you
know where
people walk*

rapidly changing environment. There is nothing to stop you doing as full a set of requirements as possible, even in an evolutionary development, but initially implementing only the most feasible sub-set. Developers then have some idea what might come next, and can design an architecture to cope, even though the actual requirements can still change.

Factors shaping evolutionary development

In an evolutionary approach, the project manager still has the choice of which parts of the system should be implemented in each tranche. This choice should be made on a rational basis – for example by:

  - cost-benefit (best-value items first);
  - maturity of components;
  - basic infrastructure then add modules (framework);
  - risk, either high-risk or low-risk first (e.g. Boehm spiral life cycle).

Even in an evolutionary development, requirements must be handled well and used as the driver for development. The requirement process is actually harder in evolutionary development, because each requirement needs to be classified as to whether it is for the initial version, subsequent revisions or for some envisaged version far into the future. Therefore in evolutionary development, **acquisition of knowledge from operations** must be a continuous, active task. This may take many different forms, such as involvement in system operations or questioning users. The development

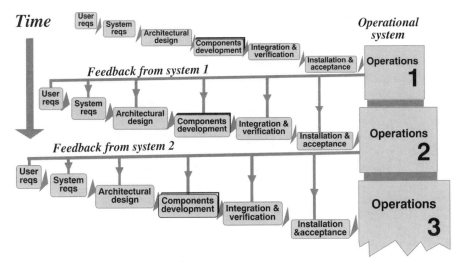

Figure 7.6: Evolutionary development

team must have access to all suggestions and complaints from users. Each suggestion has to be documented as a change request.

Figure 7.7 shows the process of capturing suggestions from those who use or support the system, and using these to drive the product evolution. All suggestions and complaints need to be classified as they come in to see if they need to be handled immediately. This sifts out the product bugs, leaving the suggestions for improvement, which are collected and grouped for the next time the development needs them. Collection of requirements can then become a continuous (perhaps low-key) process.

The release cycle should be controlled to balance the advantages of new features with the pain always involved in upgrade. The shorter the delay between a requirement being stated, agreed, implemented and tested, the better. But if new versions are released too often, the customer will suffer from 'release fatigue'. Users expect more from each release to make up for the effort of the change. Managing the progressive increase of capability is made more feasible by continuous collection of requirements, which can be used for cost-benefit analysis before deciding which features to provide next.

7.6.   Rapid application development

Rapid Application Development (RAD) combines many of the techniques already discussed – evolutionary development, short delivery timescales, concurrent engineering and intense involvement of users in providing feedback to developers. RAD is especially valuable where it is impractical to completely specify the requirements at the start of the development and the

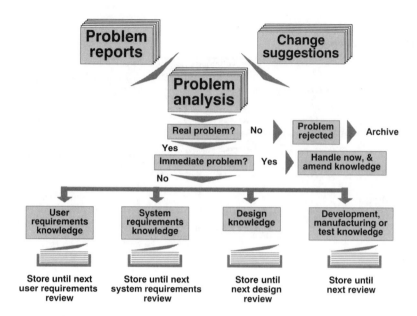

Figure 7.7: Collecting suggestions from users

real needs fully emerge as a rapid sequence of real operational products builds toward the complete system. RAD has been particularly successful when applied in the software intensive systems domain, which is well suited to rapid release of new versions.

Potential dangers of RAD include lack of discipline, the need to redevelop the architecture several times, failure to document the system as it is defined, and multiple responsibilities for defined areas of the project. To counter these, the DSDM[43] consortium has produced a non-proprietary standard for RAD with a number of key features. For example, the development is structured as a number of relatively short timeboxes of fixed duration. The objectives of each timebox are agreed with the user at its start and are influenced by the results of the previous timebox (e.g. whether preceding objectives were fully met). Since timeboxes are short, they are easier to manage and predict.

Prototyping is an important feature of DSDM, but the approach stresses the desirability of evolutionary prototypes whose quality is assured throughout the development. The issue of re-engineering a prototype to turn it from a "hacked" version to a "deliverable" one should not arise.

The customer and developer must actively share their interest in the success of the project. An adversarial approach is replaced by one of trust and co-operation. The DSDM standard has nine principles, summarized in Figure 7.8.

Advantages	*Technique*	*Disadvantages*
More likely to satisfy the users	**Active user involvement**	Destroys responsibility unless controlled
Rapid & knowledgeable decision-making	**Project team empowerment**	Must not be an excuse for abdication of authorit
Speedier time-boxed user satisfaction	**Frequent delivery of product**	Release fatigue limits the frequency
Satisfaction, but not perfection	**Fitness for purpose is key**	None
Better feedback from operations	**Iterative development**	Can increase re-work e.g new architecture
Errors can be corrected more easily	**All changes are reversible**	Extra expense How do you prove it?
A stable basis for work	**Baselined requirements**	Obviously essential
Rapid finding of faults and their source	**Testing integrated through lifecycle**	High investment in test
Compromises based on real communication	**Collaborative approach**	Relies on human nature

Figure 7.8: Principles of rapid application development

The concepts are so sensible that they can be applied within many system developments.

Like all powerful approaches, RAD can be dangerous in unskilled hands. However, DSDM goes some way towards removing the risks and if the principles are followed by an experienced team, the benefits can be great.

7.7. Framework architecture

Large systems often contain a mixture of stable and evolving components, i.e. some of the components can be rapidly improved, while others are evolving more slowly. A 'framework architecture' copes with this situation by separating the two kinds of components, and defining clear interfaces between them. For example, a warship may be expected to last 30 years, but the weapons and sensors (such as the radars) will need more regular upgrading to cope with faster, stealthier missiles. To handle this evolution, the ship's architecture needs to be defined with clear interfaces, so that new sensors can be plugged in and easily linked to the ship's command and control system. The interfaces occur at levels in the system decomposition. This approach encourages re-use of components across systems, providing clear, standardized interfaces. This will involve a systems engineering approach for at least the electronic, messaging, and electrical connections. Figure 7.9 illustrates the 'framework architecture' approach for handling large, evolving systems. This divides the system into a stable infrastructure, a clear interface,

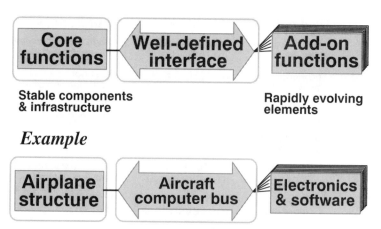

Figure 7.9: Framework architecture

and the functions that are evolving more rapidly. Functions can be upgraded as long as they conform to the interface, and the stable components can also be evolved more slowly.

Interfaces must be the most stable part of platform architectures, but even these can be upgraded as long as they remain a compatible superset of the old interface. A computer bus is a good example of a framework architecture. New boards can be plugged in to perform tasks that were never envisaged when the computer was originally designed.

Biological systems may have evolved similar techniques. For instance, the internal organs and enzymes of species are often little changed, even when the species have diverged wildly. This implies that a highly modular approach to control this information has evolved in biological systems.

The principles of a framework architecture can be extended hierarchically i.e. with a structured design, small components can be upgraded as well as sub-systems. This allows assemblies and sub-systems to be upgraded without affecting other elements that conform to the interfaces. For example, a telecommunications system can evolve at the rack level, board level, chip level and transistor gate level. In practice, any large system can be upgraded only if its components can themselves be upgraded separately.

Loose coupling between the new features and the core architecture can extend this approach. In this way, functions are initially loosely coupled and if they prove popular, they can be integrated more closely into the system (Figure 7.10). A basic infrastructure has to be provided to get the system up-and-running. Other advantages of this approach are that the core heavily-used functions will firstly be well separated, and secondly tend to get enormous implicit testing. The loosely-coupled functions will tend to be used by

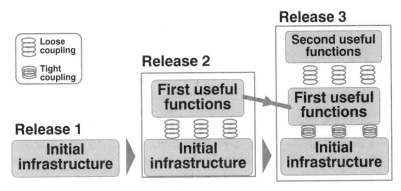

Figure 7.10: Loosely coupled evolution

enthusiasts ('early adopters'), who are often happy enough to have partial solutions to their problems. They will give feedback to improve the quality of these elements before they get heavy use.

In some cases, the creativity of users can be tapped directly to help system evolution. In another example, a scripting language on a software tool can enable users to add their own functionality. If an add-on application proves to be popular, then it can be added to the core product by the developers.

7.8.   *Competitive piloting*

In high-risk situations, it may be worth piloting parts of the system before choosing the winning design. The process consists of:

- – *defining the requirements for competing groups to implement;*
- – *picking the best two or three solutions;*
- – *operating them for a few months;*
- – *negotiating the price before choosing the winner;*
- – *pick the winner.*

A competitive approach often pushes the competing teams to new levels of excellence, and much can be learned even from the losing bids. Competition should be part of every development, and is particularly important at the design stage, where it is not time-consuming or expensive. Competitive piloting can even be used to good effect inside a company, at a high level of abstraction.

Figure 7.11 shows an example of a competitive piloting process. The two or three best candidates are selected on a paper-based approach, and then are

1402 – A piloting competition for the doors of the Baptistery at Florence. Seven sculptors are given a plate and one year to make a trial bronze of The Sacrifice of Abraham

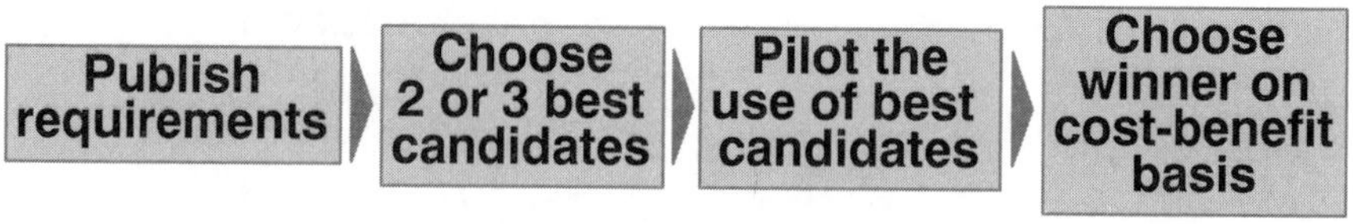

| Publish requirements | Choose 2 or 3 best candidates | Pilot the use of best candidates | Choose winner on cost-benefit basis |

Figure 7.11: Competitive piloting process

actually used in a restricted operational environment. It may well be better to pay for the pilot projects than try to get them for nothing to ensure a level, competitive playing field. The winning system could then be incrementally implemented at the different sites of the organization on a piloting basis.

7.9. Design to cost

'Design to cost' is not a life cycle per se, but an influence that pervades every development. In practice, there is always a target price that cannot be exceeded – this limit may be elastic or unstated, but it is always in the back of our minds.

Figure 7.12 shows how 'design-to-cost' influences the development approach. At the end of each stage, developers make a cost estimate and an estimation of the likely error in that estimate. They aim to drive the development to lie within the limit. This may mean going round the process again to bring it within cost targets. Making small cuts is always easier than adding new features, so 'design-to-cost' is often handled by over-specifying the system, and then deciding what to cut.

The best that one can hope for in cost estimation is an accuracy of about 30% when the system requirements are solid, and 10% with a good architectural design. If the estimated cost is outside the cost limits, the project cuts requirements and retraces its steps. Design-to-cost is very realistic, encourages modularity (so that pieces can be easily cut), and makes the choice plain between increasing the budget or cutting features. Even if the target cost is exceeded in the end, the principle of treating cost as an independent variable or, better still, as an engineering parameter, lies at the heart of producing value for money.

7.10. Re-engineering existing systems

Of all the tasks in development, re-engineering an existing undocumented system is one of the most common and difficult. Legacy systems often work fairly well, but the technology is usually obsolete, expensive to build and maintain, and clumsy to use. The user interfaces of legacy systems have often become difficult for new users to learn. However, they do the job, the users are familiar with them, and over the years, the faults have been slowly ground out.

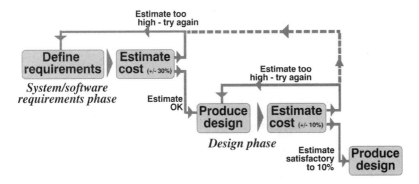

Figure 7.12: Design to cost

The natural approach is to think about documenting the old system from zero – reverse engineering the design, its requirements, the tests and so on. New capabilities could be defined in the process and then added to the old system. The software engineers at IBM's Federal Systems (now Lockheed Martin) were updating Federal Aviation Authority air traffic control systems, which were sometimes 25 years old. They had to analyze the old software and reverse engineer the system to find what it was meant to do. Only then was it possible to engineer the new system. Because of the criticality of the system, this was the only feasible approach. Trying a 'big-bang' approach is too high-risk and slow to get to the right level of reliability.

The world is made up of legacy systems

Old systems usually have a considerable amount of intelligence and experience encapsulated within them. The problem is that these features have never been documented, and so the system is essentially impossible to replicate, let alone to improve. The pressure to get the system updated means that there is rarely time to document the old system adequately. Inevitably we miss requirements and our first version will probably be less reliable than the old system and consequently rejected by users. Even if we make a better easy-to-use system, there will be a learning curve for users to handle the changes. Adopting a more evolutionary approach to legacy system development would be highly desirable.

As an example, a large and successful telecommunications system was replicated using more advanced technology. But the very first customer complained that the replacement system did not behave in the same way as the old system. Neither of the systems had a set of requirements. Several months of effort and embarrassment followed before compatibility with the old system was achieved.

Figure 7.13 shows an approach which has sometimes worked with legacy systems. Firstly, a simple functional interface is defined on top of the old system. This must define the behavioral and functional characteristics between

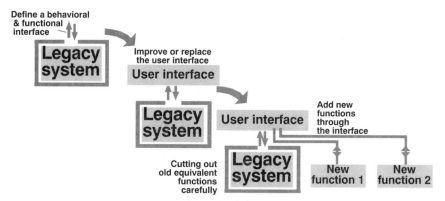

Figure 7.13: Reverse engineering of existing systems

the interface and the legacy system, and be properly documented. The user interface on legacy systems is usually outdated, and an improved version can be added as a discrete layer above the functional interface. New functions are added individually to the old system, carefully cutting out the old parts where necessary. This may be difficult, because sometimes it is simply impossible to cut out parts. Using this approach, the old system is gently evolved rather than being replaced instantly, and documentation (such as requirements) can also be added gradually.

7.11. Smaller systems

When systems are smaller, the system processes can be adjusted to avoid unnecessary documentation. A size and risk management procedure should always be used to determine the formality and number of processes for the development process.

Smaller systems can be handled with a lighter development approach, dropping some of the processes of the life cycle. Figure 7.14 adapts, for systems engineering, an approach used for handling less formal software developments, cutting down on the number of processes as the development becomes simpler[44].

Smaller systems can cut out some of the processes of the life cycle, but will need a requirements, development and integration process. However, documentation can be much smaller and handled less formally. This practice is acceptable for ISO 9001[45] certification, as long as it is defined in the business process.

In smaller systems, the size and formality of documentation can be reduced. Heavyweight documentation is pointless if the system is non-critical, can be implemented quickly, used, and then discarded in a few days. Size is not the same as risk. Even the smallest piece of software that handles railroad

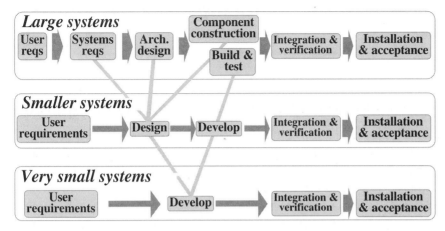

Figure 7.14: Developing smaller systems

signalling must be correct, and will therefore have to be handled formally. However, it may be handled with only three or four stages.

A large system may contain components with a range of different criticality. A plane will contain safety-critical systems for engine control, but also software to manage the video screens for passengers. As long as the components are cleanly separated, different development approaches can be applied to these different software components.

7.12. Summary on tailored development

A tailored development approach can certainly produce a better, earlier product than any 'big-bang' approach. It reflects the reality that the future is unpredictable, and tailoring the development approach can reduce the risk. The different development approaches shown in this chapter are examples of what can be done.

The more complex development life cycle also introduces problems of its own. Iteration is more difficult to control and manage, because the output products are not so obvious. Multiple versions of each document are needed, and indeed a document-based approach becomes ever more difficult to sustain (see chapter 12). Even for evolutionary development, disciplined development processes are required. We must be careful not to allow evolutionary development to degenerate into the 'build-then-try' school of development. While the sequential waterfall life cycle may be too simplistic to cope with real life, its separate steps are indispensable components of whatever life cycle is chosen.

Exercises for Tailoring the development life cycle

Exercise 28: Converting to an evolutionary approach

Choose a system you know. Estimate the net cost and time to produce the system in a single shot. Estimate the likely quality of the single shot product compared to what the customer wants (2 pages). Now define the cost and time to bring the system to the required quality.

Now define and plan a highly evolutionary development policy for the same system, stating the products produced at each release of the system. Estimate the costs and time spent on the tailored approach and compare that to the serial approach. Explain the advantages and disadvantages of the two approaches (1–2 pages).

Exercise 29: Upgrading existing systems

Your boss has requested that you replace an existing system (e.g. a telecoms system). Onew thousand of the previous version have been sold, and generally they have been successful in the field. Advances in technology mean that the system can be made smaller and cheaper for existing and new customers. The new system must work compatibly with the old system. Unfortunately no requirements were done for the original system. Many of the requirements implemented in the old system seem obvious, but might conceivably be missed if you do not state them.

Your boss says that there is no time to reverse engineer the old requirements.

You do not want to refuse the task.

Define what you will do when:

    1: The new system is a pure replacement;

    2: Enhancements are needed, replacing only some parts of the legacy system.

Exercise 30: Defining evolving elements

This exercise aims at characteriszing the elements of a system into rapidly evolving and more stable elements. Pick one of the following systems as an example (or choose a system that you have worked on in the past)

    – *video recorder;*

- car;
- aircraft;
- cellular phone.

For the system that you have chosem, define five elements most likely to evolve in the future development of this equipment. What are the their characteristics? Predict how the systems are likely to evolve.

What are the most stable elements of such systems, and again define the common characteristics that cause such stability?

Exercise 31: Logic for choosing the life cycle

Look at the following diagram for choosing the development approach for a system. The diagram purports to illustrate the logic path for choosing the optimum life cycle. Comment on the digram and its logic.

Find at least one logical flaw in the diagram.

Is it actually possible to draw such a diagram?

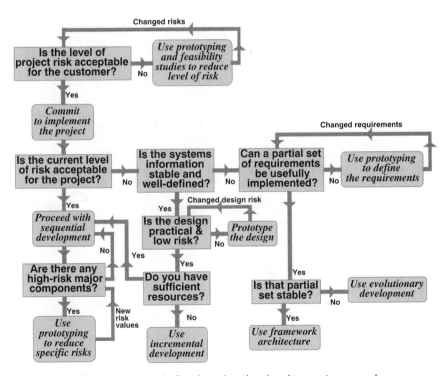

Figure 7.15: Logic for choosing the development approach

More realistic development life cycles

eight

8.1. The need for a more realistic development approach

The sequential model usefully describes how a system develops from abstract ideas to design, into definition of components, building and testing those components, and eventually produces a complete integrated system. In practice, all these serial approaches may need modification because:

- *fixing requirements for a complete system without knowledge about the design, risk and costs of implementation is impractical;*

- *a large system has to be handled as a set of concurrent smaller developments;*

- *the management of risk by different enterprises demands more sophisticated interactions than a sequential model can provide.*

To understand anything, you should not try to understand everything – Aristotle

In reality, there are always backward flows of information as knowledge about a system increases. Feedback is shown in a simple form even in the so-called waterfall life cycle (Figure 8.1). In the diagram, feedback can occur between any pair of system processes.

Often the management ethos tends to neglect the reverse flow of information, and considers a project 'in trouble' if the forward momentum is

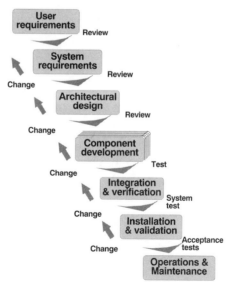

Figure 8.1: The waterfall life cycle with feedback

interrupted. An unwillingness to correct mistakes makes the early steps in the life cycle more ponderous, because *they must be right first time*.

While the requirements define the quality, the costs and practicality are determined by the architectural design. Inevitably they will feedback to the requirements and cause changes. On large systems, the feedback will also occur from lower level components (Figure 8.2).

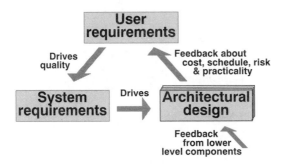

Figure 8.2: Feedback from design

8.2.   Three different processes

The overall goal of systems engineering is to provide an operational capability. In large one-off developments, such as an air traffic control system, this enables the controllers to manage aircraft flights. In mass-production, the capability enables retail purchasers to buy and use the product.

Providing a capability requires two distinct roles: one to define the required capability, and the other to provide resources to create that capability. In large one-off developments, the users and service providers define the capability, and a buying agency provides the budget and other resources to provide the capability. In mass-production, the capability needed by users will be defined by the marketing department and built by the engineering department, or perhaps contracted out.

We use the term 'customer' to represent the person with the responsibility for acquiring the capability. This customer will usually contract a supplier, inside or outside the customer organization, to meet those requirements. Thus three development processes can be identified:

- *capability development, defining and delivering an operational capability;*
- *system development, developing a system to provide the required capability;*
- *specialist component supply, constructing and supplying components at the lowest level.*

Figure 8.3 re-organizes the sequential life cycle to identify these processes. The development processes are laid out horizontally, and enclose the subsidiary processes they contain[46 & 47].

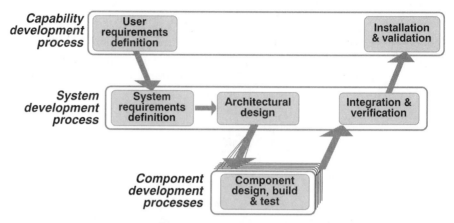

Figure 8.3: Life cycle model showing three processes

The **capability development process** aims at delivering what the users want, and so takes a user-oriented view within the development life cycle. The initial process is definition of user requirements, and when the system has been developed, it installs and validates the system ready for operations. It also manages the interfaces to the other components needed to make a success – e.g. monitoring competition, operational support, training etc. The capability development process is required once at the top level.

The **system development process** responds to the user requirements by defining a system capable of delivering the required capability. This is done by producing system requirements, followed by an architectural design. The architectural design will define the components to be developed by specialist component developers. It will also split out the operational support systems, and define interfaces to them and other external systems. The designer may need to specify interactions with components such as the operational support system or the production system, even when those are developed by external groups. When these components are finished, the system development process integrates them and delivers a tested system to the capability development process. There will be one system development process responding directly to the capability development process.

The **component development process** takes a component specification and delivers a tested component ready for integration. Many instances of component development are required, one for each component to be developed.

At the top level of the system, the capability development process writes the user requirements, and eventually delivers the complete system to the enterprise. In turn, capability development obtains a tested system from the developers. The developers partition the design out to their sub-system suppliers, and the process is then repeated through the levels. At each level, system development performs all the technical roles involved in both acquisition and supply.

Figure 8.4 indicates one capability development process at the top, only one instance of the system development process immediately below, but several levels of system development. At all lower levels there will be many instances of the system development process (one for each 'component' of the architectural design at the level above). At the lowest levels, there will be multiple component developments.

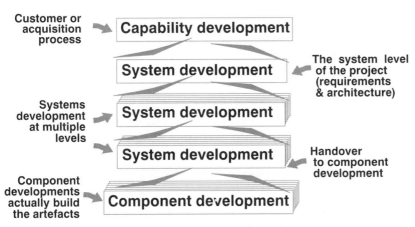

Figure 8.4: Three contexts of development

Capability development and system development both have technical authority over individual system components. The user role of 'capability development' differs from system development because it produces the user requirements, and accepts the complete system into the operational environment.

Capability development process

Figure 8.5 shows the capability development process starting from initial **agreement on the business objectives**, which controls the interaction between the project and the enterprise. All reviews between the project and the enterprise should be based on these business requirements, updated during the development. These outline the area of application, potential customers, key schedule requirements or what it must do. They contain requirements on the product, the way it is developed, plus decisions to which the enterprise is already committed. In a military system, the role is typically performed by an operational requirements branch. As elsewhere, these requirements are likely to be initially unrealistic. We may have to explore the design to arrive at realistic estimates for timescales and resources. This normally results in changes to the original requirements.

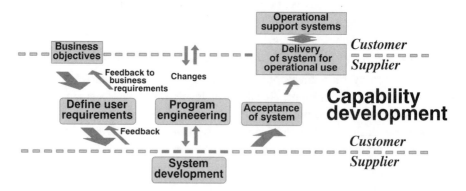

Figure 8.5: Capability development

Capability development **generates a set of requirements** to respond to the needs of all operational stakeholders. Even the process of generating user requirements provides some feedback. For example, it may become clear that users do not attach sufficient value to the product envisaged in the enterprise requirements. Enterprise objectives invariably contain managerial issues, and so they need examining to check that costs, schedules, and requirements are mutually consistent and that the skills to develop the product.

During the development, the capability development role **monitors progress** against the requirements, through traceability to system requirements, design, and then implementation. This information confirms the level of risk, cost estimates, and schedules, as well as quality. Development is monitored against the management plans generated at the levels below. Capability development manages changes flowing downwards from the enterprise and competitive environment, and upwards from design and implementation. Capability development must **plan the acceptance process**.

Capability development is also responsible for **integrating the system into the operational environment**. This task is performed against the user requirements and the contractual arrangements in the original agreement.

The user requirements and management plans are the basis of agreement with system development at the level below. Capability development uses information generated by the rest of the system to estimate the likely costs, schedule and quality of the final system.

System development

Figure 8.6 shows system development from the decomposition of a component to its eventual delivery. The systems engineering process starts by reaching **technical agreement** on the requirements for the component to be developed. This bundle of requirements is then developed into a complete set of system requirements for the component being developed. An architectural

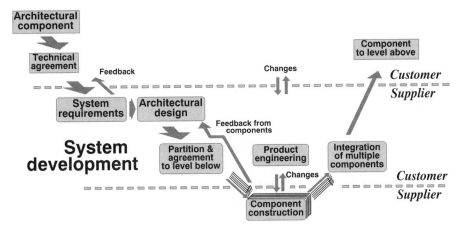

Figure 8.6: System development

design is developed against those requirements, continually supplying feedback to the customer about reality of the original requirements. The design is then **decomposed into components** at the level below, with the system development role becoming that of customer rather than supplier. Feedback from design and component construction usually results in agreed compromises about which requirements are to be implemented.

8.3. Process products and additional flows

The previous diagrams have shown the development processes, but omitted the products that they produce. For example, the net product from development is a system that gives users what they want in an operational environment. Figure 8.7 shows flows indicating extra managerial and verification checks that are needed. The dependencies which exist between

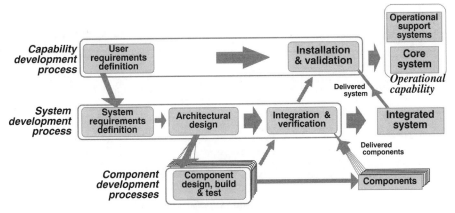

Figure 8.7: Three key processes

the processes (shown as horizontal arrows) become self-evident in this re-drawn model. For example, user requirements provide the basis for acceptance tests. Similarly, system requirements and architectural design are the foundation for verification and validation. Each top-level process generates one or more products, indicated by the square-cornered rectangles of the figure. These products are the complete system ready for operations, an integrated system for acceptance test, and components for integration.

Customer-supplier relationships

A customer-supplier interface always exists in the interactions between each of the development processes involved in a complex system, i.e. between levels. At the top level, the customer-supplier interface between capability development and system development delivers a tested system meeting the user requirements. Similarly, the component development processes provide components to system development across the interface.

These customer-supplier relationships are influenced by feedback, by change, and by the multi-level structure (Figure 8.8), which forms the basis of the customer-supplier supply chain.

8.4. Feedback before commitment

The set of requirements applied to a development must be a negotiated agreement, not a unilateral imposition by a customer on a supplier. These initial customer requests may not be immediately acceptable to the supplier. The supplier usually replies with suggested improvements based on specialist knowledge of the component. This normally modifies the customer's original

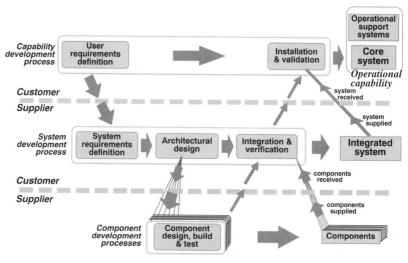

Figure 8.8: Customer-supplier interfaces

requirements, changing the requirements and improving the system design (Figure 8.9). Eventually the supplier and customer agree on the requirements and a detailed specification, with time and cost estimates for its production. Alternatively, the supplier may decide not to continue, because of unrealistic requirements, budget or schedule restrictions. This process happens at all system levels.

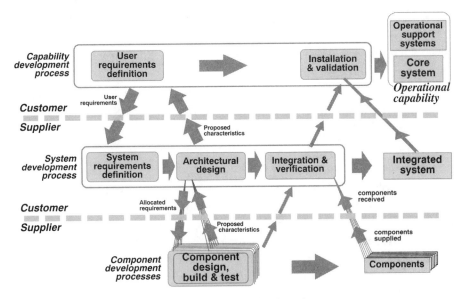

Figure 8.9: Feedback paths

Before committing to producing the component, the supplier must investigate the feasibility and risk of the customer's request. This usually involves defining the system requirements and then producing one or more potential architectural designs to explore risk. These potential designs are used to decide whether to make an offer.

These negotiations create the extra feedback paths involving the architectural design process feeding back to user requirements, as does component design to the architectural design. The information from the lower level processes influences the higher level processes. In the ideal world, the reality of design should always prevail over the aspiration of requirements. As a result, all of these processes are concurrently active, contrasting starkly with the waterfall model in which only a single process is supposed to be active.

8.5. Multiple levels of system development

For all but the smallest systems, the specialist components cannot be defined through a single level of decomposition. Instead, the system's components must be treated as 'systems' in their own right. Often the term sub-system is used to denote this type of component. A sub-system may be complex, may be an existing component, or may itself require development from different specialist disciplines.

Subdividing a large system into smaller components makes it easier to manage. The sub-division is based around the architecture, the components of which become developments at the next level down. The full-page diagram of Figure 8.10 shows how more levels can be introduced into the model. Each new level consists of multiple instances of the system development process, one for each system-level component or sub-system. Instead of receiving a set of user requirements, they receive a component specification which will consist of:

- *system requirements allocated to this component;*
- *requirements derived from the component s context within the architectural design at the system level (including performance, interface constraints, physical constraints etc.);*
- *constraints relating to the development rather than the product (e.g. schedule, allocated resources etc.).*

Customer-supplier relationships apply at each level. The system-level process agrees the specification for a sub-system level during the formative stage. The system-level process asks for a set of components from its lower level suppliers. Customers at any level are primarily concerned with progress, schedule, risk, and quality rather than the supplier's development approach. Suppliers make decisions about the development approach, based on their expertise in the problem domain.

The model extends to arbitrary numbers of development levels, depending on system complexity and the number of specialist disciplines involved. A system-level negotiates with sub-systems that must, in turn, negotiate with their suppliers. The architecture at one level defines the components which must be supplied at the next level down, and hence shapes the managerial structure.

The multi-level approach increases the interactions which must take place between these processes. The introduction of concurrency and the need for negotiation between levels allows ideas to evolve over time. At all times, system engineers must keep a holistic viewpoint as specifications are negotiated across the customer-supplier interfaces.

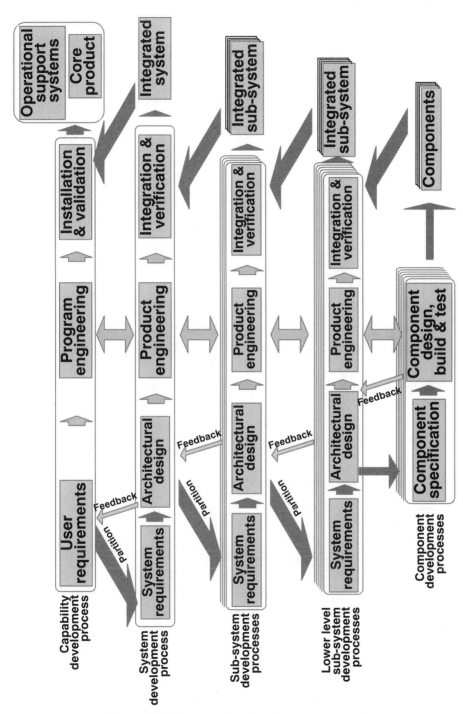

Figure 8.10: The complete development approach

The model can be re-drawn to emphasize the interaction between requirements and design, unifying the requirements and design structures (Figure 8.11). This view illustrates the interaction between requirements and design interactions, with the former leading. A piece of requirements work is followed by a design, which will confirm or change those requirements. Another piece of requirements work follows. Although it looks very different, it is completely compatible with the multi-level view.

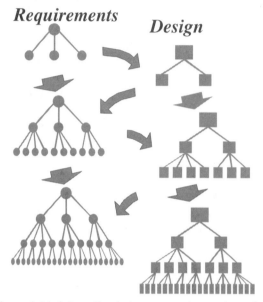

Figure 8.11: Interaction between requirements and design

8.6. Change in complex systems

The more realistic model copes better than the waterfall model with the changes that occur in the real world. The initial customer-supplier agreements are open for review throughout a project, as changes occur. Since change is inevitable, it is essential to plan for it, although the cost of making a change rises remorselessly through the course of a development. Changes can arise from variations to the user requirements, the environment of the product, (top-down change) or from difficulties in producing or buying a component (bottom-up). Changes may also arise from better technology or the available resources may change. Changes must therefore be simultaneously assessed from a systems engineering, management, and risk viewpoint. This must occur at each of the levels that could be affected by a proposed modification. Two additional processes of program and product engineering are needed to handle the engineering impact of proposed changes (Figure 8.12).

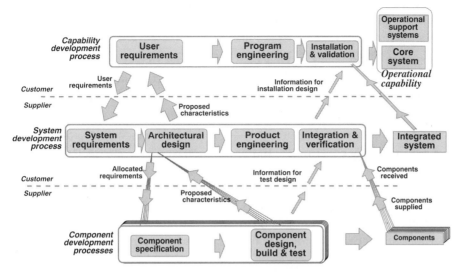

Figure 8.12: Reality of change

Product engineering process

The product engineering process is added to system development to handle changes from both the customer and supplier levels. The first step in responding to a proposed change is to assess its impact, initially from a technical perspective. Changes will almost inevitably have an impact on time and cost and hence these aspects must also be assessed. Whatever its scope, a change may lead to modifications being required to the system baseline information, to modifications of the build information or real end products. Product engineering updates the system baseline, while the main development processes update the build information and artefacts.

Change impact may be localized or wide-ranging. A change may also have an impact on the customer-supplier interfaces and agreements. The decision on whether to implement any change is made on a cost-benefit basis. When a change has been authorized, any of the following actions may be necessary:

- — *negotiate changes in the user requirements;*
- — *change the system requirements;*
- — *change the system test strategy and/or plans;*
- — *change the architectural design;*
- — *change the integration and test strategy and/or plans;*
- — *change component specifications and/or the interface specifications;*
- — *negotiate changes in the component specifications for component suppliers.*

These actions involve both systems engineering and project management to some extent. The engineering actions involve updating the relevant technical information. The project manager handles the resources and schedule implications on the development plan, and negotiates changes to the customer-supplier agreements.

The actions to be taken depend upon the impact of the change. If the impact is small and localized, changes may be implemented without recourse to wider consultation. As the magnitude of the change increases, the project or even the product manager becomes involved (see Chapter 9).

A holistic approach to assessing changes keeps requirements, design, plans and risks mutually consistent – the prime motivation for introducing this extra process into our model. This encourages a complete and thorough approach to prevent the system baseline and build information gradually falling into chaos. Management plans and technical information must be kept mutually compatible. All too often the plans are changed without reference to the decisions and technical information used to derive them.

Changes at the capability development level

Program engineering handles change at the capability development level once the development process is underway. For this process, there is no 'upward' interface, although it is influenced by changes in the working or business environment. Change suggestions will come from users of the proposed system. The program engineering process is responsible for assessing the cost, time and risk impact of changes to the requirements proposed by the users. In assessing the change, the program engineering process relies on information generated by the lower level product engineering process.

Changes can also emerge from the system development process, and program engineering must cope with these suggestions by interacting with the real users or their representative. Changes can flow inward through variations in the available finance or market conditions.

8.7.   A generic system development process

Similar processes are happening at multiple levels in the project structure. The same generic development process, applied recursively and concurrently, describes the whole development. The generic process starts with a request from a customer and responds by generating an abstract solution (system requirements) and an architectural design. This enables the developer to negotiate with suppliers to determine the practicality of proposed designs. With this information, the developer can negotiate the agreement with the customer, and start to generate the agreed system. This views the world from the perspective of each separate development; it is a systems engineering view of the customer-supplier relationship (Figure 8.13).

The generic process is 'context-independent', and applies at the overall systems level and at all lower level sub-system development levels. In each

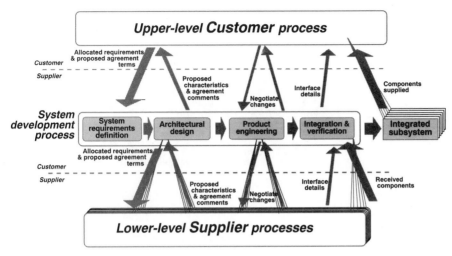

Figure 8.13: Generic system development process

context, it has one customer and many supplier levels. The customer process triggers the process into existence; the supplier interfaces are developed as work proceeds. This process can be applied repeatedly to define the overall development process.

The interactions taking place across the customer-supplier interface during the formative stage are:

- *request/proposal cycle* – to establish the scope and content of what should be done;

- *negotiate agreements* – to agree the exact specification, delivery terms, cost and timescales for the artefacts to be developed.

Interactions across the customer-supplier interface during the build stage are:

- *receive details of lower level interfaces (required to specify detailed test procedures etc.);*

- *receive the developed components from suppliers against the agreed specification;*

- *supply integrated components to the customer according to the agreed specification;*

- *negotiate changes as required with customer and suppliers* – changes can be instigated by the customer, suppliers, or within this level of system development.

Components at many levels

In practice, components will not always appear at just one level of the system development approach (Figure 8.14). One person's system is another person's

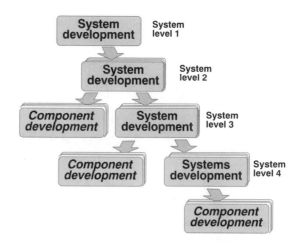

Figure 8.14: Components appearing at different levels

component. The decision to use either the system or component development process should be taken by the supplier, not enforced from above. From the customer viewpoint, the key factor is the level of confidence in the estimates of cost, timescale and performance from the supplier. The customer must be assured that the supplier has properly identified, assessed and quantified all the relevant risks.

Example of a derived requirement: 90% of powertrain faults shall be locatable through built-in test capabilities

An industrial example for a car

Figure 8.15 applies this life cycle to a car, showing the vehicle partitioned into sub-systems such as the engine, bodywork or interior. In turn, the engine separates into the mechanical component (the 'base engine') and the powertrain controller (mostly software) which manages the engine functions. The powertrain controller in turn splits at the next level into the software and hardware elements. The 'hardware' in this component might involve circuit boards, custom chips, connectors and cable harnesses. This diagram was derived during an industrial workshop in the automotive industry.

The model allows requirements to cascade down to any sub-component. For instance, the software for the engine is four levels down. Without this linked cascade of requirements, engineers cannot determine what the software must do. The user and business requirements should define the countries in which the car will be sold. If the car is to be sold in Ecuador, the roads may go to up to 11,000 feet, where there is less oxygen, and special control strategies are needed for the engine. In India, fuel may be sold in bottles at the roadside, and be highly variable in its octane rating and cleanliness. Third-world car repair shops cannot afford expensive diagnostic equipment. Software engineers need all this information to allow them to design the software for built-in test, timing control, response to engine temperature, engine revolutions etc.

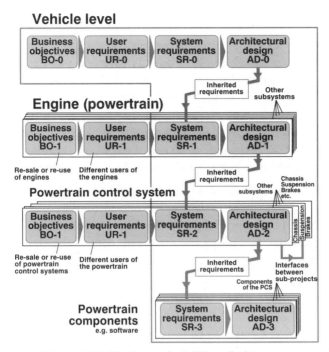

Figure 8.15: The layered model applied to a car

Although the user requirements will not mention software, it is impossible to write this engine control software without knowing what users want.

The diagram illustrates the possibility of user and business requirements occurring at each level, particularly when components are re-used in different developments. In practice, the business may well re-sell the engine separately from the vehicle, for example for use in boats. As a result, there are business requirements that are not derived from the original vehicle requirements. They have to be injected in lower down, at the level of the engine. This approach needs to be carried down another level, because the engine controller is re-sold for several different applications, such as specialized road-cleaning vehicles. Wherever there is re-use, any development therefore has more than one 'parent'. User requirements may be injected at different levels, e.g. the different user requirements from the boat will influence the engine.

8.8. Consequences of a more realistic approach

Organizing the development into distinct levels has numerous advantages such as reduction of document size and complexity, provision of a framework for interfaces, and the ability to postpone design decisions to the correct level. This approach also encourages sub-system definition by engineers with the right domain skills, rather than at the system level. It allows concurrent specification of the overall system rather than freezing the specification and passing it from one level to the next. The approach allows rapid iteration before the design is fixed.

Using a leveled approach also helps control the partitioning, because the whole system is contained in every level at different levels of abstraction. Any component is equivalent to the integrated set of its children. Traceability and control are much easier, in this more structured approach. Organization into levels also makes re-use much easier, because levels correspond to interfaces, which may survive across many systems. For example, in electronic systems the levels could correspond to racks, boxes and connectors. Each level provides a stable framework for definition of interfaces between components.

The multi-level hierarchy meets the need for parallel development of multiple sub-projects. At the lowest level, each component development can proceed separately, within any scheduling and risk constraints required for integration. Similarly, subordinate projects can proceed independently, delivering integrated sets of components to the level above.

There are however disadvantages, especially in the complexity of control that is demanded. Systems engineering is needed at multiple levels, and the feedback between levels can easily be interrupted by contractual or organizational boundaries. These factors are however produced by reality of the world, which the model attempts to capture.

8.9. *Summary*

Complexity, novelty and size combine to make a sequential approach unrealistic. This drives a multi-level approach to ensure that the requirements, design, costs, schedule and risks are always mutually consistent. Component development is undertaken within the context of a specialist discipline using its specific procedures.

Sequential development approaches fall apart when confronted with the complexity of the real world. Finishing a phase and tossing the results 'over-the-wall' is simply not practical even for the smallest systems. Commitment can be safe only when quality, cost, schedule and risks are known to an acceptable tolerance, and mutually acceptable. The project information needs to be organized into multiple levels, which has consequences for the sub-contracting structure and managerial responsibility. The top role of capability development (customer acquisition) occurs once, while systems engineering is repeated for each sub-project.

The more realistic system development model therefore results in:

- *feedback from design before commitment to requirements;*
- *concurrent exploration of design options at many levels;*
- *a multi-level recursive structuring of the system into separated developments;*

— *additional engineering processes to cope with the inevitable changes at all times.*

Despite the complexity of this more realistic model, the component processes of the sequential life cycle still survive almost unchanged. The model is permeated with the basic ideas of traceability and consistency of the sequential life cycle. All requirements must still be consistent with design, and traced to the validation system.

Exercises for A more realistic life cycle

Exercise 32: Inherited requirements

Define 10 requirements that you wish to apply across all software developments for a complex system, such as a plane or a car. Justify each requirement.
Ideally, who should be responsible for stating these requirements and ensuring they are implemented?
What skills are necessary for the group imposing the requirements?
How can a business ensure that these requirements are followed on every project?

Exercise 33: Cascaded requirements

You are producing the software for the ambulance command and control example. The following business and user requirements apply.

The total running costs for the service shall be less than $4.5m per year

The death rate for ambulance patients shall be lower than the national average for equivalent cases

The mean time from receipt of call to collect the patient shall be 8 minutes or less

Write two requirements that could be derived from each of these requirements.

'The mean time from receipt of call to collect the patient shall be 8 minutes or less'
'The mean number of available ambulances shall be more than five'

anagement in multi-level ojects

Introduction

The 'enterprise'

Customer-supplier relationships

Delegation and escalation

Program engineering and product engineering

Different kinds of acquisition

Summary

9.1. Introduction

This chapter covers the management structure and customer-supplier relationships within real-world systems. It shows how the management structure of a project is affected by the design process. In large systems, the component providers must expend systems engineering resources before commitment to a development. A generic model that can apply at any level is then developed.

In a complex system, separate development projects for each subsystem are usually necessary. Each project can lead to the creation of further development projects at a level below. The overall structure of these sub-systems is primarily based on the architectural design, with each sub-system normally becoming a distinct project (Figure 9.1). The management structure at one level is determined by the systems engineering work at the level above.

The system architecture, the set of projects, and contract structures are highly correlated but not exactly one-to-one, so the structures are not identical. Each project will have a single project manager, and as a result, there will be multiple project managers across the development. Of course, some managers may control more than one project.

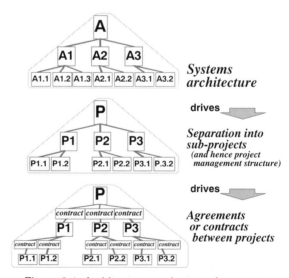

Figure 9.1: Architecture, projects and contracts

Components are therefore defined and developed concurrently, not sequentially. Decisions in one component may interact with many others, and the sequential approaches to management (as described in chapter 6) will not work. Requirements have to be negotiated in the light of design knowledge possessed only by lower level suppliers.

In a concurrent development, the management plan evolves as the system architecture gels. Risks, feasibility, cost and timescale are under constant analysis by multiple projects. As the development proceeds, changes cause interactions across the development structure. Control, delegation and the handling of problems between sub-system developments become essential.

The core management disciplines of configuration management, verification and validation, quality assurance and project management remain, but extra tasks are needed to handle interactions with other development projects.

9.2. The enterprise

Until now, we have used the well-understood term 'business' for the organization that spawns and resources a project. But of course, a business may itself be organized as a set of 'business units' or 'profit centers'. The concepts of a 'business' can be reapplied recursively at many levels throughout an organization. The term 'enterprise' is substituted for 'business' under these more generic circumstances.

Each project in the multi-level structure is handled as an 'enterprise', which authorizes and resources it. Authorizing a project is typically be the responsibility of a business manager within it (see Figure 9.2). The enterprise must hold resources to be able to do work before commitment to a project. The enterprise handles the business, project, and technical issues.

The business manager handles all enterprise issues, and empowers the project manager to plan the development, authorize the work, and monitor progress against this plan. The project manager informs the enterprise about progress, and handles changes to the objectives and/or budget.

In a multi-level development, enterprises at each level authorize their projects. The enterprises must also negotiate agreements (or contracts) with the other enterprises (their customers or suppliers). Thus an enterprise contains three distinct sorts of activity:

  — *the enterprise or business aspects;*

Figure 9.2: Projects are authorized within a business

– *the project management;*

– *technical areas.*

The enterprise handles sales, marketing, finance and contractual issues, defines working practices, and monitors their application across all its projects. The development behaves as if it were a 'mini-enterprise', receiving a bundle of requirements and resources, and in return delivering a conformant component (Figure 9.3).

Figure 9.3: The 'enterprise' function

A complete development can be thought of as a 'super-project' that contains the set of projects authorized by the enterprises, and linked by customer–supplier agreements. All intermediate levels, 'enterprises' act both as a supplier to the level above and as customers for components from the level below (Figure 9.4). Each enterprise is effectively a partially independent agent, running its own business and treating all other elements as if they are external.

9.3. Customer-supplier relationships

Relations between enterprises can be thought of in classic customer–supplier terms. Of course, this process is not indefinitely recursive, but even the customer for the complete system usually supplies that end product as part of a larger system. At the lowest level, the end of the supply chain might be the material suppliers, but even these may acquire the raw material in bulk from their own suppliers.

An enterprise may itself initiate sub-projects (Figure 9.5), performed by external or internal suppliers. For external suppliers, a request for proposal (RFP) for components is then sent to external suppliers. For internal supply, a less formal approach such as an inter-departmental memo or tasking form may be used. This triggers negotiations between the customer and supplier, which may eventually result in a firm contract. Before this happens the

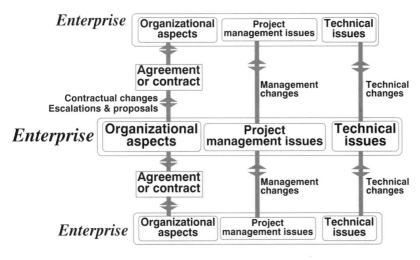

Figure 9.4: The enterprise function

supplier will in turn negotiate with other suppliers to check the feasibility of the proposal.

When a product is being developed and marketed for sale, the stage-gate approach described in chapter 13 will be used to trigger the project. When the end component is a part of a larger system, the first step will usually be to prepare a proposal. This requires systems engineering work to determine potential solutions and their cost and risk. Work is also necessary to establish suppliers for components which must be bought in or separately developed. Work to generate proposals will not be funded by a customer, but by each enterprise. Enterprises at each development level must therefore have the resources necessary for the work needed before commitment.

Everyone is a customer – everyone is a supplier

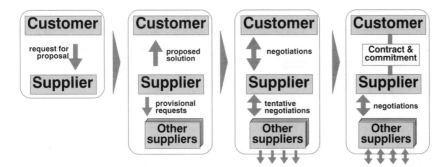

Figure 9.5: Commitment between levels

Figure 9.6: Selecting suppliers

Customer view

Customer–supplier relationships cascade down through the multiple development levels, and generally start long before full commitment. This interaction involves business, project and technical issues. Figure 9.6 indicates the customer's view of the customer–supplier interface.

The project manager has to determine what is required, then establish a set of potential suppliers. As we have seen, this involves systems engineering effort to identify the components and produce an outline specification. This foundation work establishes the overall system requirements, an architectural design and component identification in enough detail to estimate cost and risk. After establishing an initial specification, the project manager issues requests for proposals (RFPs) to potential suppliers. Suppliers eventually respond with an indication of cost, delivery time and specification. This necessarily involves negotiation between the supplier and the project manager, who relies on technical assistance from system engineers.

The project manager, plus team members, evaluate the proposals and select the best suppliers. These decisions will involve trade-offs between the technical specifications for the proposed components, plus their cost, delivery time and assessed risk. Negotiations with each chosen supplier can then complete the best deal possible.

Supplier view

Suppliers do not start serious work until the RFP arrives, and even the preparation of a proposal is itself a project, absorbing resources, and needing a degree of commitment. Unless this work is done, the supplier is bidding blindfold. The project manager (or bid manager as they are often called at this point) prepares a plan for the bid.

To produce a proposal with an acceptable level of risk, the supplier will usually need to generate system requirements and an outline architectural design for the required component. Where the component is unusual or complex, intensive risk management work may be needed by the supplier. External suppliers may supply components more efficiently than internal developers, and these should be identified and selected. Thus the communication model must include the supplier's relationships with its own suppliers (Figure 9.7).

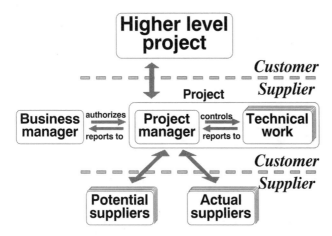

Figure 9.7: Suppliers can also have suppliers

Agreements are made to proceed if the higher level enterprise wins the bid. The higher level enterprise can then respond to its potential customer with a proposal that incorporates realistic information about components from lower level enterprises.

The project view

Once all the supply agreements are in place, lower level projects in the supply chain can be triggered. The communication model can be redrawn as indicated in Figure 9.8. Each level is authorized by its own enterprise,

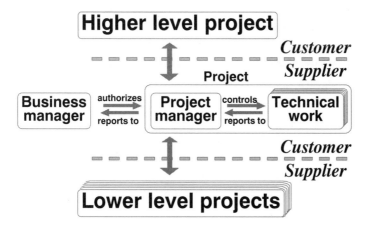

Figure 9.8: Communication paths for the project manager

empowering the project manager to proceed. In a multilevel development the project manager interacts upwards to customer projects and downwards to suppliers.

Figure 9.9 shows the contractual and technical communication paths. For instance, complex systems demand in-depth technical discussions between engineers across the enterprise boundaries. These interactions should happen only with the approval of the project managers at each level, although the project managers are unlikely to be deeply involved. Interactions between enterprises primarily concern contractual issues between customers and suppliers and inevitably involve the project manager.

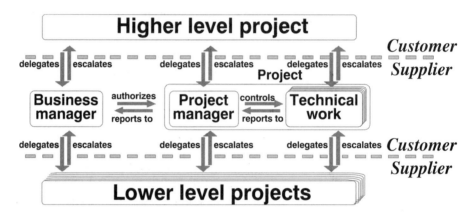

Figure 9.9: Business, project and technical interaction

9.4.   Delegation and escalation

Although project managers have overall responsibility, the whole project must work as a team for success. As a result, authority must be delegated through the levels of a project, and from the enterprise to the engineers who perform the work. When problems arise that cannot be handled locally, they must be escalated to the levels that they affect. Figure 9.9 shows the interaction between the business, project and technical roles in a multi-level development.

Enterprises delegate authority to their suppliers through customer–supplier agreements.

Technical interactions take place between all levels between system engineers. This allows them to make technical decisions in the best interests of their development. the issue is primarily technical, consultation is needed with the system engineers in the higher level system (Figure 9.9). When the issue primarily affects cost, timescale or commercial aspects, it escalates to the project manager.

If a problem does affect the contract, the project manager handles it directly. Problems involving project management issues normally escalate to the project manager at the level above. In other cases, a contract amendment may require changes to the original specification, payment terms, or schedule. As problems escalate, they shift left in the diagram, from technical areas to project management and then to business issues.

9.5. *Program engineering and product engineering*

In chapter 8, two variants of technical management emerged as necessary to handle complex systems – *program engineering* and *product engineering*. These technical roles handle all the technical issues as components are developed by lower level suppliers.

At the top level of the system, program engineering is the technical authority that acts for the acquisition role of the system. This role occurs only once in the project.

The product engineering process **controls all the issues lying above the single component**. This includes resolving interface problems between two components, monitoring the key parameters such as cost and risk, change management, and the planning of integration. This role occurs at many levels in the development.

Handling change during the component definition and implementation is the key role of product engineering. Change can be driven from above e.g. through alterations in the enterprise or working environment may force a re-evaluation of a design. It may turn out to be impossible to produce a design to meet the requirements, forcing changes on requirements at the levels above. Change may even be driven by related components at the same level, when an interface becomes problematic. As components are manufactured, feedback provides detail about the actual costs of implementation or operation, risks, more detail of the predicted schedule, and the possibility of implementing new requirements. As the design solidifies, the estimated costs may escalate.

While the components are being developed, *planning for integration* is performed by system development. This becomes more detailed as the components are defined.

When the components are delivered, system development integrates those components (see chapter 5), eventually delivering an assembly to the level above. Thus system development acts as a supplier to the level above and a customer for the levels below. Because the processes of system requirements, architecture, and integration have already been defined in earlier chapters, this section restricts itself to the additional areas.

The major variant of the system development role occurs at the system level, where system development covers the complete system as an entity, rather than multiple components.

Component construction

Component construction is performed at the lowest level of the system, using specialist disciplines, and lies outside the domain of systems engineering. A variety of skills such as integrated circuit design, mechanical engineering and software development may be needed even to build an individual component. System development occurs at many levels, and hence one person's component may be decomposed into further sub-components. The amount of visibility and control on component development may vary widely according to the policy, level of trust, and the number of staff available.

Contractual agreements between system levels

Figure 9.10 illustrates the nature of the contract between system levels. This may be a less formal agreement ('work order') when the work is performed inside the same enterprise. In turn, each development interacts in a similar way with its own suppliers. Requirements are imposed both on the product to be produced and also the development processes (e.g. schedule or reporting). There is effectively an 'agreement' between the systems engineering and each development below containing both requirements on the product and the way it is to be developed. The agreement also contains the commitments from the upper level, such as the available resources, or the time to be taken for decision-making.

The managerial requirements on a sub-system may include:

- *schedule – start date, required date;*

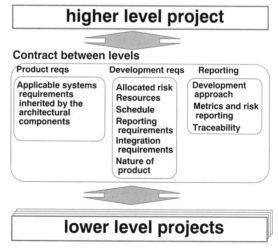

Figure 9.10: Agreement between projects at different levels

    — *risk level applied to the package;*

    — *available resources for the development.*

During development, the project reports back to the enterprise, detailing the costs, risks, and the current status of the requirements. The project can then calculate the 'benefit' to the enterprise. The project uses the system development process to define and control its own sub-systems.

The primary flows under the agreement are the information and the delivered configuration items. Other flows are concerned with the important aspect of change management. Change can come from either side, and a change proposal from above causes the project to respond with a proposed change. If agreed, this is eventually bound up in a contractual change. Change suggestions coming from below must be accompanied by a proposal.

9.6. Different kinds of acquisition

Variations in the nature of the acquisition will affect the development processes (Figure 9.11). Consider the differences between mass-production (e.g. a cellular phone) and the acquisition of a single system (e.g. an aircraft carrier or a Channel Tunnel).

In mass-production, users are represented by the marketing department. The actual purchase of the system may be affected by rival products, by errors in market intelligence or value of the market. Where a product is custom-made, a representative handles the interests of users. This role is needed throughout

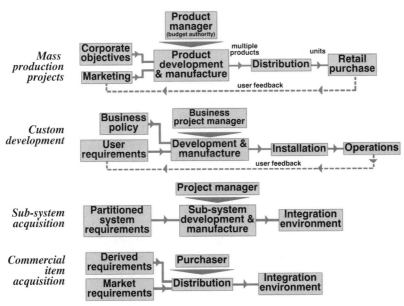

Figure 9.11: Different types of acquisition

the development process. In custom development, as for a military aircraft, the customer is (nominally) pre-determined. The customer pays for the development, or reimburses costs even if the development is cancelled.

In some cases, the product exists already, and is typically purchased from a distributor. Even these existing commercial components should be chosen against requirements, and be implemented into a larger system. A typical example might be the elevators in a building or the hydraulics systems on a plane. These 'components' will be bought from specialist manufacturers, and integrated into a hotel and an airplane respectively.

Each of these types of acquisition can be considered as a variant of the generic acquisition cycle, which includes users, acquirer, and developers working within their own environments. The major differences between the types of acquisition lie in:

> ***risk sharing;*** *a custom-made development has a commitment from the purchaser. Even though this commitment may not be as firm as it seems, it does not depend on open competition in the marketplace.*

> ***evolutionary production or one-off developments;*** *evolution enhancements of an item such as a cellular phone mean that there is a continuous flow of information that helps improve the equipment. A single item like a tunnel or a bridge has to work first time, and is difficult (but not impossible) to upgrade. However, knowledge of how to build better bridges is held within the enterprises involved to improve bridges yet to be built.*

9.7.   Summary

In complex systems, the architecture drives the management structure across the sub-projects. Architectural components tend to be split out and handled as individual developments. The architectural design therefore also drives the information structure for the system, showing the deliverables and their inter-relationships, and defining the managerial responsibilities. The roles of program engineering and product engineering are essential to coordinate complex developments. These roles perform the technical control as the project decomposes into multiple projects. A good methodology is therefore essential if these roles are to be performed properly.

The roles of program engineering and product engineering are essential to control component developments. Program engineering is often poorly handled and perceived as being a non-technical role, but the customer-side role is critical to success. Producing a structured set of user requirements, managing the reality of development and successfully accepting a system requires a disciplined engineering approach from the customer and supplier.

From the customer's point of view, the project is controlled by the program manager, who controls the user requirements and the resources to ensure those requirements are implemented. The designer may however think of himself/herself as controlling the project. After all both are specifying the design, and how the system is implemented. In reality, both claims are true – one controls the user requirements and releases the funds, the other manages the design and the way the money is spent.

Exercises for Management in multi-level projects

Exercise 34: A project to build a vehicle

A vehicle designer decides that all intelligent electronic sub-systems will communicate with a standard messaging system based around a fiber-optic LAN. In which document should these requirements be stated?
Where is the detailed design of the messaging done?
Half the components for the vehicle are supplied by outside contractors. You are a major customer for them. Define how to would cope with this situation.

Exercise 35: Levels of control

An enterprise manages the acquisition of large systems simply by controlling the user requirements. It will accept (and pay for) the systems on the basis of conformance to the user requirements. What are the likely problems of such an approach? What must the enterprise do to reduce these problems?

Exercise 36: Contacting the end-user

You are building a telecommunications switch, a sub-system which is integrated by your customer as part of a telecommunications system. You want to sell this switch around the world. The working environment for the telecommunications systems is changing rapidly, with end users demanding more functions. The customer passes you well-organized requirements, but tries to prevent you from contacting its users. As a result you never see a set of user requirements and are suspicious that they do not really exist.
Define why you need to know the user requirements and define an approach to find out these requirements, without offending the customer.

Software and systems

10.1. The information economy

All new systems, even those regarded as 'physical,' now contain large amounts of software. Most of the new functionality and added value of financial services, aircraft, digital television and cars are implemented through software. A modern car may contain 20–30 microprocessors, with software controlling aspects such as engine ignition, pollution control, security, air-conditioning, car radios or even the seat position. New financial services, such as pension schemes and phone-based insurance are totally reliant on databases and communication software. Even a building such as a hotel will be littered with software for controlling reservations, managing phones, billing the guests, and managing the elevators. Analysis software increases the amount of oil that can be extracted from a complex oilfield. Information technology is now the largest US industry, ahead of construction and the automotive industry[48]. Software has become critical to the industrial success of almost all modern products.

In most developments, software is also the component on the critical path, and takes the blame for system development problems. The fundamental reasons for this have little to do with software, but are related to size and complexity. Modern products are more complex than before, and most of that complexity is implemented in software. These features would not be remotely feasible without software. Typically we are trying to build new features into products such as cars, cameras, or telecommunications systems to make them more competitive. As an example, the braking system of a modern car detects the onset of skids, senses the dynamics of the driver's foot on the brake, and works even with the complete failure of one hydraulic system. The brakes are far more complicated than they used to be. Software represents a substantial, often dominant, part of the overall complexity of the vehicle.

Companies that do not manage software development efficiently are destined to fail. If your software strategy and development processes are strong, you can add extra functionality to almost any product before rivals can respond. The development cycle for products has been reduced, and products can now be rapidly deployed worldwide in months. You do not need a big factory to mass-produce software and send it around the world. Companies can dominate a world market with a few months' technological lead over their rivals, especially for easily replicated software-based products.

In the past, software engineering was a small element of the system, and any problems could be cured by the injection of more resources. Almost invisibly, software now controls the fate of companies. This dependence on software leads to novel requirements for availability, integrity and security. If its information systems fail, a financial company may not survive a single day. Enterprises have become so dependent on software that there are major risks involved in computers breaking down, information being lost, stolen, or interfered with. This generates major (and expensive) requirements for reliability and upgradeability.

10.2. Software and market leadership

When new technology is introduced, most profit comes from being at the leading edge of the market. Whenever a new, better product is released, the unit profits are high because there is little competition. If a company can reach a reasonable level of sales before rival technology emerges, it can extract most of the available profits (Figure 10.1)[49&50]. According to a McKinsey report, a six-month delay in introducing a new product costs 33% of profits, whereas over-running the development budget has only a minor impact on the eventual profitability[51]. Many modern products have short cycle times, and this is probably an under-estimate. The leading company gets the patents first on new technology, with all the opportunities that gives to block competitors or license intellectual property.

As the technology becomes commonplace, the product becomes a commodity, an updated version is released to renew the cycle. By repeatedly releasing improved products with this cycle, a company can absorb most of the available profit and starve rivals of the funds that they need to close the gap. The improvement carries on until the technology limits are exhausted, and the effort shifts to process improvement.[52]

Hewlett-Packard provides an excellent example of a strategic approach to software in a 'hardware' industry. When Canon produced print engines for

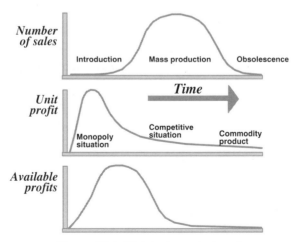

Figure 10.1: High-tech product cycle

laser printers in the early 1980s, Hewlett-Packard fielded products a few months before rivals, because it already had software available from its plotters. By the time Canon produced their first color ink-jet, Hewlett-Packard who had already sold millions, responded with an improved version and cut their prices. More than a decade later, Hewlett-Packard still had 55% of the ink-jet market in a multi-billion dollar industry, holding on to the start given by software. They have maintained that lead by continually releasing improved printers, keeping them ahead of rivals such as Canon and Epson.

Hewlett-Packard managed the tricky feat of keeping their lead through a discontinuous change of printer technology, i.e. from laser jet to ink jet. Normally the market leader loses out in such a transition, as Epson had with dot-matrix printers a decade earlier.

Hewlett-Packard had learned this lesson the hard way. Two decades earlier, they had an equivalent market lead in hand-held calculators, but lost it with an inappropriate marketing approach. They aimed to sell their 'better' calculator at a high price, and leave the commodity market to Japanese producers. But gradually Casio and Seiko matched them technically at a fraction of their price, and took the market from underneath. Hewlett-Packard were determined not to repeat this marketing mistake with printers.

Software as the soul of the system

Software is quietly assuming another key role with system-level implications. In many modern products, software now controls the interactions between the sub-systems. Software has become the 'soul' of the system, often as the central 'data management system' (DMS). Where the same information is required across many different sub-systems (e.g. temperature or time), the software-based data management system coordinates the whole task. The DMS handles the sensors, co-ordinates actions and timing across the system, controls the overall status, and copes with the faults.

As an example in banking, it is the bank's financial systems that determine when to buy and sell stock, and how to interact with the customers. If the computers broke down, the bank would not survive more than a day. As systems grow more intelligent, this central role grows more significant.

Even this representation of the importance of software is insufficient. In a typical modern product, software handles the key tasks of user interface, management of the overall system, and implements most of the functionality. Architectures for software-intensive systems, such as a car, a cellular phone or a satellite, are often dominated by the data management system and the user interface. At the top level, the user interface is full of software, although it also involves hardware aspects such as dials, steering wheels, a mouse, and displays. The data management system at the level below acts as the coordinator of all the sub-systems – the software is 'first-among-equals'.

Below this, embedded within the sub-systems, are many software components, often closely tied into hardware components (Figure 10.2).

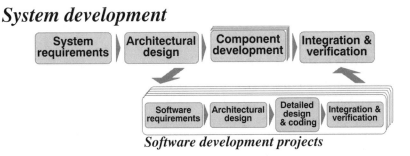

Software development projects

Figure 10.2: Embedded software within a system

10.3. Problems of software in systems

Types of software-dominated systems

Two types of systems, both highly dependent on software, need to be distinguished:

Software-intensive systems (SISs) – large systems that are essentially software-based. To handle software correctly they will need to use systems engineering principles. Examples include information systems, command and control systems, and financial systems.

Software-shaped systems (SSSs) – complex systems containing mixtures of software, hardware, and people. Software is, however, the critical element in terms of cost, added value and risk. Examples include cameras, cars, planes, and cellular phones.

In SSSs, the need to apply systems engineering principles is clear. The problem is relating the software to the system development. When the systems are almost totally composed of software, an obvious starting point is to imagine that any problems are caused by software. These projects need to handle decomposition, risk management, interface control, and integration – i.e. systems engineering. The problems of software-intensive systems cannot however be solved through software engineering alone.

For a variety of reasons, SISs and SSSs – especially for large systems – are plagued by problems. The tough job is making very large (>1,000 person-years) software-dominated products, which are known to be difficult to develop. We have all seen well-publicized examples of software disasters – the Denver Airport baggage system, Ariane V, or the UK Taurus stock exchange system. Closer examination of these software-related disasters

The difficulty in large software development is primarily systems, not software engineering

often reveals problems at the managerial level. In the Ariane V proto-flight rocket launch (1996), the launcher exploded just after take-off. Software for the inertial platform had been re-used from the previous, different launcher – Ariane IV. It had not been validated for Ariane V flight conditions, and a module of software that was not even required for Ariane V drove the rocket to destruction[53].

10.4. Software shaped systems

In an SSS, software will not appear in the requirements or early design stages (Figure 10.2). After all, there are no user requirements for software – it may or may not be part of the solution. The same applies at the system requirements stage, because only the functionality is defined, and a function could at this stage be implemented by software, hardware or people. For example, a vehicle may need to meet new standards for reduced pollution.

Individual packages of software start to appear at the architectural design process on a small system, and several levels down in the architecture of a bigger system (Figure 10.3). Until this point, there are no software components per se, i.e. each component is an indeterminate mixture of software, hardware, and people.

Example system-level requirement for software– All software components shall communicate using the standard messaging protocol

In a modern system, pieces of software will appear in many separate places scattered across the design. In a car, for example, software controls the engine, vehicle security, brakes, air-conditioning and dashboard displays, and even equipment such as the mirror and seat position. Components such as automatic braking systems are often bought in from specialist producers, and need to be integrated into the vehicle. They inevitably contain large amounts of embedded software. Manufacturers often buy in components from several different producers to ensure a safe supply, but then have to interface several different external components to the single internal component.

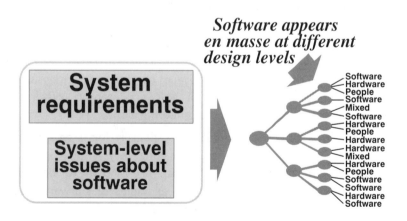

Figure 10.3: Software within system projects

Enterprise and system-level issues of software

Because software is so dispersed and important, many issues about it need to be considered outside the individual software developments. Examples include development standards, security, software engineering methods, resources, messaging, data integrity and freshness and control structures between the packages. The two factors that are immediately leapt upon – tools and programming languages – may be possible candidates but are usually over-emphasized. These 'system-level' issues are defined in a section of the system requirements. They demand appropriate expertise and resources at the system level to prepare for multiple software developments.

Software is critical to enterprise success, and therefore needs to be driven by enterprise requirements. Managers then need to supply the resources and managerial structures to develop software to meet these needs. The modern enterprise needs to drive and manage its software engineering efficiently to meet its goals.

10.5. The software engineering process

As the system breaks down to its component parts, each element can be labeled as performed by hardware, software or people. A single piece of software implements some of the functionality required at the level above. Some non-functional requirements (e.g. reliability) will be tied to that functionality. Effectively an agreement forms between the system and software engineering roles – the former the customer and the latter the service provider.

The software engineering process takes the package of requirements from the level above and implements it as a piece of tested software, ready for integration. Figure 10.4 shows the software development process, covering an individual software component. Normally there are **no** direct user requirements for the software package.

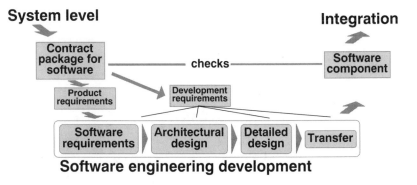

Figure 10.4: Defining a package of software

Partitioning and packaging these requirements into individual software components is a systems engineering task. The allocation is based on criteria such as cost of implementation, cost of replication, speed of implementation efficiency, ease of change, and error rates during operation.

Small-to-medium software systems (< 50 person-years) are much easier to handle than huge SISs. Large SISs therefore need to be decomposed into less intricate, more manageable, components. Systems engineering occurs at multiple levels until the software components split out at the bottom of the system decomposition. Of course, this demands overall systems engineering control for aspects such as the overall performance, resource utilization and performance.

Linkage between systems and software

Eventually a package of requirements will be allocated to software. It will consist of a set of functions, plus the related non-functional requirements for the developing system and the software engineering role. Figure 10.5 illustrates the information structure that allows communication between the systems and software engineering roles. The function to be implemented in software is determined by negotiations between the system engineer and software engineer, and the appropriate set of requirements marked out in the system requirements document. This is sent from the system requirements set to the top level of the software CASE tool. The system and software engineers eventually agree a package of requirements to be implemented, along with schedules and resource limitations. As the software engineer

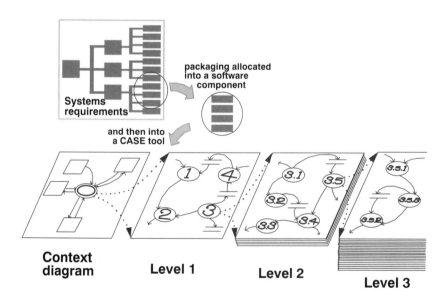

Figure 10.5: Linking system requirements to CASE tools

implements the functions through different levels of hierarchy, they can be marked off as complete in the software tool. If the interface exists, this traceability information can be fed back automatically to the system engineer. The system engineer can then monitor progress of the software development. Most CASE tools (currently) have almost no capability to handle non-functional requirements, but usually have a notepad which allows requirements to be ticked off as each function is implemented and tested.

The software engineer will also need to understand the system context of that software – the related hardware elements, and the system and user requirements that lead to the need for that software.

Software-intensive system process

Figure 10.6 shows the systems engineering processes applied to a large software-intensive system (SIS), for example a command and control system or the set of IT projects within an organization. The principle of organization of the software into components is essentially the same as for hardware. Above the level of software implementation, the technical work is about decomposition, feedback, and risk management. At the lowest level, the components are all software or predominantly software. Software engineers perform the development of these components. Figure 10.7 shows the full systems engineering model applied to a SIS, and it is fundamentally the same as for any other development.

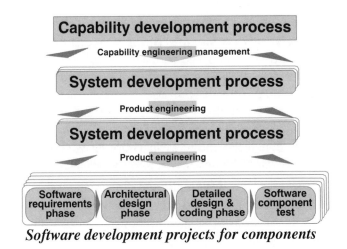

Software development projects for components

Figure 10.6: Organization within SISs

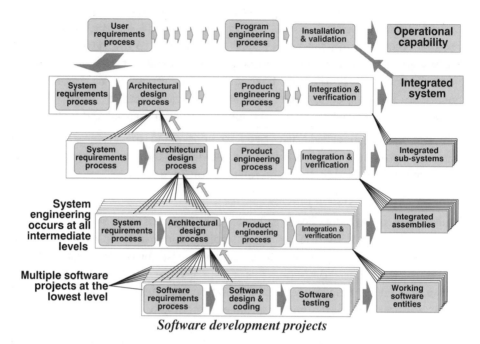

Software development projects

Figure 10.7: Software-intensive systems

10.6. Differences between systems and software

The software and systems engineering processes overlap considerably but there are significant differences between software and systems, such as:

Software (effectively) has no manufacturing process. Replicating a million copies of software is trivial compared to making a million copies of a vehicle. Software is also cheap to reproduce for test or for configuration management. The disadvantage is that software can also be easily pirated. Configuration management of software can also become a nightmare, because of multiple versions. You end up with dozens of copies of marginally different information ('just-in-case'), and then make mistakes in choosing which copy to use. In software but not hardware, the designer is also the manufacturer.

Any change to software is a design change. Repairing a car returns it to its original state – we need only test that the repair was done correctly. When software is 'repaired', it always changes the design. Hence it needs re-testing – perhaps the whole system needs re-testing even if only a single line of code is changed. A producer would never accept an unfinished design for manufacture, yet we constantly face this risk in software systems.

Systems engineering is multi-disciplinary, software is a single discipline. System engineers are regularly involved with trade-offs between disciplines, contradiction, flexibility, and intervening in arguments between specialist disciplines. Software engineering is a single discipline, and technically each project receives requirements from above as a starting point. Some software engineers work in a fantasy world of zero gravity and infinite performance, where nothing ever decays or needs maintenance. Experience slowly teaches them to take a more realistic and practical view.

Systems are analog and concurrent, software is serial and digital. The nature of computers means that software programs distort reality in ways which may be obscure to users and programmers. The real world is analog, but software models this world with discrete zeros and ones. At some invisible point between the real world and the software, there is a transition from continuity to discrete values. We never know when this may cause critical failures in models which appear to work well most of the time. If we test a bridge with a ten ton weight and then with twenty tons, we naturally feel it need not to be tested with fifteen tons. But a software program may need to be tested for every possible input value. Normally a small change in input values in a system causes small changes in output, but this is not necessarily true in software. Also the underlying model is a serial process, which may map uncomfortably to parallelism of the real world.

Software is usually inherently complex. Software is particularly suitable for handling some types of complexity – behavioral and dynamic. As a result, the system complexity is preferentially put into the software. A software program may contain hundreds of thousands of lines of code, and thousands of active fragments of code. A fault in any one can kill the system. The mechanical components of a complex system have fewer parts, more uniformity between those parts and – critically – those parts are usually passive, not active.

Failures in software tend to be immediate and total. Hardware often groans before it fails, allowing time to detect and repair problems before disaster strikes. A failure in one area does not usually break the whole system. Software rarely fails in this way. The effects of a software defect are often immediate and catastrophic. A different approach to testing and defending against malfunction has to be adopted.

Once software is perfect, it does not wear out. Hardware needs replacement parts, logistics support, servicing, changes of oil, and logistics. At least in theory, software is not damaged by use or testing, nor does it need 'support'. However, software (or the system containing it) may well need to be designed to cope with hardware failures or deterioration, or even faults in critical pieces of software. This may involve built-in test, or redundancy in hardware or software so that failures are isolated before they cause disasters.

Interface penetration is much higher for software than hardware components. A physical system can be protected with guards and a wire fence. But the slightest computer link to the outside world presents a risk of external leakage or internal corruption. A software interface can carry complicated commands as well as pure data, and these commands can affect behavior on the other side of the interface. Higher interface penetration makes modularity more problematic for software than for hardware, i.e. it is difficult to isolate elements. This usually requires standardization of commands across the whole system, and validation of the data ranges across interfaces. We need to avoid or perhaps minimize common areas of data that multiple programs can access.

Software normally **contains more novelty** than physical systems. A house that contained more than, say 10–20% of novel components would rightly be regarded as a prototype, likely to fail. Software programs, even when they are updates of existing systems, contain a large percentage of new code. The combination of novelty and intrinsic complexity makes for high risk.

Comprehensive **testing of software** can easily be impossible, for all except the smallest programs. There are typically too many combinations of inputs, decision paths and tests to check out every permutation. Asynchronous software introduces a new element of uncertainty because system paths are governed by the random events generated by the environment. This makes repeatable tests difficult to organize and tracking down the origins of known faults is painful. These factors make it expensive or perhaps even impossible to use software in areas of extreme criticality. In 1990, the AT&T signalling network ran amok, taking the whole telecommunications network down. The fault was a missing character in a line of code for a minor upgrade feature deemed not to require testing. Even a simple non-concurrent system can generate very difficult testing problems. For instance, it would take several hundred years at a million tests per second to test all the possible input combinations for a 9–digit floating-point multiplier.

Emphasize the data, de-emphasize the non-data – Edward Tufte

10.7. The user interface

The user interface (UI) is a major component of many modern systems. The UI presents the current state of the system to users, and allows them to control the system. The concept of treating user interface as a single entity is familiar to software engineers, but user interfaces are just as important in physical systems. For example, the user interface of a car consists of the **set of controls** (*steering wheel, pedals, switches), and* **feedback** (*lights, dials, windshield, vibrations, noises*). The concept of a user interface can however be extended further to consider the labelling, styling, coloring of paints & fabrics, and all display elements which require a consistent approach. For example, the engine parts that need user servicing, such as oil, water, and anti-freeze can all be marked in yellow. In a plane, the user interface will include all the screen displays, dials, views out of the windows, and other aspects such as vibration of the control stick. The typical user interface is therefore composed of many elements such as the display and controls, on-line help, manuals, telephone help-line and training.

In many modern systems, the user interface absorbs most of the processing power and most of the computer memory. The interface shows the state of the system to users as clearly as possible and hides unwanted information. Feedback on the current system status has to be given, and emergency warnings supplied.

The user interface of the vehicle should consistently help car drivers handle every problem, but never distract the driver. Similar tasks should be approached in a consistent way, and similar information shown in the same format. The text on dials and all forms of lighting should be consistent. The user interface should help to avoid user errors, such as attempting to start the car when the engine is already working.

Modern cars can potentially keep the driver in touch, giving information about traffic jams, handling the music on a CD and radio or warning about the engine and fuel status. The challenge for the designer is to convey this information clearly without distracting the driver. The 'information load' on the driver must be minimized, especially when driving. For instance, detailed maps should not be visible to the driver at 70 mph, but any passenger should be able to access them. This creates difficult, sometimes impossible, problems about how to inform drivers without disturbing them.

The computer and the visual metaphor should be invisible to the user

Tufte's books[54] show techniques to present information clearly and reduce clutter. Although they are not about computers, these books should be mandatory reading for user interface designers. Tufte also shows excellent presentation techniques drawn from a wide variety of sources – maps, sculptures, and buildings. For example, Tufte clearly shows which colors to use to convey different kinds of information.

The London Underground (subway) map is a superb example of presenting information clearly through abstract graphics design[55]. This 1930's map presents the readers with everything they need to know about the Underground network, and nothing else. The map strips away all the irrelevant detail in a normal map, is far smaller than if it were a faithful representation, and much clearer to read.

The fundamental rules of presentation are to emphasize data and suppress non-data. This involves stripping away information junk, such as pie-charts, clip art, or unnecessarily strong borders. Anything conveying real information should be emphasized. User interface designers need to become humble. If their presentation techniques are obvious, they have failed. It is worth taking a lesson from typographers, who have learned that their job is to make text clear, comfortable and elegant, but never intrusive[56]. The perfect user interface is invisible, letting the user see the task transparently, unencumbered by the presentation technique.

The visual metaphor

A system presents itself to users through a 'visual metaphor', a key concept and one that is often completely misunderstood. The visual metaphor for a word processor is a sheet of paper through which we scroll. The visual metaphor for a car is a steering wheel, the control pedals and switches, the dials and gauges, the view through the windshield, and more subtle feedback such as noise and vibration. The more familiar and 'physical' the visual metaphor, the quicker the user can start to work. For example, the computers on the Boeing 777 shake the control stick to warn about stalling, a simulation of the effect with which pilots are familiar.

Historically (on systems) the user interface has been defined by sketches, which have been turned into a variety of prototypes, and gradually more representative implementations. Creating a good visual metaphor requires understanding of the user task, artistry, design skills, humility, and some knowledge of what is possible (and not possible) with computers. These skills are rarely combined in one person.

From a systems engineering viewpoint, the design of the user interface is driven through non-functional requirements and graphical sketches, both as part of the system requirements. From a purist's viewpoint, the user interface provides no system functionality, although it makes the existing system functionality more visible and easier to control by users. As a result, it may not figure too much in the system functionality, but will be a large component in the architectural design. Where the visual metaphor is fundamentally important, it should form part of the system requirements document (see chapter 3 for an example). At this stage, the images can be created with a drawing package or even by sketching. These initial sketches are **not** a definition of the interface, but illustrate and explain the elements required in the user interface.

Development process for the user interface

Some of the work of designing an interface can be done with a graphics user interface (GUI) toolkit. These software programs simulate, then help implement, the user interface. Early in the development, the user interface can be the most tangible element to the user. Modern tools make it easy to generate some parts of the interface.

In software systems, the command structure produced by the GUI kit may form the framework for the code. The functional code can be tied on to the buttons, windows and selectors. Figure 10.8 shows the development cycle for the user interface. In general, the user interface will 'lead' the development of

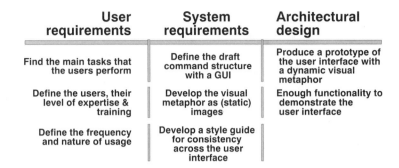

User requirements	System requirements	Architectural design
Find the main tasks that the users perform	Define the draft command structure with a GUI	Produce a prototype of the user interface with a dynamic visual metaphor
Define the users, their level of expertise & training	Develop the visual metaphor as (static) images	Enough functionality to demonstrate the user interface
Define the frequency and nature of usage	Develop a style guide for consistency across the user interface	

Figure 10.8: Developing the user interface

the rest of the system. The interface helps users visualize the whole system and supply feedback.

In the user requirements process, the nature and experience of users and their domain should be defined. The user interface will also be affected by whether they use the system continuously, or perhaps only in emergencies.

Sketches in requirements

In both software and systems, the user interface forms part of the system requirements and is best defined through a combination of pictures, textual requirements and comments.

During the system requirements process, sketches, command structures, and a style guide for the user interface can be generated. A prototype user interface can also be produced. An annotated sketch is an excellent start. Figure 10.9 shows a real-world example of a sketch as a part of the requirements, then later translated into a real interface. This sketch used small, triangular icons to illustrate the existence of 'links' needed between a requirement and other information.

Figure 10.10 shows the eventual result of the user interface produced as a result of that sketch. Most of the concepts have been implemented, and the eventual implementation is different, but still recognizable. Only the core

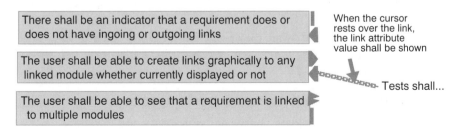

Figure 10.9: Original requirements sketch for the user interface

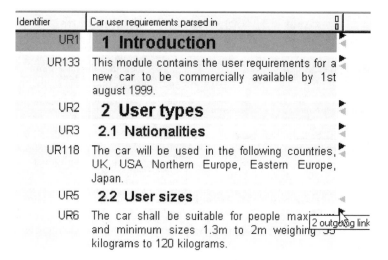

Figure 10.10: Eventual user interface

concepts need be covered in these sketches, because the end product will inevitably look different. Once those core ideas are reasonably settled, the user interface can be prototyped with a graphical user interface toolkit.

During architectural design, the architecture of the final user interface should be defined, and a fully working prototype of the user interface should be produced. This can be used as a prototype for the whole system, or used simply to improve the user interface itself. You must choose your GUI toolkit by this point at the latest. GUI toolkits are of little use in defining the visual metaphor, but do provide the frame for it, and connections to the commands.

During the architectural design process, we should have a good simulation of the user interface by having developed:

- *the architecture and appearance of the visual metaphor;*
- *interfaces to sensors and controls;*
- *the command structure;*
- *interfaces to coding modules.*

One of the authors attempted to prototype the user interface during the user requirements process. The result was an abject failure. You have to understand the users and what they want before even starting to prototype the user interface. This work has to be the initial task of the user requirements phase.

10.8. Summary about software and systems

Considerable overlap exists between software and systems but the differences are much too great to treat the two disciplines as identical. As software grows more complex, it behaves more like a system and has to be managed as a systems engineering problem. At the management level, however, the development processes for software and systems are similar. The manager must avoid the siren lure of getting dragged into the detailed technical issues and focus on meaningful deliverables and schedules.

Software is so important, pervasive and time-critical in almost all modern systems that it must be handled as a key system-level issue, despite the fact that the individual software components are developed at a lower level. In turn this requires well-defined systems engineering processes which show how to structure the software within systems. The software and system processes must be consistent across the enterprise. Software must be understood and resourced from the management and systems engineering levels.

Not surprisingly, the problems exhibited by software-intensive systems are mainly due to systems engineering, not software. Focusing on the software issues alone can rarely solve them. Software engineers therefore need to understand the systems engineering processes to see their own work in the context of the whole system.

Software packages are just as critical for the development of systems as for use in the end product. Software is the main mechanism in reducing the development cycle and improving performance through tools such as CAD/CAM, requirements management, project management, test systems, chip design, and software design.

The user interface is a critical element in most modern systems, and emerges progressively as the lifecycle proceeds. This is the most tangible element of a software system and is ideal for early prototyping to produce a good visual metaphor.

Exercises for Software and systems

Exercise 37: Development approach for software projects

You are the project manager for a large system development for a complex vehicle, which has a considerable amount of software within it (a software intensive-system). More than 40 pieces of software are needed throughout the vehicle and in external systems, such as diagnosis and testing tools. Software will be 35% of the total cost for the project and is on the critical path. You approach two design teams to see how they will implement this system.

The **first** design team has a large amount of software experience and works together in a specialist center. One design proposal collects all the software together as a major design component. The software will be produced using a single specialist software group.

The **second** design team proposes that vehicle design proceeds down through the specialized sub-systems as normal, and implemented by the domain specialists. Functions are classified as either software and hardware once the detailed design is complete. Each individual piece of software will be produced by the different sub-systems groups. This team tends to be hardware-oriented.

Write five good reasons for grouping all the software under a single part of the architecture, and implementing this with a specialist software group.

Write five good reasons for leaving the software spread out amongst all its components, and implementing software components within the sub-system to which they belong.

Define the optimum approach to adopt for developing software for such large systems developments.

Exercise 38: Consistency of user interfaces

You are designing the 'driver interface' for a vehicle. Consider two tasks for the driver of clearing the fogged front and rear windshields of a car. Analyze and draw the controls that are provided in your current vehicle for these tasks.

Are the two tasks handled consistently?

Describe a user interface that would allow the user to employ a consistent approach across both tasks.

Draw icons which would reflect this approach.

Exercise 39: User interface in a car

A car has duplicated braking systems. One of these has failed, but the other is working well. If drivers are told about the failure, they will be reluctant to drive the car back to the garage, though it is as safe as any car with a single braking system.

On the other hand, the driver who is taking a long journey would welcome feedback about the potential problems with the vehicle before even starting out on that journey.

How will you handle this situation when designing this braking system?

Define five requirements relating to the braking system for each of the
following two states.

- *the driver is starting the vehicle;*
- *the vehicle is currently doing 50 mph (80 kph).*

Prototyping

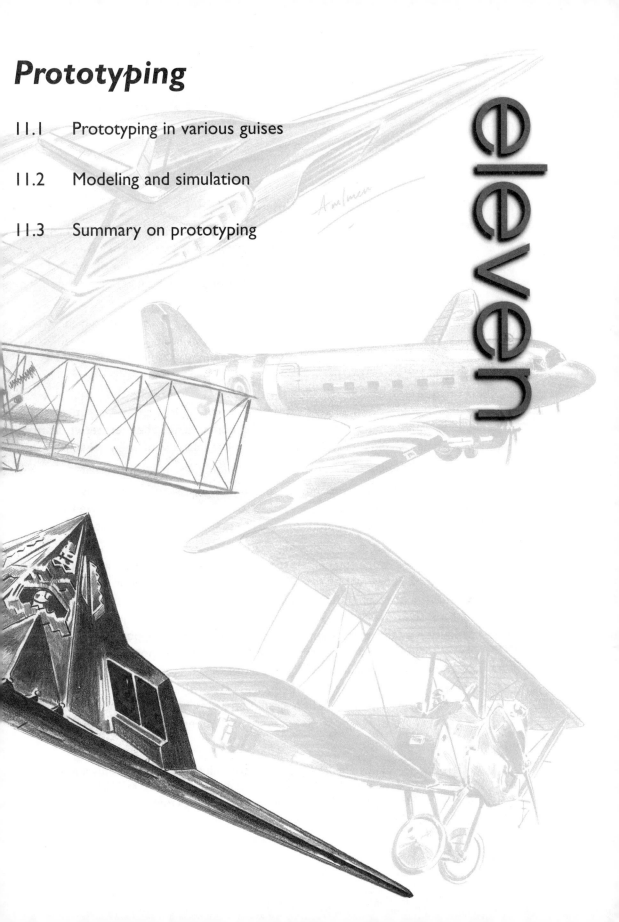

11.1. Prototyping in various guises

This section covers a variety of prototyping methods, including feasibility studies and modeling and simulation (M&S). These are all risk-reduction techniques, distinguished by the nature of their output products. They can also be used as part of the verification process for the design or end product.

Prototyping is a very old concept, used where the risks are too high or too uncertain. The technique may be used at any level, i.e. for the whole system or for a small, but risky, component. Prototyping may be used to reduce risk in requirements, design, manufacture, or test. The net product from a prototype is therefore clarification of risk – by improving the requirements, design, manufacturing or test system. A prototype may show that a product is not sensible or cannot use a specific component. The net result from a prototype may be a single negative statement that is immensely valuable:

Titanium alloy type 237 is unsuitable for use as a fan blade

We are culturally pre-conditioned to think of such a result as a failure. Actually, the prototype has served its purpose because it has saved us from wasting an enormous amount of money designing around the material.

The end product of prototyping may be knowledge in a variety of forms; better user requirements, system requirements, design knowledge, or information about test or manufacture. Although (by definition) prototypes do not have a true operational phase, they will often be assessed by users to capture their feedback. This feedback can improve the information being produced in the current process of the life cycle. Suppose we are in the design phase and are concerned that a design component is high-risk. A prototype may be built to verify that a particular design approach will work. Perhaps a second design will be constructed as a back-up in case the first approach fails. The information should be ready before the end of the design phase because the objective is to improve that design.

> The Master Shipwright of the yard is to transmit to the Board not only a Model of such ships as to their dimensions, but how they propose to finish them
> *Perrin, W.G. from the Royal Navy Archives, Greenwich 1715.*

In all its forms, prototyping is distinguished from evolutionary development because the net product of the former is information, not a working operational system. For example, a cardboard tank used to test camouflage patterns is a prototype, as is a virtual reality version of the same vehicle. The end product from these two different prototypes is design information about the camouflage, and neither can fight a real battle. An evolutionary development could, however, generate an operational version of a tank, perhaps with limited night vision capability and an engine that will later be upgraded. This tank could be (carefully) usable for example in exercises.

Many prototyping techniques are used throughout the life cycle in risky industries. For example, the cinema industry will demand scripts, reject most offerings, perform read-throughs, marketing tests, and film tests. They focus on successful stars and standard formats (e.g. Westerns) to build a series of films, and re-use directors with a history of success. Even after a film is made there will be trial releases in limited areas, with cuts, script changes, or even cancellations before general release. This blurs prototyping into incremental development. Figure 11.1 shows examples of prototyping techniques used in a variety of industries.

Confusing prototypes with valid operational products can be expensive. The Apple Newton personal digital assistant was launched with a fanfare but never lived up to expectations. The handwriting recognition was not as good as users wanted and the processor was too slow. The Newton was a prototype and should have been treated as such. Yet clearly the market for the product (or something similar) exists, and the technology was immediately useful for some specialized applications. Apple would better have built a few hundred Newtons and spread them around friendly users to get feedback. Once the problems were ironed out, mass-production could then have started.

Industry	Number made	Design cost	Unit cost	Prototyping characteristics
Cars	100,000-10,000,000	very high	high	Stable functional requirements Intense design prototyping effort (>500 man-years, >500 prototypes)
Airplane	50-1,000	very high	very high	Safety in design and manufacturing Prototyping with rigs and qualification models
Satellite	1-10	very high	very high	Variable mission and user requirements Design prototyping and reliability Prototyping costs more than flight units
Publishing	5,000-1,000,000	medium	low	Intense prototyping before full design High failure rate tolerated
Software	1 to 5,000,000	high	close to zero	Very variable user and functional requirements No manufacturing process High failure rate in practice

Figure 11.1: Prototyping in different industries

Nature of prototypes

A prototype may be anything from an artistic sketch to an expensive, 'close-to-final' system. The former are used in the early stages, for example to shape the basic concepts. Users supply their comments on the sketches to improve future versions. In the later stages, the prototypes become much more representative, i.e. more like the end product and much more expensive. For instance, as a car gets close to production several hundred prototypes are produced. Each prototype costs about $250,000, and the net product of an investment of $125M is design verification – confirmation that the vehicles meet their requirements and are ready for production.

The different kinds of prototypes could be classified as *imagination*, *simulation*, *emulation*, and *partial implementation*.

Starting from the end of that list, *partial implementation* actually creates the part of the final system involving the highest risk. This can be tested on a rig or used as part of current operational equipment. For example, if you were designing a new electrical motor for a car, it could be tested and used on the current version of the car a long time before mass-production starts. Some aspects of a complete system are very difficult to simulate by partial prototypes, for example the overall look-and-feel of the car interior. For instance, the reflections off a car body are important in the users' overall perception of the vehicle – pictures or computer models are not sufficient. These are best handled by full-scale prototypes. The manufacturing process must also be prototyped, and before mass-production, a few vehicles will be assembled to test the process and the manufacturing tools. Obviously this form of partial implementation is 'representative', i.e. the component is close to that used for the final system. It is also expensive to perform, difficult to change and can really be used only to identify minor changes.

Focus on the real output of prototyping – knowledge

In *emulation*, the final design (or part of the design) is implemented, not necessarily using the final technology. For instance, if some software will eventually run on board a vehicle, we can test it by having the software run on a microprocessor development kit sitting on the front seat. This allows bugs to be flushed out from the software under operational-like conditions, before the special chips and boards have been constructed. When building a new design of chair, cabinet makers often construct a full version out of softer, cheaper pieces of wood nailed together. This allows them to look at the aesthetics, and gingerly test the chair for comfort.

Simulation (also called analysis, animation or modeling), is normally performed through software programs. For physical systems, analysis will usually be centered around a three-dimensional modeling program. These software programs model aspects such as volume, stress, vibration, center-of-gravity, rotational stability, materials, and can analyze potential 'clashing' between moving parts. The 3–D model also forms the framework for many other kinds of analysis. Particular concerns for a satellite are, for example, thermal behavior and radiation protection. Because there is no air to diffuse heat, parts of the satellite can get extremely hot or cold. When part of a satellite is shaded from the Sun, the temperature drops rapidly, moving joints get frozen and so the thermal behavior of the satellite has to be carefully analyzed. Similarly, bursts of radiation from the Sun in outer space can destroy electronics or even kill astronauts outside the space vehicle. The satellite is designed to protect the electronics as far as possible, by placing them in the heart of the satellite, behind absorbent material. In both cases, the engineer will subject the 3–D model to simulations of the thermal and radiation environment to see how they impact on the satellite. The net products of this analysis work are improvements to the system requirements or adjustments to the architectural layout of the satellite. As computer modeling techniques improve, they are slowly but steadily displacing physical prototypes.

Imagination is the most abstract and creative type of prototyping, suitable for the front-end of projects. In this case, the prototype involves a few sketches, manually stepping through the whole process, or combine simulation with some physical components. A structured animation can step through the use of a system, providing the user with as much realistic feedback as possible. For instance, an air traffic scenario could be prototyped by showing images or video recordings on a monitor, and using external telephone callers to represent the messages from aircraft. Vehicle designs often start off as sketches on the designer's notepad, gradually transforming into three-dimensional computer-aided engineering representations.

Vertical and horizontal prototypes

A vertical prototype (Figure 11.2) explores a small area in detail for a particular risky area, and may well produce a fairly representative part. If a jet engine manufacturer wants to see if a carbon fiber blade really will work, a few can be built and tried in an existing engine on a ground test system.

A horizontal prototype allows a broad-brush view of the system, even when there is no functionality underneath. For instance, a prototype for an air traffic control system may simulate the user interface for the whole system. The system may be animated manually, allowing air traffic controllers to comment

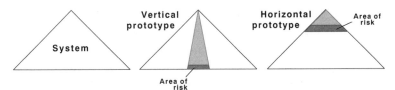

Figure 11.2: Vertical and horizontal prototypes

on clarity, response time, and interactions with other users. Horizontal prototypes are particularly useful for user interfaces, and the front-end stages of systems.

Requirements for the prototype

Prototypes should be developed to be good enough to produce the required output information, but no better. They should be built against a set of requirements. Some requirements will relate to the information that the prototype must produce, while others will be needed to make the prototype safe or make it durable enough for the job. If the prototype only has to last two weeks, this should be detailed in the requirements. The prototype must however not be dangerous, even for this limited period of 'operations'.

Explaining prototypes to management

A prototype often looks very believable at first sight, and can easily fool people into imagining that it is real. For example, you may have generated the user interface for a system, and a small amount of supporting software that lets you step carefully through one or two key areas of functionality. A piece of wood may have been painted to look like a real control button. The system behind the interface is simply not there yet, but you avoid venturing into those areas in your demonstration. This type of prototype is extremely useful for obtaining feedback. However, when managers or potential customers see this sort of demonstration, they can easily imagine there is a complete system behind the facade.

In explaining prototypes to management:

- *always make it clear that it really is only a prototype;*
- *declare its scope and purpose up front;*
- *have a short, costed, plan available to convert from prototype to an operational system, detailing the limitations and risks of operational use;*
- *make sure you collect and document the feedback as changes to the requirements (the real deliverable from prototyping).*

You should always make clear the reality of the prototype to people outside the system. Despite this, your customer or management may demand that this component be put into use immediately. This is an opportunity as well as a challenge, and you never want to say 'no' to your customer. You should be prepared by writing a concise plan on how to convert the prototype to an operational system. The plan should include costs and schedule for converting the prototype to an operational system. When the manager wants the prototype for real use, produce the management plan, ask for time and money and show that you have considered the costs of the transition in advance. Above all, state the scope and the operational limitations of the prototype.

Industrial trends in prototyping

Prototyping is very realistic and useful, but producing the models is expensive and time-consuming, particularly toward the end of development. The industrial trend is to do as much as possible by simulation, reducing the need to build physical prototypes. For instance, when the Boeing 747 was developed in the early 1970s, many kinds of prototypes including full aircraft were built [4 & 5]. These aircraft never flew a paying passenger. But the Boeing 777 was designed and tested in the computer, and the first aircraft off the production line was certified and now flies passengers – after two years of design verification of that first plane. The same computer information models the integration, prevents clashing, measures cable runs, and produces the tooling for mass-production. This eliminated errors caused by manual re-entry of information. Parts produced from around the world slotted together perfectly. In comparison, the older Boeing 747 has typically required 100 pounds of packing material (shims) to align the parts during assembly. Computer modeling software is gradually displacing the physical rigs and prototype equipment, especially where the fundamental architecture is stable.

11.2. Modeling and simulation

The word 'model' can refer to anything from a simple sketch to a live exercise involving representative equipment[57]. Requirements or management plans are themselves models – abstract representations of the future product or development. A model is any physical or mathematical representation of a system, and a simulation implements the model. Modeling and simulation (M&S) are used throughout the project for many different purposes, such as:

- *improving requirements;*
- *improving design;*
- *performance prediction;*
- *training;*
- *checking out potential changes;*
- *generating acceptance criteria;*
- *assembly strategy.*

> *When we mean to build,*
> *We first survey the plot, then draw the model,*
> *And when we see the figure of the house,*
> *Then must we rate the cost of the erection;*
> *Which if we do find outweighs ability*
> *What do we then, but draw anew the model*
> *In fewer offices, or at least desist to build at all?*
> *Bardolph, Shakespeare, Henry IV, Part II, Act 1*

The starting point for modeling is the current reference information for the system, i.e. what is fixed, and what other options exist. The information is typically transformed as it moves to the modeling tool to make the information suitable for the modeling task. For example, to perform stress analysis on a satellite, the analysis tool accesses the master set of three-dimensional information, plus details of the materials to be used.

But to perform the analysis, the system information also requires a surface mesh of lower resolution to enable stress calculation to be performed in realistic time. In the process of modeling, the fine detail of the reference information is thrown away. The valid result from the analysis is about over-stressing in part of the reference information, but the 3–D model information has been degraded for the analysis process. Unfortunately, this process cannot be automatic because of the loss and transformation of that information. Even worse, each different type of analysis (thermal, mechanical, radiation, stress) tends to need a different kind of transformation. For instance, to examine the thermal performance of the satellite we must build a model of the heat flow from sunlight, internal heat generation and radiation of heat. Figure 11.3 illustrates the process of extracting the information, modeling and then replacing the changed information back in the project database. Many of these steps are necessarily manual. The clear conclusions are that modeling depends on information generated by the systems engineering process, and that seamless modeling will require the transformation process to be automated and loss-less.

All models are false.

Some are useful.

A change is occurring from live to simulation environments at the system level. This process is driven by the enormous increase in processing power, and also the (much slower) improvement in the quality of the models. This reduces the number of physical tests and prototypes that have to be

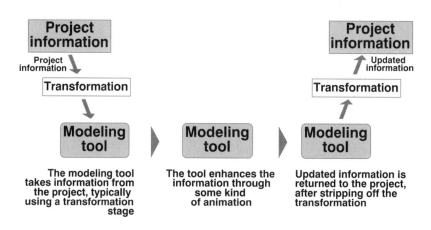

Figure 11.3: Modeling and transformation

produced. For example, the Sidewinder missile program has seen a 6–fold decrease in the number of live firings needed over a thirty year period of development. In the initial development (1960–4) there were 129 test firings, but on subsequent versions this was steadily reduced to 29 firings (1991–3). The timescale involved shows the long learning curves which have been needed to build accurate models.

Characteristics of good models

A model should capture the essence of a problem, while excluding all the clutter. An ideal model has characteristics[58] that include fidelity, simplicity, validity bands, resolution, clarity, neutrality and tractability.

M&S is one form of prototyping, providing an abstraction of the real world, only needing to cover things that are necessary for the analysis. Models must be *predictive* and *explanatory* – i.e. they should show the essence of what is being analyzed, hide the irrelevant, and reveal information that we would not see without the benefit of the model.

Decisions have to be made using the results from the modeling, and this always leads to problems of trust – does the model really represent what it claims to represent? A *faithful* model represents the essence of the area that we are trying to model. This does not mean the model is complete, but we must be clear which elements are **not** being modeled. We must not build in artefacts which lead us to unrealistic conclusions. A good check is to test the model against information that was not used to set up the model. The model must therefore be *verifiable*, and must be verified against reality. For instance, when using satellite information to model what is happening on Earth, the results need to be checked out against what is actually happening on the ground ('ground truth'). Models must therefore demonstrate that they faithfully represent the aspects being modeled. Because of the long life of many models, verification may need to be repeated at intervals.

Resemblance to truth is not truth –
Aristotle

A model should be as *simple* as possible, but no simpler. 'Ockam's Razor' tells us (in everyday terms), that the simplest model that explains the facts is likely to be the correct one. A model should discard any elements in which we have no interest.

Clarity is essential – the model must show unequivocally what will happen in the real world. Perhaps most difficult of all, a *neutral* model should avoid building in the investigator's prejudices. Any viable solution should be able to emerge from the model – prejudice toward one solution must not be built into the model, consciously or unconsciously.

The model must be *tractable* enough to provide the results with reasonable effort, i.e. it must not be time-consuming and painful to use. Being able to generate tomorrow's weather forecast is not too useful if it will take two days to produce.

Modeling and simulation are not an end in themselves, but have to add value by improving the final operational capability. They do this primarily by changing the system information, typically clarifying the risk. Producing the M&S system must be treated as a project, with proper objectives, verification of the model quality against reality, and configuration management. This is often not the case, and modeling projects sometimes drift for years without defined objectives.

Different uses of modeling

At the requirements stage, M&S can animate the user scenarios, plus any extra scenarios needed to explore failures. This can provide a useful environment for users and developers for mutual interaction, and is much clearer than a document-based approach. Ideally, the information needed to run the simulation would be produced automatically or semi-automatically from the requirements. The net product from this work is an improved set of requirements.

During development, many different system aspects will need to be simulated, covering aspects such as weight, center of gravity, thermal performance, mechanical behavior, 'clashing' of moving parts, throughput, and resistance to electro-magnetic interference. For example, on oil platforms, the massive runs of pipelines cause problems of 'clashing' i.e. interference between pipes. An oil platform can cost $1.5bn, and involve more than 1,000 pipe layouts. The industrial average for clashing was about 7%, but on one example project this was reduced to <0.5% by extensive use of CAD/CAM[59]. Beta-testing is another form of protoyping, because we cannot perfectly simulate the operational environment by normal testing.

Ideally, the same simulation information and environment would be used from beginning to end of the project. This is impractical without the unifying structure of a system process producing a defined set of information. In practice, most current models and simulations are stuck behind functional barriers, and information from one model cannot be used directly in another type of M&S.

Organizations such as the US DoD aim to overcome these problems by unified modeling environments, based on common data representations. The objective is to acquire systems specified through synthetic environments ('simulation-based acquisition').

Dangers of prototyping and modeling

The potential dangers of prototyping include:

  - *not incorporating the results of prototyping into the main project (perhaps through weak contact with the main project);*

- *confusion between the prototype as information generator and the prototype as an early design model;*
- *loss of discipline within the development process;*
- *not keeping clear objectives for the prototyping activities;*
- *over-design of the prototypes;*
- *not knowing when to stop prototyping;*
- *belief by others that the prototype is real .*

Synthetic environments for simulating system behavior are becoming steadily more important. They can allow a really good view of many system characteristics – particularly physical and performance aspects – at an early stage. However, they are complementary to good systems engineering and not a replacement for it. No model can come near to showing all the requirements for a system. Although simulations are more and more, in practice the more intricate or subtle aspects are immune to modeling. For instance, the aesthetics of a car, its overall 'feel', and the non-functional requirements are difficult to simulate. Software is particularly problematic to model because we can deduce little about its behavior from its requirements or structure. In the automotive industry, the engineering model is still the biggest influence in changing the end product[34]. Hard-headed racing car developers still spend money to build wind tunnels, because they are not able to rely totally on their CAD/CAM models. Engineers find, for example, that the system loading of a radar demands knowledge of the detailed architecture, which is far too subtle for any model. Subtle algorithmic compromises to a design can enhance throughput enormously, but can be introduced only during component design. This information is not available at the system requirements stage, where simulation is really useful. Unfortunately we can build really faithful models only when we understand systems in detail and, by definition, the models have then become less useful. Synthetic environments are becoming more useful all the time, but we must always recognize and live with the limitations of modeling.

11.3. Summary on prototyping

Prototypes come in a variety of flavors from sketches, paper-based studies, software analyses, ranging up to full-blown exercises involving real equipment. As a developer, the key factor to remember is that the end product of a prototype is information, not an early version of the system, i.e. prototyping is quite distinct from evolutionary development. As computer-based models become more faithful to reality, they are slowly, gradually replacing physical prototypes. Although many engineers are still cynical, simulations are slowly growing more multi-purpose, for example the same CAD/CAM model can be used for design and for production of tooling. This saves effort and reduces errors introduced through re-entering information. System engineers face the challenge of unifying M&S to the information generated by the development process. Gradually the separate M&S activities should become more integrated, by using the system information model. This would allow modeling tools to access project information directly, analyze and improve it, and then return the results automatically to systems engineering model. In this way synthetic environments, modeling and systems engineering are growing closer, and affecting one another intensively.

Exercises on Prototyping

Exercise 40: Convincing the customer about the prototype

A project produces a highly successful prototype, which shows users a simple system quickly. It is not reliable enough or practical to manufacture, and the documentation is ad-hoc. Your customer sees the prototype and immediately demands to use it operationally.
This is too big an opportunity to say 'no'. Define four actions to bring this prototype into engineered production.
How should you have prepared for this event?

Exercise 41: Characterizing prototypes

For each of the following systems, define whether it is a prototype or a full development. If it is a prototype, define what type of prototype it is, and what is the intended output product of the prototyping activity. Define the phase of the main project in which the prototyping should be performed.

1: A prototype for an air traffic control system, that consists of a user interface that can be manipulated manually to give the appearance of a real-life situation.

2: A full-scale radar system is constructed and tested by a government research lab as the basis for later manufacture of one thousand systems by industrial companies.

3: A computer simulation of a large-scale integrated circuit.

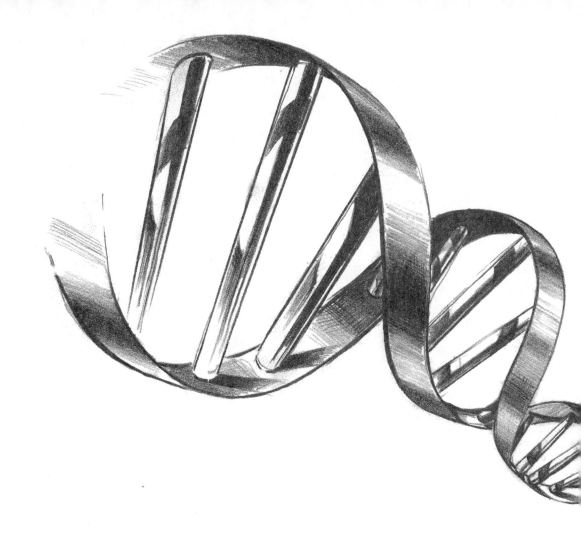

Information modeling

12.1. A project as an information system

Projects are moving from being controlled through paper to being information-based (Figure 12.1). System information is now increasingly handled in a database, and once this happens, paper is only a carrier of information, not the storage medium. A document then becomes a partial view of some fraction of this information. This approach can potentially be applied to all areas such as requirements, design, text, management plans, and even descriptive material. The system processes provide the starting point for the information model, before it is tailored; the act of tailoring the information model is equivalent to modifying the process.

Handling information in a database has many attractions – better control, a single master copy, information written once and used many times, and far easier management of inter-relationships between information (see chapter 7). The objective of all systems engineering work is to provide the information for successful decision-making. Information can be selected or filtered for specific tasks and changes of information can be controlled more sensibly. Many development tasks, such as change control, cost-benefit analysis or

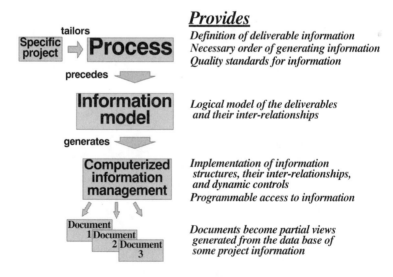

Figure 12.1: Derivation of the system information

requests for quotations can become much more disciplined. The information needed to perform the tasks is available, without re-typing or re-invention. For instance, cost-benefit analysis involves the benefits (requirements and their value) and costs (components and their attached costs), plus the relationships between the two elements.

Developers can now work on up-to-date information, without having to re-type or imagine the underlying system information. We need not even lose the advantages of documentation, and can easily produce specialist paper documents.

But a simplistic approach of moving documentation into a database and using 'data-mining' is not enough. Information must be well structured and correctly inter-related.

To summarize, some important objectives in handling information are:

- *writing information once;*
- *using the same information many times;*
- *finding information easily;*
- *naming information by convention;*
- *selecting subsets of information;*
- *detecting missing information;*
- *replicating and improving traditional styles of documents;*
- *keeping a history of changes to the information;*
- *handling relationships between pieces of information;*
- *producing metrics of development effectiveness from the information.*

System information has to be generated and checked in a logical order (e.g. user requirements before system requirements) and this has to be reflected in the information system representing the product.

12.2. Defining an information model

The control of a project demands the creation of an 'information model' or 'schema', organizing the information, its inter-relationships, and dynamics. This model supports the development, construction and integration of the product. Once this is produced, implementing a project database is relatively straightforward. Essentially the model defines an 'entity-relationship diagram' of all the information defining the product. Historically this has been the set of product definition documents.

In a typical case, the model starts from enterprise objectives leading through requirements, design, construction, integration and verification, i.e. it implements the systems engineering life cycle. Information is considered as atomic units rather than a continuous flow. These information objects have attributes attached to them, and link to other objects through relationships.

They are organized in hierarchies linked to other hierarchies, each representing a coherent set of information (e.g. user requirements). The objects may be joined to produce a document, or filtered to provide specialist views. They may even be animated to show dynamic relationships. Information is handled as coherent sets of small 'objects' related to other pieces of information.

Generating an initial information model is an early systems engineering task, a mini-project which may be completed in a day or two of intense interaction, typically centered around a whiteboard. The information model was traditionally referred to as a 'document tree', which performed a similar role in a document-based approach. The systems engineering life cycle is the starting point for defining the information model, because it defines the information involved from enterprise requirements to design. Experience shows that the model is never the same between two systems. For a standard project, the model indicates the key information sets, and the dynamics of how they are produced.

The information model is the control framework for who can read and write information. Most project information is freely available for developers to read and comment on. However, the capability to write information must be tightly coupled to responsibility within the projects. Loosely controlled 'stakeholder' or 'integrated project team' concepts need responsibility for managing different sections of information.

Each object is a member of a hierarchical set of similar objects. During development, these pieces of information may need to be created in a specific order, and the order can be represented as a state diagram. Each set of information (such as the system requirements) is produced as an end product of one of the systems engineering processes. The pieces of information produced within the development have to conform to the mandatory rules of the processes being implemented. Each mandatory requirement in the system process should cause a change to some piece of information, otherwise the mandatory statement is not verifiable. For example, a requirement may tell us:

All system requirements shall be marked with the system level at which they will be verified (e.g. unit, assembly, system)

For the requirement above, one could automatically check to ensure that the correct attribute had been applied to each requirement, and check the system-level testing needed.

Checking that the correct type of information has been added is straightforward, provided that the processes check output deliverables. Of course, we can say nothing about the quality of engineering judgement. A good engineer will make good decisions and a bad engineer will make bad decisions, but the checklist provided by the system engineering process at least reminds us what tasks really are necessary.

The basic logic of this book is about the creating information that defines and controls the project. An equally valid and complementary view is to see that information as being generated simply to make decisions. Information is good enough if it allows the necessary decisions to be made sensibly. Decisions cut off some options and decide which direction the project takes.

The mandatory statements in a systems engineering process are the natural source of these rules to check the system information[60]. They will for example demand traceability between requirements and design.

To summarize, a business process can be represented as (Figure 12.2):

-   *a concurrent, hierarchical state diagram representing the order in which the information is created;*
-   *an information model of the outputs of each system process;*
-   *a set of decisions linked to input and output information;*
-   *a set of rules for the characteristics of information.*

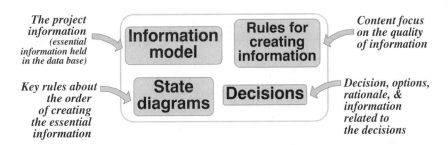

Figure 12.2: The project as an information model

Figure 12.3 shows the principles applied to two processes in a project. The user requirements 'state' generates a set of information, i.e. the user requirements document. This can be checked against a set of rules contained in the process about user requirements information. When this information is cleared as satisfactory, the next 'state' – the system requirements process – can be triggered. Thus each step of the development processes is a 'state'. The events that move the system from one state to another are the approval of deliverables, such as a set of requirements information. That approval is triggered when the requirements information conforms to the mandatory requirements of the process. A tailored development approach will clearly modify this simplistic approach.

Before going further, we should emphasize that any model of a system development is a small sub-set of reality, and no more. As long as we are well aware of what is and is not being modeled, this limitation need not matter.

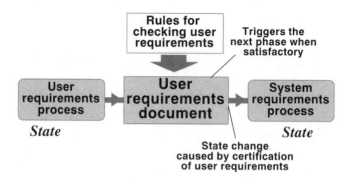

Figure 12.3: State diagram with output products

Reality is always much more intricate, concurrent, and conditional than any model would suggest, and this is particularly true for the creative tasks of development. Some software tools try to impose rigid behavioral processes on developers. Prescriptive approaches generally fail in creative areas, because developers need freedom to do tasks in any way they want. Why impose, when imposition may be detrimental?

What is not modeled is often as important as what is modeled

State diagrams need to be able to express hierarchy to cope with size, and concurrency to handle parallel activities. Each systems engineering process can be partitioned into sub-processes, producing subsets of the information. For instance, producing a list of user types is a small milestone during the user requirements process. At times there will be concurrent activities, each producing their own components. These sub-products are usually integrated into one composite 'document' (i.e. set of information) which is reviewed at the end of a process.

The information in the database has to be handled as multiple, linked hierarchical sets of information, with each piece of information treated as an 'object'. Hierarchy is needed to cope with size, and the 'object' approach is needed to maintain configuration information on individual pieces of information.

Ownership of information

We tend to think that the author of information has the permanent right to control and change that information. In practice, this is not always the case. In a project, information may be created and retained by one party but, after it is baselined, it may not be changed without approval by others who are then using it. For example, the customer may be using deliverables as the basis for measuring progress. The prime contractor will have defined these through the configuration item structure, but once it is agreed, it cannot be changed without agreement from the customer because it destroys the ability to monitor progress.

Conversely the customer should not make arbitrary changes that may have huge impacts on downstream information. For instance, a small change in user requirements may have a huge design impact The impact of proposed changes should be evaluated formally before committing all parties to the change.

12.3. Example applications

If system information is well structured, a range of other applications can become much more disciplined (Figure 12.4). Indeed it is difficult to imagine how many of these tasks can be handled properly without access to a coherent set of information. These tasks have traditionally been handled using a document-based approach, with all of the obvious problems. Handling parts of the information in single tools is not much better. The following list of applications provides examples of key processes which rely on system information. Most of these applications relate one set of system information to another, and therefore demand a coherent information-based approach. Examples of important processes are covered in more detail later in the chapter. Many applications such as review, tender evaluation, change management are cost-benefit analysis in one guise or another.

traceability (see chapter 12.4) – a whole variety of needs are served by different kinds of linkages between system information, such as communication of user intentions, relating test to specifications, proving that the design meets the requirements and linking responsibilities to the tasks to be done.

management planning and reporting (chapter 12.5) – meaningful metrics about project progress need to be based on the real status of projects. Management planning relates deliverables, schedules, work, responsibility and contracts, to the requirements.

technology management (chapter 13.7) – technology should be developed to fit into an enterprise's projects, which in turn should be tied back to the goals for the enterprise. As the projects and the enterprise's goals evolve,

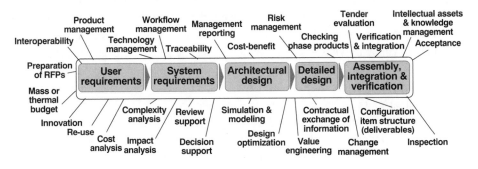

Figure 12.4: Applications above system information

technology developments need to be reviewed against these changing objectives. Technology management therefore relates technological development, product development and enterprise objectives.

prototyping, modeling and simulation, & feasibility studies (see chapter 11) – Prototyping, modeling and simulation and feasibility studies are variants of the same process of risk mitigation. Modeling extracts information from the current system information, analyzes and improves that information before re-injecting it back into the system definition. Modeling relates any part of system information to the tools used to animate that information.

request for proposal – when an enterprise needs to acquire products from an external contractor, it issues a request for proposal (RFP), typically a composite of requirements, management plans and contractual conditions. Potential contractors reply with a compliant bid traceable to the RFP, with the winning bid is chosen through cost-benefit analysis. This normally consists of a provisional architectural design with attached costs. The process of tender evaluation then relates the values of requirements to the costs of design.

verification and validation (chapter 6.4) – the verification system compares products with their requirements (or design). The test system is therefore a related system, driven by the product. Similar principles apply to the production system for a mass-produced product. The verification system relates products back to their original specification.

Measure twice, cut once – old carpenter's maxim

decision support (chapter 6.6) – almost all of these processes involve decisions, made consciously or sub-consciously against a set of evaluation criteria (i.e. requirements). Similarly each decision will generate derived requirements. Decision-making is often invisible and the decisions are not communicated, and we need to tie the decision-making process into requirements information. The decision support system relates input requirements, possible alternatives, decision rationale and derived requirements.

metrics and process improvement (chapter 13.6) – measurement of efficiency across multiple projects is impossible before defined processes are in place. Metrics should be generated automatically by developers through the application of the processes, i.e. if the processes are followed, the metrics information must inevitably be produced. The metrics are then incorporated into the information model, which then offers the potential for automatic or semi-automatic generation of some metrics. For example, the percentage of user requirements met at different stages through development (a good metric of user satisfaction) should be simple to produce. Clearly we can only improve the process efficiency once there are some basic metrics for the process. This is an example of an enterprise management task.

cost estimation – cost estimation becomes sensible only when we know what elements are to be built, and the requirements attached to each element. For instance, the technique of function-point analysis attempts to measure size by looking at numbers of functions, their interfaces and controls[61]. For aircraft, the traditional approach has been to estimate cost through the likely weight of the airplane. This seemingly naive approach has been relatively successful historically. Cost estimation therefore relates components and their requirements to estimated costs.

change management and impact analysis – a sensible decision on whether to implement change requires knowledge about the costs, benefits and risks associated with the decision. For example, deciding to reduce performance when a design turns out to be too expensive may impact upon user requirements, and also require re-work on an alternative design. Making a rational decision under these circumstances will demand traceability back to user requirements.

maintenance and upgrade – during the maintenance stage, documentation is required to repair and to make small upgrades to the system.

re-use across the enterprise (chapter 13.8) – successful re-use demands that components are linked to specific requirements. Such components must be developed to the right standards for re-use. Re-use relates components and their requirements to the multiple projects in which they are re-used.

Some of these tasks have already been covered because they are so integral to systems engineering. A few of these examples – traceability, management planning, and technology management – are now discussed as examples of what can be done through an integrated information model.

12.4. Traceability

System information is highly intricate and inter-related. The whole system can be thought of as a set of organized information, linked to minimize duplication. A requirement should ideally be stated once and applied to many different areas, by linkages, rather than repeating the requirement. If a change is required, only one item needs to be updated, and the result is cloned to many different places. For instance, relationships can link test results to the specification to allow the overall test status to be calculated. Traceability is the complete set of relationships or linkages between information.

Once traceability is in place, the consequences of change become more obvious. For instance, any attempt to change a user requirement should warn us about the potential impact on any design elements that would be affected. Documenting these relationships between components is however expensive and time-consuming. Traceability uses resources and tends to slow down our ability to make changes. We should strive to minimize the necessary traceability, because of this restrictive effect. Traceability should therefore always be a compromise reflecting the costs and benefits of linkages. Not everything need be traced; only do it where the traceability information is useful. Ask the questions 'why am I putting this link here?' and 'what questions will this link answer?'.

Traceability is therefore not an end in itself — it exists to help us perform project tasks. Typical questions answered by traceability might be:

- *are these user requirements met by the current design?*
- *are these user requirements met by the current implementation?*
- *what is the level of criticality of this piece of equipment?*
- *what is the functionality of this equipment?*
- *which requirements are to be met in the next release?*
- *which user requirements have not been tested?*
- *what is the likely cost of this proposed change?*

All the above queries are concerned with the product. But traceability is also needed for development and test issues such as responsibility for verification, the amount of work necessary to build specific components, and the test status of an item.

*Take care of the means and the end will take care of itself –
Mahatma Gandhi*

Internal interfaces between functions (e.g. in data flow diagrams) or relationships between user requirements are simply relationships that occur within a single set of information.

Different kinds of traceability

Many kinds of relationships are needed to handle different tasks. The most obvious relationship type is between parents and child information, normally generated automatically when a function is decomposed. Relationships need to reflect the characteristics of the information they represent, such as their cardinality (e.g. one-to-one), inheritance, and completeness.

This includes:

- *coverage relationships showing that one process covers the specification of a previous process;*
- *applicability relationships to show how non-functional requirements apply to functional requirements;*
- *relationships to show how tests are related to components and the requirements for those components;*
- *relationships that show who is responsible for performing specific tasks;*
- *relationships to show how structured information is related to descriptive information;*
- *relationships of generic engineers to specialist engineers, usually working with specialist tools (data flows, control flows).*

Coverage relationships are the most basic type of traceability. They ensure that (for example) the system requirements meet the user requirements, or that tests cover the requirements. Users are normally interested in finding which upstream elements (e.g. requirements) will be implemented, or which downstream components do not do anything useful.

Applicability relationships relate non-functional to functional requirements, in the system requirements for example. A relationship is normally inherited by all the children of the applicable function. For example, a requirement about the thermal environment might state:

The engine shall operate at 120 degrees Centigrade

In a large system, applicability relationships allow information to be stated once, and re-applied to many elements. By default, making a function safety-critical makes its children safety-critical through inheritance. This technique reduces the information to be managed and makes subsequent change analysis much easier.

Test relationships link requirements or the design to the test system, and the components being tested. These relationships may be many-to-many i.e. one requirement can be related to many tests and vice-versa. Typically the test criteria should be attached to the requirement, the test results attached to the test relationship, and the overall test status attached to the requirement. These relationships allow us to see which requirements are to be tested, at which system level and by what method. When the tests are actually run, the status of the requirement can be updated through communication across the links (Figure 12.5).

Development relationships tie the product into the management plan, or define the management plan itself as an information model. The configuration item structure (CIS) is a bridge between the product and the development process. On one side the CIS is attached to design, and the other side is

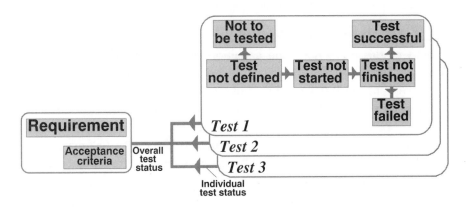

Figure 12.5: Relationships between requirements and test

attached to the work breakdown structure. The configuration item therefore bridges the product and the system that develops that product. This illustrates how the development model may be as complex as that for the product.

Relationships to **unstructured information** such as studies and reports need to be created and maintained. These will be used to report on how many of the requirements in the unstructured information are accepted, and to document why requirements have been changed or rejected.

Relationships to **specialist disciplines** allocate bundles of requirements into work done by specialist areas, and allow monitoring and control of specialist skills. Examples are relationships to CASE and CAD/CAM tools. The system engineer allocates a set of requirements to the specialist for implementation, then checks progress as these are gradually implemented.

Cloning relationships allow the same pieces of information to be re-used in several different places. For instance, the same components may be replicated across the system, or the same tests can be re-applied at different times. To implement these ideas in an information model, the concept of 'cloning' groups of information is required. A variety of different cloning types are needed, depending on how information can be changed. Sometimes the cloned information can be changed centrally, and the changes are reflected everywhere (e.g. schedule information). At other times, any user of the cloned information should be able to modify the information, without affecting other replicas (e.g. for re-use). Cloning must leave an audit trail of origins and changes.

Summary of traceability

Traceability is expensive but essential to show the connections within projects. Enthusiasm to do a complete job of traceability needs to be tempered by an understanding of the intrinsic costs. Traceability should be restricted to those areas where it adds value, such as reducing the amount of information, checking sources, or linking to tests.

12.5. Plans as information models

The focus of this book is on the definition of the product through systems engineering, but the same techniques can be used to control the development process. This approach defines the management plan as an information model, which demands that different structures − such as the configuration item structure, organizational breakdown structure − need to be defined and inter-related. When complete, this forms an 'information model' of all management information i.e. the management plan has been organized into a database.

The starting point for all management planning should be the set of deliverables, organized as a hierarchy, and showing their inter-relationships. (Figure 12.6). By attaching the schedule to this configuration item structure,

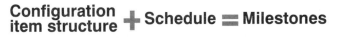

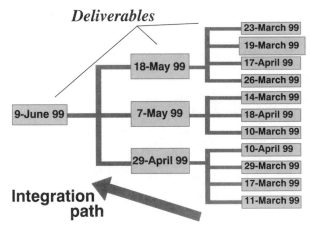

Figure 12.6: Milestones and the configuration item structure

we define the project milestones. All payments must then be tied to acceptance criteria, defined in the customer/supplier contracts. If a deliverable is accepted, payment is made, otherwise payment should not be made.

The **schedule** is the set of planned dates, tied to the completion of deliverables. The actual delivery date is when the deliverable meets all of its requirements, forming a milestone.

The **work breakdown structure** (WBS) consists of all the work that absorbs resources, organized by similarity of work. The WBS is therefore a functional hierarchy of work, with details of how much work is needed to build the system. Nodes on a WBS might for example include programming, managing, or quality assurance and the amount of work needed shown as an attribute of each element of the WBS (Figure 12.7). For instance, we may need 350 hours of coding or 50 hours of management to make the deliverable.

The **cost breakdown structure** (CBS) shows the cost for each unit of work, such as the different skill or resource that is used. It tells us, for example, the cost of one day's programming effort, or the monthly cost of offices. The CBS is normally linked to the WBS to allow the total cost to be calculated. Costs cannot therefore be defined until the deliverables and the WBS are known. At this point, for the first time, a realistic estimate of overall cost can be made. Even then, the full detail of the deliverables has not been defined.

The **organizational breakdown structure** (OBS) organizes the people and/or organizations that actually perform the work. The OBS is structured by organizational position. On a large system, the different companies building

A structure must have an organizing principle and define the kinds of components involved

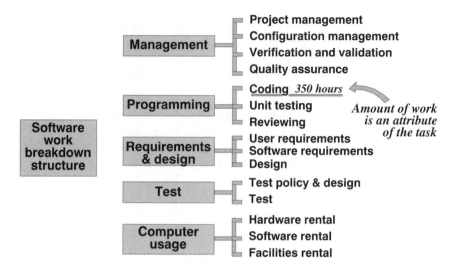

Figure 12.7: Work breakdown structure (WBS) for a software project

parts will form parts of the OBS. Relating the OBS to the WBS links the people to the work they are doing.

The management plan

Together this alphabet soup of development acronyms tells us:

- — *what will be made (deliverables);*
- — *when it will be ready (schedule);*
- — *what work is needed to make it;*
- — *what it will cost (totally and by sub-division);*
- — *who does the work (responsibilities).*

This total set of information makes up the management plan. Figure 12.8 shows this management information as an entity-relationship diagram, which allows the inter-relationships to be shown. Much of this relationship information is normally lost through expressing a management plan as a document. If the system information is organized in this way, the management plan can be printed out directly from a database. Because there is traceability back to requirements, the management plan is directly tied to the requirements (through the design). Planning information can be written once but can be viewed from several managerial perspectives e.g. by time, by deliverables, by responsibilities, by amount of work, by cost or any combination of these factors.

Documents are weak at showing relationships, such as those between work and responsibilities. Trying to maintain a management plan through documentation also restricts us to a single structural viewpoint e.g. time

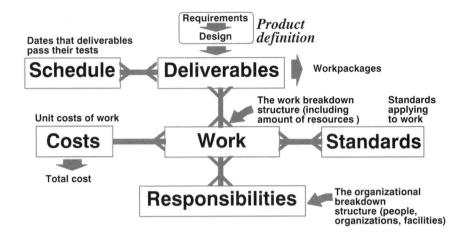

Figure 12.8: Core components of a management plan

(schedule), or deliverables (configuration item structure), or work (work breakdown structure).

The biggest problem in changing to information models from paper documents is the need for a more disciplined approach to defining information. We may get away with documents that are slightly ill-defined and poorly structured. This is simply not possible where the information is organized into databases, in which we have to be careful about what is exactly being organized. A structure is meaningless unless we understand the principle by which the structure is arranged, and the nature of the components that are being organized. For example, the work breakdown structure is often a hapless mixture of dates, deliverables, and tasks. A coherent definition of WBS comes from the US Department of Energy:

> *Work that absorbs resources, organized by similarity of work.*

Thus the WBS is a functional definition of the types (and amount) of work needed to produce a deliverable.

12.6. Summary

The traditional approach of control through paper-based documents requires super-human discipline. In practice, a document-based approach tends to focus effort on the format and outlines of the document rather than on the intrinsic quality of the information[62]. The key trends are to represent the system information electronically and to organize and control that database through the rules defined for the organizational processes.

In one form or another, this knowledge is the most valuable asset of a company, and information therefore needs to be handled to maximize its value. The transformation demands resources, but opens the opportunity of increasing the value of a company's information assets.

Although the discussion in this chapter has been largely based around the sequential model, the same ideas apply in evolutionary or large, multilevel developments. In these cases, the information model will be more complex.

Systems engineering tools will improve as our understanding of the systems engineering processes increases. The starting point for constructing an integrated tool set must be well-defined and practical systems engineering processes. This knowledge is an essential foundation for any attempt to construct a suite of systems engineering tools.

Exercises for Information modeling

Exercise 42: What is the structure?

Two definitions of work breakdown structure are:
1: 'The WBS defines the products to be developed or produced and relates the elements of work to be accomplished to each other and to the end product' – Mil Stand 881

2: 'Work that absorbs resources structured by similarity of work'

For each definition, attempt to draw the 'structure', stating the organizing principle which groups similar elements together, and define the nature of the components that are being organized.
Take a project that you know and draw the work breakdown structure – do not include elements other than work.

Exercise 43: Processes and Information

For each of the following tasks, define in a paragraph the types of system information being handled and the process being applied to that information.
1: Cost-benefit analysis.
2: Impact analysis.
3: Interoperability.

Exercise 44: The limits of modeling

Comment on the following statement:
'The ability to model systems through virtual reality techniques allows them to

be presented to users early in the system life cycle. This gives early feedback to the developers. As a result, the systems engineering processes can be condensed, and for example, we no longer need requirements documents'

Exercise 45: WBS, OBS, and CBS

Draw a sample WBS, CBS and OBS for a small project and relate them to one another showing the relationships to each other.

Projects and the enterprise

thirteen

13.1. Introduction

Projects start and develop within an environment provided by an enterprise. The enterprise tries to ensure that projects operate together, are adequately resourced, staffed by trained staff, sensibly partitioned, and initiated at reasonable risk. The enterprise itself should have its own business objectives and apply these to individual projects. Systems engineering processes need to be defined, applied and audited across all projects. Systems engineering skills will be needed for current and future projects, and this will require training. Supporting systems for test, design support, or technology management cannot effectively be constructed within a single project, which does not have the resources or the time. The enterprise must be innovative enough to keep up with the changes in its environment. Management of the intellectual assets of a company also benefits from systems engineering discipline. These issues all demand systems engineering effort at the business level or more generically, within any enterprise (e.g. a business unit within a company) that controls its own resources.

To make a success of a specific project, the enterprise must build or re-use a number of development and support systems such as simulators, tools, operational training, marketing, pricing, and sales strategy. Figure 13.1 shows the totality of projects which might be needed for a core product. For example, developing a successful Space Shuttle also requires ground systems, training and simulation facilities, and technology development. The complete set of all projects needed to deliver an operational capability is sometimes

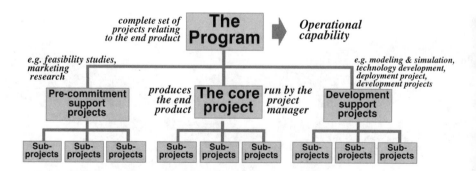

Figure 13.1: The Program and The Project

called the 'Program'. Other kinds of projects are needed for the organization to explore the feasibility of the project, before total commitment. These support areas lie outside the 'core project' but essential for overall success.

Although these ideas are most familiar and most stable at the business level, many can be applied below the corporate level. For example, a department of Motorola may itself be almost a self-standing entity, acting as an enterprise, generating some of its own technology. Systems engineering at the enterprise level is likely to be needed for any activity which:

- *lies above the single project;*
- *has to be prepared in advance of the project that needs it;*
- *needs to be carried through or across many projects;*
- *provides independent or management support to the customer.*

Many of these ideas also apply above the business level, e.g. at a national level, when governments implement infrastructure projects or training programs.

13.2. *Managing through stages*

The enterprise needs processes to manage products from cradle to grave. Before committing to full development of an expensive system, enterprises must perform systems engineering work to explore risk. A large-scale project is ideally initiated through a string of low-cost risk reduction exercises. These processes must allow for progressive reduction of risk, and reduction of uncertainty in the time, cost and performance estimates. It must also allow for steps of gradual commitment, with approvals to proceed further. This is called stage-gate management, which is described in the following section.

Each stage is a real project, whose purpose is to produce information, not a real end product for the users. The objectives are to define the system well, and to reduce the risk exposure to an acceptable level. This work may involve paper-based analysis, modeling and simulation, building physical prototypes or producing a detailed design and analyzing its likely costs. The early stages may even be handled by a 'future studies' department, with some of that initial team being taken into the core project later on.

A project steadily passes from an idea, through conceptual analysis, to a small project, a prototype, and gradually steps toward full development. The number of stages should not be rigidly pre-defined, and the whole process must be as speedy as possible. The enterprise process is divided into stages separated by gates, at each the system is evaluated simultaneously against:

- *enterprise objectives;*
- *technical feasibility;*
- *marketing or operational need, roll-out and distribution risks;*
- *capability to manage the project to success.*

As it passes through each stage, the whole product is defined in greater levels of detail, and hopefully with a lower risk exposure. The stage-gate process is a decision-making process, which accepts, rejects, or modifies the proposals for the next stage. What was originally the complete life cycle has become a 'stage', a partial process of development repeated several times. The system information needs to be high enough in quality to make the correct decisions. In the early stage especially, a prototype may encompass a whole stage.

In exploring the risks in a system, the project passes through the 'complete' development life cycle several times, evaluating the risks. Figure 13.2 shows this represented as a spiral cone of increasing investment and definition. This section applies systems engineering to stage-gate management and also brings in ideas as discussed by Garz[63], Farncombe[64] and Gorchels[65].

The histograms of the figure illustrate the relative effort on different systems engineering processes as the project proceeds. (Most representations of the life cycle show a commitment, but do not illustrate the exploration effort being performed at any time.) Initially the bulk of the effort must be spent on refining user requirements, to form a foundation for the later work. This will inevitably involve iterating through system requirements and design. As the user requirements solidify, the focus of attention shifts to system requirements, then design and the same principles carry through

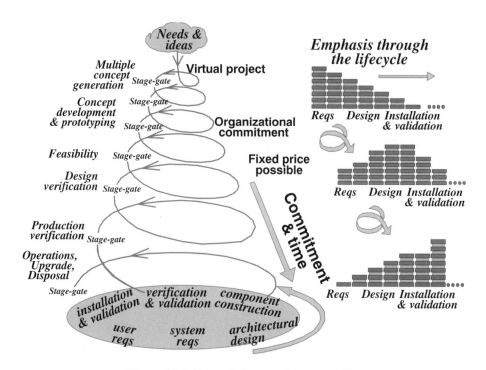

Figure 13.2: The spiral cone of a system life

implementation and operations. Only after exploring several stages in sufficient detail is there a commitment to full product implementation. At any time, the system engineer is exploring every aspect of the development.

At the time of system conception, a stage may be traversed in a single person's head, or through conversations between ad-hoc groups. We mentally step through these processes before we buy or build even the smallest product. The early stages may require little or no resources, and an enterprise may not even know they are happening. Gradually the system becomes formalized through computer analysis, market or operational analysis, passing to computer-based and physical prototypes that grow closer to the final system, and then the full implementation. Risk is explored virtually at first, then with steadily more representative end products. When the level of risk is acceptable, i.e. the costs, schedule and quality are acceptably consistent, the enterprise can trigger the full development of, for example, an aircraft and its production.

The number of stages and the amount of time spent on each stage will vary depending on the nature of the project and the industry. Figure 13.3 maps the spiral cone to a linear timeline.

Commitment is progressive rather than being a single one-off event, and may involve exploring the design architecture several levels down. The meaning of 'commitment' varies between enterprises. Some may release sufficient budget at an early stage to enable the project to be completed. In other cultures, projects are completely re-evaluated each year even if they remain on target. This latter approach effectively imposes a financial stage-gate on the project every year, which may encourage micro-management and undermine project responsibility.

Workshops that cover a complete stage are particularly valuable at the start of projects. They can explore one complete stage covering user requirements, system requirements, design, management plan, costs and risks in a few days. This can lead to several system concepts being evaluated, exposing the high-

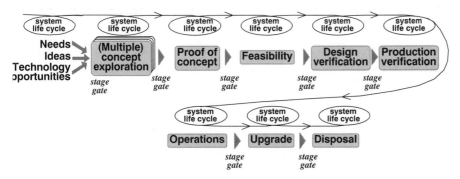

Figure 13.3: Commitment through the stages

risk areas, and showing inconsistencies between likely costs and the available funds. In one example, the initial budget allocated by management for a project was $3M, but when the design was defined and costed, the projected expense was $10.2M. This resulted in intense activities to cut costs, but also to provide a more realistic budget. The Web site (www.complexsystems.com) accompanying this book contains a plan used in such workshops.

The purpose of such early feasibility efforts is not normally to design the product, but to show that the requirements are practical, i.e. can be met at least one practical design at reasonable cost. They may show consistency between costs and requirements to a level appropriate to the current project information. For instance, the enterprise may define the requirements, provisionally design the system, produce cost estimates, examine the potential marketplace, check out the available enterprise resources for development, and be satisfied with the level of risk. Only then should the company commit to proceed with the product, using the requirements as the basis for development. Even then commitment may happen in multiple stages. The 'virtual design' may show that at least one design is feasible, but not necessarily that it is the best design. Designers may well think of an even better design later on.

Figure 13.4 shows an example of a complete set of stages in a life cycle from its initial concept to eventual disposal. Progressive commitment proceeds through feasibility and design verification, until a full development can be launched, resulting in a delivered product. The spiral cone may continues beyond the first operational fielding, merging into an evolutionary upgrade process. Each stage-gate must represent a true milestone. The particular set of stages used will vary from project to project, and depend on the maturity of the original concept, product type, and the acceptable level of risk. Each successive stage narrows the options, shapes the product, and bounds the overall costs, and the business and operational benefits. The goal of the initial stages is to reduce uncertainties to an acceptable level to commit to build, or perhaps to create a few evaluation units ahead of full production. Later stages will typically be concerned with designing and approving evolutionary upgrades of the product.

Ideas behind the spiral cone life cycle are also to be found (for example) in the staged life cycles employed by large defense acquisition organizations. In the UK, the Downey cycle[66] calls for one or more feasibility and project definition stages, conducted multiply and in parallel, resulting in at least one fully-costed development proposal. The original guidelines suggested that initial feasibility should cost 0.5% of the likely total cost and successive stages 5% and 10% before full commitment. Downey pre-programs the number of stages, and specifies the exit criteria for the stage-gates only in financial terms.

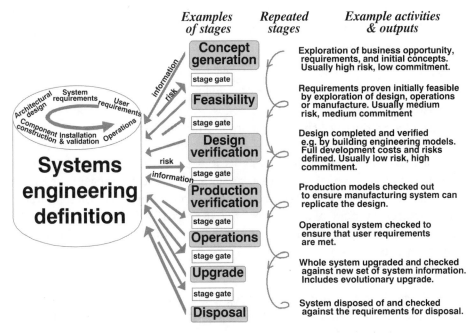

Figure 13.4: Examples of stages making a complete life cycle

Equivalent stages can be seen in the US DoD[67]. The stages concluding in milestone approval are concept studies, concept demonstration, development, production, major modification and finally disposal.

Both organizations recognize similar practical difficulties in applying such processes: the frequent reviews can lead to bureaucratic delay, it can be difficult to revisit early decisions mid-way through, and different organizational responsibilities (and possibly different contractors) in successive stages leads to discontinuities in project and product information. However, there is no reason that this spiral-cone lifecycle cannot be made to work effectively in these environments if clear stage-gate criteria are applied.

13.3. Stage-gate management

The creation of new systems is a high risk, high reward activity exhibiting all the characteristics of Darwinian evolution. Good ideas are very precious, but most new proposals will inevitably fall by the wayside. Most ideas will come from a small number of people, who will often be continually creative. We always need to encourage the people capable of true innovation, but even the best idea needs enhancement to be even vaguely practical. Only a small fraction survives the first rounds of evaluation. Most of the profits in any field go to a small minority of the products that are launched. The objective is to maximize the success of the launched products within a defined set of resources.

Most companies imagine that innovation comes solely from internal experts. Von Hippel[10] indicates rather disturbingly that the two major sources of innovation are through:

-   *improvements made by users of equipment;*
-   *exchange of information between competitors.*

The latter source of ideas perhaps needs some explanation. Sometimes the release of a product will show the innovation to the world. In these cases, it is impossible to hide the innovation, and even the strongest competitors will permit information exchange as long as it is bi-directional. However, where the innovation can be hidden (e.g. an internal manufacturing process) this information is usually well hidden. Ideas from users are often ignored: manufacturers should make it easy for users to make enhancements, for example by supplying details of interfaces, and then actively collect those improvements.

Evaluation through stage-gates

Each stage forces the system through the whole life cycle, with tasks undertaken concurrently rather than sequentially[4]. The output deliverables at each stage-gate include (Figure 13.5):

-   **a plan that covers full roll-out**. *This plan provides an overall management plan for complete roll-out into the marketplace (or into operations), resources, schedule, overall development approach, an enterprise-level evaluation, and a market or operational analysis. This plan is updated from stage to stage, and may be very approximate at the early stages. The plan defines the life cycle proposed for full development.*
-   **current product definition**. *This defines whatever is known about the quality of definition of the proposed product. It defines the current levels of risk for enterprise, operational, marketing, technical and managerial aspects, derived from the last stage-gate.*
-   **a plan for the next stage**. *This plan covers the output products to be delivered in the next stage, the resources and timescales for that stage. The output product of the stage is not necessarily the end product, but any combination of a roll-out plan, a prototype, operational analysis or market research. The stage-gate plan should aim for pre-defined targets for enterprise, marketing, technical and managerial feasibility at the end of the next stage.*
-   **risk evaluation**. *This evaluates the project against key risk criteria based on current knowledge about the product.*

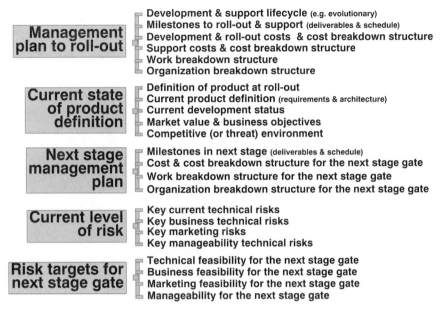

Management plan to roll-out
- Development & support lifecycle (e.g. evolutionary)
- Milestones to roll-out & support (deliverables & schedule)
- Development & roll-out costs & cost breakdown structure
- Support costs & cost breakdown structure
- Work breakdown structure
- Organization breakdown structure

Current state of product definition
- Definition of product at roll-out
- Current product definition (requirements & architecture)
- Current development status
- Market value & business objectives
- Competitive (or threat) environment

Next stage management plan
- Milestones in next stage (deliverables & schedule)
- Cost & cost breakdown structure for the next stage gate
- Work breakdown structure for the next stage gate
- Organization breakdown structure for the next stage gate

Current level of risk
- Key current technical risks
- Key business technical risks
- Key marketing risks
- Key manageability technical risks

Risk targets for next stage gate
- Technical feasibility for the next stage gate
- Business feasibility for the next stage gate
- Marketing feasibility for the next stage gate
- Manageability for the next stage gate

Figure 13.5: Contents of a stage-gate evaluation

At each stage-gate, the initiator produces a simple version of the information for the whole system, so that an overall risk analysis can be performed. The early stages must be low formality, low cost, approximate estimates, and with little bureaucracy needed to trigger a development. In the initial stages, ideas must be allowed to bloom and be explored before being too intensively analyzed. Initially, management should be light or non-existent, and exist primarily to encourage the innovator to explore the core concepts[68]. High-risk developments are acceptable at this stage. Small amounts of money can improve ideas and clarify risk enormously at this stage.

After the first low-cost stages, each stage-gate must flag up the current status and define the danger areas from a balanced perspective. A technically excellent, but financially foolish project (or vice-versa) should be stopped or re-worked. As far as possible, everything is prototyped, not just the product but even the sales cycle with a 'trial sell' to limited numbers of customers or within a small area. The later stages increasingly focus on marketing, finance and analysis of practicality. A financial analysis based on return on investment is obviously essential, but we must also allow ideas to gather a little strength before evaluating them too rigorously. Crushing new ideas before they can blossom is all too easy. The first stage-gates can be technically oriented, but should fairly soon balance enterprise, marketing, and management with the technical issues.

As the investment becomes larger, the risks must be squeezed from the project to allow it to continue. Figure 13.6 shows the general characteristics

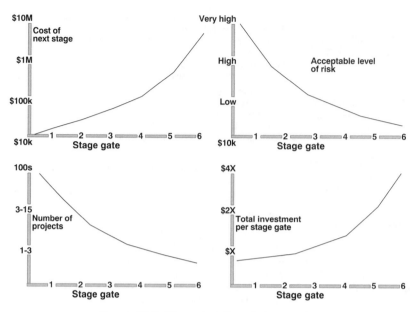

Figure 13.6: Characteristics of stage-gates

of new projects passing through the stage-gates. The number of surviving projects falls, the acceptable level of risk declines, and the cost per stage rises. The cycle time for the early stages must be short enough to reduce the overall time to deliver a quality product, not increase it. The exact values depend on the level of acceptable risk and the research policy of the enterprise. For example, the 3M Corporation has two key rules: spend more than 6.5% of sales revenue on R&D, and generate more than 30% of company income from products less than four years old.

Systems that fail to meet the criteria for the gates are modified or cancelled without criticism, and gradually the hurdles become greater. A multi-functional team with delegated authority headed by a program (or product) manager takes charge of the project. The person who conceived the original idea rarely has the talents to take it to launch, and must be rewarded and gently separated from the development. The investment gets higher at each step, until eventually the enterprise decides whether to implement the system.

Criteria for evaluating proposals

At the stage-gates, projects should be evaluated against criteria which have been demonstrated to be critical for success or failure. Proposals should be evaluated against criteria structured around enterprise, market, management and technical feasibility. The relative importance of these factors may vary depending on the development state and the acceptable level of risk. The books by Cooper[4] and Gorchels[65] both contain criteria for evaluating developments. Stage-gates therefore act as filters, removing the weak proposals, and improving the survivors. The criteria that separate successes from failures are (statistically) well-known, and these form the basis of reviewing proposals through the different gates. Figure 13.7 summarizes the important factors for success or failure across 203 projects, demonstrating the key factors as[69]:

- **Product advantages** While this factor will come as no surprise to creative people, many people still think that 'ideas are cheap'. A good idea for a product can make or break a project. Products that copy rivals or merely respond to them are unlikely to succeed. The best design may not always win, but it is really helpful to have on your side.

- **Process advantages (especially pre-development activities)** An enterprise needs good processes for initiating, developing and launching products. Innovation must be encouraged, within a logical process for initiating, improving and evaluating products. A good pre-development process, including user requirements, is as critical to success as a healthy development process. Bad proposals must be eliminated unemotionally, and scarce resources focused on the best, which should be remorselessly exposed to constructive criticism. High quality, relevant development skills, distribution channels, and related products reduce the risk in product introduction. In-house skills in technology and marketing can be leveraged to produce innovations with only marginal set-up costs.

Importance ranking

Product superiority	**1**	*Is it a better product with real advantages or just a me-too response ?*
Product well-defined before development phase	**2**	*Are the requirements, practicality, resources, & risks well-defined in advance and mutually consistent?*
Quality of development execution	**3**	*Does the organization have good development & production processes for such systems?*
Technological synergy	**4**	*Does the technology fit in with existing successful products and developments?*
Quality of execution of pre-development activities	**5**	*Is the project set up well from a managerial, organizational & requirements view?*
Marketing synergy	**6**	*Is there a close fit between the project s marketing needs and the existing distribution system?*
Quality of execution of marketing activities	**7**	*Are the requirements well researched & realistic? Is the introduction planned & resourced?*
Marketing attractiveness	**8**	*Is there a growing, world-wide market for this product.*
Competitive situation	**9**	*Is there little competition, is the product better than its future competitors?*
Top managerial support	**10**	*Is senior management committed to introducing this product?*

> Doesn t improve the product, but helps get it launched

Figure 13.7: What makes a product successful?

- *Compatibility with enterprise objectives* Management commitment is essential to launch a product successfully, although it makes little difference to success after launch. If the enterprise has defined strategic objectives and the product fits within these goals, then management support is obviously much more likely.

- *Financial and market feasibility* Short payback times, real profits, a real marketplace, low development costs, and lack of competitive products all increase the chances for a new product. The company must be able to get the resources needed for a full launch. Realistic cost estimates of development and launch should become available after the first stage of product initiation and then become increasingly firm. From the beginning, the whole development must be based on user requirements and estimation of customer demand. The market must be attractive, i.e. growing and open for the new product, but as closed as possible to competitors (e.g. through patents or time to market).

- *Risk to any of the above* Each of the core areas needs to be quantified for the level of uncertainty.

These critical success have been organized into criteria for evaluating new projects (Figure 13.8)[70]. Choosing the factors on the left-hand side allows the user to scale the relative importance of enterprise, technical, marketing and managerial issues. The 'impact' column indicates the size of the risk. Each

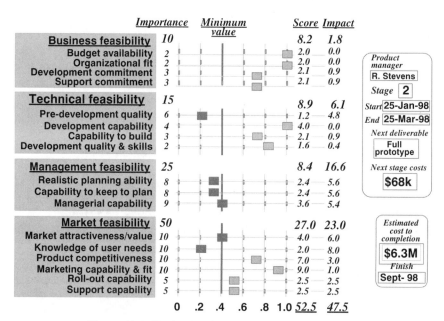

Figure 13.8: Evaluating feasibility through risk analysis

factor is marked for risk on a scale of 0 to 1.0 by the squares. These factors predict whether the enterprise can build the product, can develop the product, manage the development, and can compete in the market. The factors are broken down one more level to end up with 15–20 key risk factors, which have been derived from real-world statistics on project success or failure. Each proposal can then be classified against all these factors, giving an overall rating for risk.

Minimum acceptable values for any factor can be pre-defined, below which the project will be cancelled or re-directed. For instance, when an investment of more than $100k is needed, the minimum for every factor might be 0.5. The proposal evaluated in the diagram is high-risk on knowledge of users' needs, in all three areas of management, and in its pre-development quality.

As with any arbitrary scale, the results of this risk analysis should be used for guidance, not control. If the project is approved for another stage, the objective is to get higher scores, particularly in the weak areas. While the scale means little in absolute terms, it can be used to compare proposals. The relative importance of success factors may vary across different types of systems, as those shown are composites derived from overall statistics.

Figure 13.9 shows the process of choosing between innovative proposals during the early development stages. Proposals are evaluated against the stage-gate criteria, with the pass criteria growing higher through the development. A proposal may be approved for the next stage, sent back for improvement or cancelled. Because the proposals are competing for

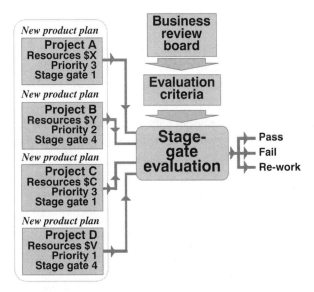

Figure 13.9: Choosing between multiple proposals

enterprise resources, they often have to be aligned in time to be reviewed together. The calendar should not however be used as a straightjacket and, if a proposal needs an immediate review or decision, then this should be provided quickly. In particular, the front-end stages which cost little, should not be tied to the calendar.

All of these stages may generate useful information as a by-product of risk evaluation. For example, they will need to define user requirements to produce prototypes. This information should not be discarded.

13.4. The product manager role

In industry, the **product manager** handles all aspects of the product from the business point of view. The product manager role starts at the ideas stage, encouraging the innovator and providing any support needed to make the ideas more realistic. After the first step, a more balanced evaluation is used. In the early stages, the product manager co-ordinates all system information, requirements, marketing, manufacturing, scheduling, cost estimation including all the support activities that impact on the enterprise. The product manager collects all the information for use later in the development, especially the requirements and the size of the market. During the initial stages, the product manager handles all issues, for the product as well as costs, marketing and other support projects.

Once the enterprise commits to build the product, the core development is handled through a core project, with a dedicated project manager (Figure 13.10). Many different roles still need handling outside the core development, such as marketing and operational planning and these tend to remain under the control of the product manager. During the build stage, the product manager is concerned with roll-out, timing the launch, publicity, and organization of the installation and operations. For production products, the product manager organizes the sales approach, discounts, distribution arrangements, and marketing to potential customers. The product manager acts for the customer in controlling these issues above the individual project.

In this chapter, the term 'product manager' has generally been used, because it is already common within mass-production industries. Large one-off developments have tended to use the terms 'program manager', 'procurement manager', or 'acquisition manager' for what amounts to a similar task. In such one-off projects, an operational requirements department may take the place of a marketing department, but the role is intellectually similar.

The product manager role is difficult, not least because it is normally a matrix role, without direct authority over the people doing the work. Companies often use marketing staff in the product manager role, and this can create friction with both technical staff and end users. In the early stages, the role is inevitably fairly technical, but when the development is underway, a marketing

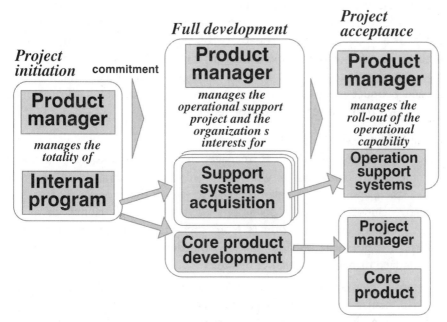

Figure 13.10: Product management during initiation and development

bias becomes steadily more appropriate. By necessity, it is a single-point role, i.e. each product must have one and only one product manager.

The product manager role is critical to enterprise success, but it needs experience, tact, technical understanding, and good human relationships. The role encourages healthy internal competition between overlapping products in a company. Procter and Gamble were first to formalize the product manager role during the 1930s to pit one brand of soap against another. This concept of product management was so successful that it is has been copied and enhanced ever since.

Continuity is important because the product manager role spans the whole development from beginning to end. Good documentation is therefore essential to carry the message through the whole life cycle.

Ownership of the user requirements

User requirements are 'owned' by the end users or the product manager representing them. In a commercial company, the marketing department takes this role, working for the product manager. Marketing's job is to capture intelligence from the marketplace and use it to drive development. In an acquisition-oriented environment, such as defense or a government health agency, there is typically an operational requirements branch, writing the requirements and a procurement agency organizing the acquisition of systems from outside contractors.

There is often a disconnect between user needs and the reality of development, especially during the long interval between requirements and delivery. The product manager needs to be highly professional, organizing a structured set of user requirements, driving the developers hard – but always from a user perspective. The product manager must understand how the proposed product is to be used in detail, but also understand the technical issues enough to make sensible cost-benefit decisions.

The product management plan

At each stage-gate, the product manager is responsible for the product management plan, consisting of two major components – detailed definition of the next stage, and an overall plan through to launch the product. The second plan also includes a process definition, i.e. the intended launch date, the number of stages and the products from each stage leading to launch. This overall plan is gradually updated through the development. These plans can use a standard management plan template.

The essential element of the product management plan is that it integrates enterprise, management, marketing, and technical issues, along with the risks that link them. None of these key issues can sensibly be considered in isolation.

Large developments may split up into multiple separate projects, performing basic research prototyping, or studies. The product management plan drives and synthesizes all the separate sub-project plans. The plan for an individual sub-project may go into more detail, but must be compatible with the elements in the product management plan.

13.5. The organizational process

To undertake business developments, an organization needs to have defined system processes. In defining a business process, an organization may draw on a number of sources, which are depicted in Figure 13.11. These include:

- **research**: *large systems engineering or customer organizations may invest in independent research into systems engineering processes; universities are entering the field, albeit slowly;*

- **industrial best practice** *is increasingly defined in the open publications and the proceedings of professional associations, in particular the International Council on Systems Engineering (INCOSE);*

- **national/international standards** *lay down norms for systems engineering processes (see chapter 15);*

- **benchmarking** *as direct comparison of systems engineering processes and best practices with equivalent organizations, either singly or in clubs; this occurs informally between organizations when they conduct joint projects, but may be formalized in explicit benchmarking exercises.*

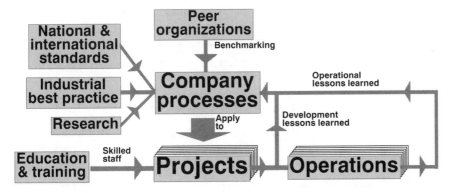

Figure 13.11: Influences on the organizational processes

Naturally, these processes will have to be rolled out to the professional staff, who will need to be trained in their use. Metrics are collected to drive process improvement through the analysis of lessons learned from development and operational experience of the product.

Capability maturity

An organization may assess the overall state of its systems engineering processes against a capability model (CM). The concept originated with the Capability Maturity Models of the Software Engineering Institute[71], now being extended to systems[72]. Typically, a CM model defines a number of levels against which the maturity of an organization's processes may be measured, along with criteria to check whether it has been reached:

- **level 1 (Initial)**: *No definable processes in place; projects are conducted by competent people and heroics;*

- **level 2 (Repeatable)**: *Basic project management processes are in place to track cost, schedule and functionality. Planning and managing new products is based on experience with similar projects;*

- **level 3 (Defined)**: *Processes for management and engineering are documented and integrated into a standard process for the organization. All projects use an approved, tailored version of the organization s standard process;*

- **level 4 (Quantitative)**: *Detailed process and product quality metrics are fully employed. Meaningful variations in process performance can be distinguished from random noise and trends in process and product qualities can be predicted;*

- **level 5 (Optimizing)**: *The organization has quantitative feedback systems in place to identify process weaknesses and strengthen them pro-actively. Project teams analyze defects to determine their causes; processes are evaluated and updated to prevent recurrence of known types of defects.*

Such definitions can only provide crude guidance, and an organization often aims for different levels of maturity in different parts of the systems engineering processes, depending on the nature of its business. Level 3 represents the onset of real systems engineering capability, and is broadly equivalent to the levels of definition called for in ISO 9001.

13.6. Metrics for the development process

Metrics for the efficiency of system development need to be managed at the enterprise level, i.e. above the level of the individual development. The objectives for metrics are to help improve the efficiency of all developments, and to detect malignancy at an early stage within a single development.

We collect metrics to make better decisions – for example, to re-direct or cancel a project, inject more resources, review a project's goals, or determine the effect of a process change. The metrics must provide information to improve the quality of those decisions. Martin[73] says that the objectives for metrics are to measure and improve processes, provide information for planning and monitoring, and for comparison between projects. The process is to define the goals for metrics, define the questions that metrics will answer, and only then define the metrics[74]. A good fraction of the metrics information currently collected is wasted, because no-one has thought through what questions need be answered.

Choose the metrics carefully by asking questions such as:

What are the requirements for these metrics?

What decisions do I need to make about this project?

What information do I need to make these decisions?

Can the development process demonstrably meet the enterprise objectives?

Example requirements for metrics are that they should be meaningful, easy to collect, predictive, provide current not historical information, and be intellectually acceptable to those supplying the information. Each metric should be both useful and minimal, i.e. measurements should be taken only if they answer a question or enable a decision to be made. The metrics must meet the needs of both the project and the enterprise controlling multiple projects.

Metrics should not be an add-on to the systems process, but be built integrally into the process. The act of following the development processes should generate the metrics information automatically. It should not be possible to proceed through the processes without supplying the correct metrics information. Metrics should encourage good practice i.e. the act of producing a metric should reinforce good development practices. These factors also shape whether sampling is good enough to produce the metrics or whether everything will need to be measured. If metrics are not chosen correctly, they can locally optimize a single factor while degrading overall performance. For example, by focusing solely on the throughput of a supermarket check-out counter as a metric, we might alienate customers by not giving them enough individual attention.

Metrics for systems engineering processes could include:

- *percentage of user requirements met* − this encourages user requirements to be created, and measures how well they are being implemented, throughout the life cycle;
- *conformance to planned resources and schedules* − this factor measures the ability of the team to plan and predict;
- *amount of re-work* − this metric can be subjective, but measures the effort being wasted. The value covers unplanned work, not planned iteration of a product: only one formal review should be needed for each process step;
- *problems caused to users by product faults* − this represents the pain caused to users by products that do not meet their requirements, plus the costs of replacement and/or re-installation.

13.7. Technology management

An enterprise needs to control:

- *the products being developed;*
- *requirements on the development processes for products (e.g. cycle time);*
- *technology for those products;*
- *competitive position relative to its competitors;*
- *enterprise objectives for the company (e.g. market penetration).*

Even if all of these elements are managed well, the inter-relationships between them are rarely handled rigorously enough. Technology development must be driven by the needs of future products and the enterprise objectives. Managing technology requires access both to technology development information and the projects that need to use that technology.

Technology management is another task which uses the techniques of systems engineering outside the individual project and therefore driven from the point of view of the enterprise. Figure 13.12 shows the technology management process, starting from a set of business objectives which, for example, define the opportunities that the enterprise wishes to exploit, its development budget, or the policy for risk.

Information needs to be structured and inter-related to handle technology planning. This connects the products to the new technology which they will

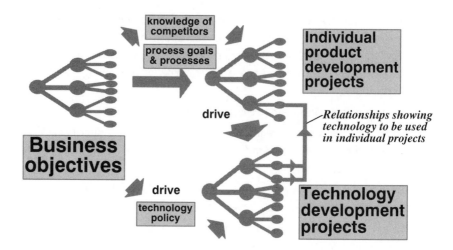

Figure 13.12: The management of technology

employ when released. Figure 13.13 shows an example roadmap for the technology for a gasoline dispensing system. This roadmap is a timeline which classifies the risk involved in a technology versus the time. Others will show the relationships between business objectives, technology, competitors, and business opportunities.

Each development project should be linked back to the enterprise objectives. The schedules of technology developments are then tied to the particular projects demanding the technology. Changes in priority or schedule in projects can then be reflected immediately in the associated technology developments[62]. The enterprise goals for improving the development processes should be tied into technology management to explain the investment and risk policy of the organization. For instance, a reduction in the development time of 30% may be worth several hundred million dollars, by improving take-up of the business opportunities. The objective is to systematically manage the evolution of core technologies. This information shows how much it is worth spending to improve the systems engineering processes.

Philosophy for technology management

Technology projects usually start off as small, low-cost and high-risk, and gradually transform into more expensive projects with the technology closely tied to one or more industrial products. As the technology gets close to being injected into commercial products, the risk must be very low because of the expense involved if the technology fails. An automated system for managing technology can therefore allow rapid access to strategic and tactical planning information, with automatic generation of technology roadmaps. If this

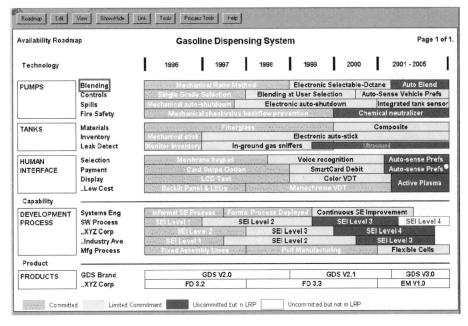

Figure 13.13: A roadmap view of technology management

information can be modeled electronically, the technology and enterprise plans can be viewed across the enterprise. The real metric is the added value from technology injected into the final products.

Our attitude toward developing technology has undergone a revolution in the last decade. The major sources of innovation are seen to arise from customers and production, not from pure ideas. The old concept was a quiet, greenfield research park or university site, where scientists developed brilliant ideas which were then passed to companies for 'engineering' into products.

This illusion simply did not compete with the Japanese approach of putting technology development close to customers and the production line. For example, the video recorder was an American invention, and US companies such as Ampex produced the first commercial studio equipment. But Japanese companies flattened their US rivals to turn the video recorder into a consumer product. Research parks such as Xerox Parc spawned brilliant computing inventions, such as the workstation, mouse, and icons, but repeatedly failed to bring these to market. Compare this with the Lockheed 'Skunk Works' approach, where a small team designed and even assembled a sequence of planes such as the U-2, the 2,000 mph SR-71 Blackbird and the Stealth fighters[75]. Invention, product innovation and technology should be as close to production as possible.

Enterprises have gradually realized that technology can be a commodity, and can sometimes be both bought and sold. Attempting to develop all the technology in-house can be very inefficient. An enterprise can make a considerable amount by licensing technology, perhaps even to rival companies.

Technology development may sometimes be started before the products that will need their outputs or may sometimes be targeted for use within several products. To drive such technology development, the enterprise may need to define 'virtual products' to use the technology when it becomes available.

The technology policy determines the overall level of expenditure and risk which the enterprise will shoulder. The policy might dictate whether the emphasis will be on internal development or purchase of technology.

Management of intellectual assets

In many businesses, knowledge is the critical corporate asset and represents a substantial part of the company value [68&76]. For example, companies such as Microsoft, Universal Studios, Virgin, and Netscape have little 'book value' in terms of visible equity. Microsoft's prime asset (perhaps 90% of its share value) lies in its customer base of tens of millions of users of Windows products. This is not confined to hi-tech companies, and the asset values of advertising agencies, fashion labels, or the Coca-Cola Corporation are primarily knowledge-based[77]. Their market value is primarily derived from intangible intellectual assets. This may be in the form of the knowledge of its staff, customers, experience, the ability to manage complex processes, technology, design algorithms, patents, software code, research expertise, customer lists, the ability to re-use elements across the organization, or knowledge of competitive businesses. It can easily be lost when people leave a company. Knowledge can be expressed outside a company, as customer or supplier relationships or inside a company as processes or research knowledge.

Systems engineering is both a generator and a consumer of many of these intellectual assets. Systems engineering processes and knowledge are prime intellectual assets of an organization. The application of this knowledge can enable a company to develop products more effectively and dominate a marketplace. The discipline is particularly important in documenting knowledge for re-use, in the form of experience, or rules. For instance, introducing a new product one year earlier than planned may present a business opportunity of $200M, but require an investment of $25M to improve the development process. To produce such figures, the company needs to be able to link projects, process improvement, enterprise objectives, and technology development. Technology management is an example of organizing information into knowledge.

Human beings are the origin of all of these assets, but the value of intellectual assets can be enhanced (or destroyed) by sharing and distributing critical information across many projects. Documentation is a poor mechanism for leveraging such knowledge, because of all the problems of multiple versions, finding and linking information. To be valuable, intellectual assets must be communicable, saleable, easy to find, easy to group, and be well structured. Intellectual capital takes disorganized information, and packages it into knowledge that enables action to be taken[78]. The principles used for organizing system information can be re-applied to manage intellectual assets.

13.8. Multiple operational systems

Re-use across systems

Re-use of elements across multiple systems is another task for the enterprise rather than for individual projects. Re-use can involve physical components, but also may involve tests, designs or requirements. For example, a car engine or body panels may be re-used across a range of cars, software can be re-applied across a range of telecommunications switches, or test requirements used for many radar systems. Re-use across multiple projects requires investment and support from the enterprise. An individual project will rarely want to spend the extra resources needed to enable re-use.

The first step is making sure that any re-usable element is of sufficiently high quality to be re-used. Projects need to be able to see and identify those elements, and to see the requirements tied to them. Figure 13.14 shows some of the features needed to encourage re-use. Organizing information for re-use for real-world systems takes discipline and investment over several years. The rewards are high, but the task is far from easy.

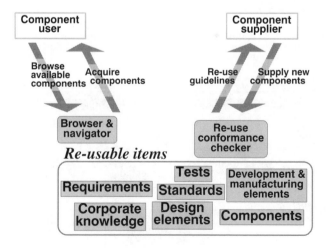

Figure 13.14: Re-use

Systems of systems

Until now, the impression might be that systems come into being individually, then interact with their immediate environment and support systems to generate a single capability. In reality, it is possible to couple large systems together to create large meta-systems, or *'systems of systems'*. These meta-systems fulfil functions greater than the set of coupled systems from which they are built.

Examples are already around us, such as air traffic control systems which have for several decades integrated the individual surveillance, communications and data processing systems into a complete service. National air defence systems have followed similar paths. The trend is clearly towards the creation of larger assemblies of this nature. The so-called 'Digitized Battlespace' and wide-area transportation systems will provide the backbone of future operations in the defense and civil arenas respectively.

Because 'systems of systems' are, in effect just 'systems' at another level of abstraction, most of the earlier concepts should be applicable. Figure 13.15 shows a model of how the information underlying the creation of a system of systems − or system of projects − might be linked. In this model, stakeholder requirements are derived for the meta-system, and linked through the system requirements to the 'systems of systems architecture'. Exploration of this triangle leads to the overall system concept. From this, the requirements for individual projects are defined, and related to existing legacy systems within the overall architecture. Individual system projects are integrated into the 'system of systems' to provide an operational capability. Projects here could

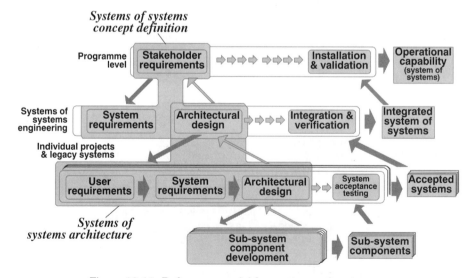

Figure 13.15: Reference model for systems of systems

be aimed at the provision of infrastructure, such as communications services, as well as products for end users.

The term 'systems of systems' is perhaps misleading, because many systems are in effect systems of systems. The trend towards *systems of projects* extends the boundaries of project management outside the domain of the single development project. This calls for management disciplines and controls beyond those of the simpler world of isolated systems, although the are in principle described by the model described in chapters 8 and 9.

What is emerging is a move towards developing operational capability above the level of an individual project. The decision to develop a particular system, such as a plane or ship, has always implied architectural judgement in the owning organization. When the individual systems are not linked, integration is trivial and the architecture of the overall system probably never expressed. In modern federated systems, the interaction between the systems is far more intense, and architectural issues are becoming explicit. Managing at the capability level would allow the design of the plane – or even the judgement as to whether to develop a plane or an unmanned vehicle – to emerge from trade-off studies at the operational capability level.

Figure 13.16 shows an example 'system of systems' for organizational information technology. Each separate project is a component of the total system, which should meet the organizational objectives for IT. Organizational IT policy (such as re-use, interoperability and use of COTS) can be stated once at and applied across all projects. Project can never work together successfully if this architecture is not constructed.

In another less conventional meaning of the term 'systems of systems', an automotive manufacturer may decide to produce, for example, four sizes of vehicle with maximum re-use of components and development facilities across that range. This defines a 'system of cars' in this case optimized from a development perspective, rather than how the parts interact operationally.

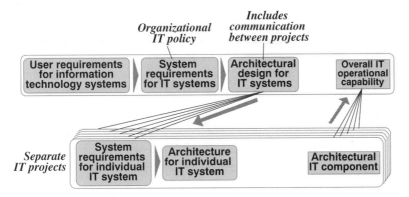

Figure 13.16: Example 'system of systems'

Again, an organization may procure a family of systems which interact only through their operational support. An example would be a fleet of military support vehicles made up of modular, reconfigurable sub-assemblies, from which the organization could assemble ambulances, tankers, and other general supply vehicles. The overall architecture would be derived from customer requirements, and describe how the component parts might be built and assembled in multiple configurations. 'Systems of systems' are therefore becoming increasingly common as a means of improving operational and development effectiveness.

Although the underlying systems engineering model is no different in principle from an isolated project, the added dimensions of complexity and expense constrain the system of systems architecture. For example, a closely-coupled architecture would be inappropriate for an operational system of systems, because all design changes would call for multiple changes in different projects. Continuous, iterative changes in all constituent projects could easily become unmanageable. Architectures for systems of systems must therefore be loosely coupled (as discussed in Chapter 4), with a strong dependence on interfaces and behavioural definition. Because of its impact and longevity, the 'systems of system architecture' has to be based on stable principles, expressed and held at the highest level of the organization.

13.9. Summary

The principles of systems engineering carry up to the business level, where projects should be driven by objectives. The enterprise is itself treated as a system. The advantages of 'time-to-market with the right product' are potentially available to the whole business, but also require discipline at the management level. The business must itself employ expertise in systems engineering to handle the technical issues above the level of individual projects. This is becoming especially important with the increasing trend towards systems of systems, that is products or systems linked in operations, during development or through their support systems. Experience shows that a good, staged, innovation process is particularly important. This ensures projects can be created at acceptable risk, they fit together and work together correctly. This requires investment from the company, and perhaps more difficult, demands intense interaction between systems engineering and the managers setting the enterprise objectives.

The term 'business' gives a hook on which to hang many of these concepts. However, many of them are applicable recursively above and below the individual project, i.e. to the customer or sub-system level. They fit into the generic enterprise model at every level.

Exercises for Projects and the enterprise

Exercise 46: Applying enterprise technology

A technology that is key to the future of the enterprise has been developed in-house. The technology is far from perfect but now needs to be applied to get it out of the laboratory and into use. A new project that might use the technology has evaluated it, but decided on a rival commercial option on the grounds that it is cheaper. The director of research says that you, as company CEO, must impose the technology for the long-term good of the enterprise. Define how you would handle the situation.

Define, from a systems engineering point of view, how you would ensure that these decisions would be implemented through the life of the project.

Exercise 47: Novelty and risk

A large organization is aiming to build and sell a new product in which it has only partial experience.

Pick one of the following areas and write a plan for what the organization needs to do and how much it should spend before it gives full commitment to proceed with the project.

    1: An electric hair dryer;

    2: A cellular phone;

    3: A new brand of lager.

In each case, define what you think will be the major risks of failure.

In your plan, show how you would reduce these risks.

Exercise 48: Different approaches to commitment

The following policies represent the way in which an enterprise 'commits' to financing a development project (these represent the cultures of different nations).

Write a paragraph on the advantages and disadvantages of each approach.

Define what project tactics is likely evolve in response to the policy being imposed on them by the organization.

> *1: The project gets the full budget allocation on a yearly basis. In the last two months before the renewal, the complete project is reviewed financially and technically. The budget for the next year is announced two weeks before the financial year starts.*
>
> *2: The project gets the full budget for the development of the project at an early stage of the project. The organization tracks the project against costs and the deliverables defined by the project. The project may re-define the deliverables. As long as the project does not exceed a projected cost-to-completion of more than 120% of the allocated budget, it is allowed to proceed.*

Now define a better enterprise commitment policy.

Define key requirements for commitment that will allow the enterprise to commit to the project.

Define the key products that the project must produce to reach that level of commitment.

Exercise 49: Defining the danger signals

You are the manager of ten projects in an organization. The company has a history of several product failures either during development (when it became clear they were too expensive) or of failure on introduction to the marketplace.

The company needs to reduce the risk of this happening, but it still needs to produce innovatory products.

Define a process and a set of metrics that will enable you to monitor the status of these projects to flag up these dangers at an early stage or to suppress them before they happen.

Exercise 50: Who owns the architecture?

A major defense system is to be procured, with a projected service life of 20–30 years. During the course of its operational use, it is expected to be upgraded a number of times. During the lifetime of the system, the customer wants maximum freedom to select and add new subsystems, inject new technology, and to work co-operatively with other systems in a wide variety of scenarios.

Should the customer control (and keep updated) the requirements during the development?

Should the customer take control of the architecture to do so?
What systems engineering resources (if any) does the customer need to control in order to handle this role?

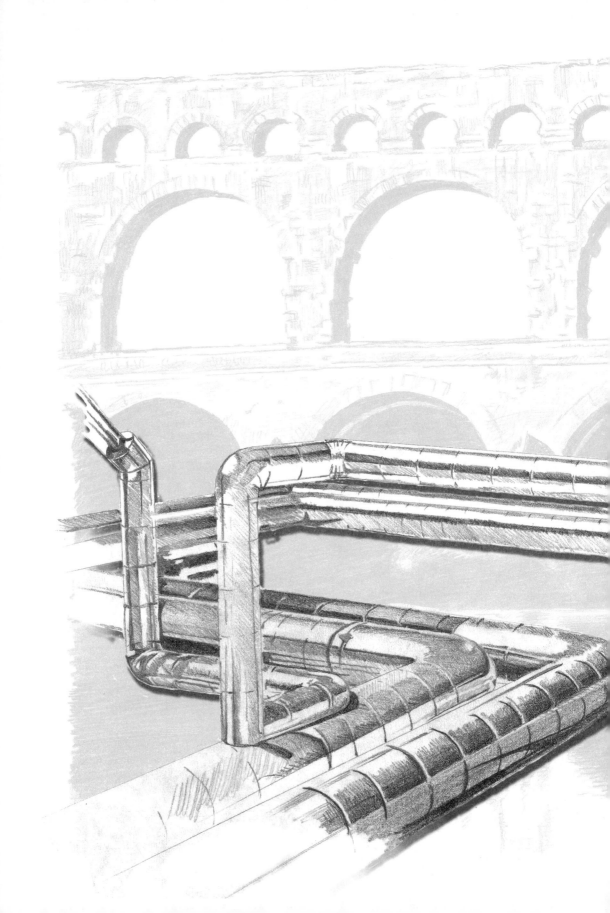

Improving the systems engineering process

fourteen

14.1. Agents for change

In many enterprises, the systems engineering processes are currently fragmented or non-existent, despite valiant attempts from individual enthusiasts. For example, few companies have a solid connection between the marketing and development departments, or apply a consistent set of system and software processes. Good requirements documents are relatively thin on the ground. Many companies spend a fortune on R&D and product development, but are reluctant to allocate a fraction of that on improving their development process. Yet the rewards for delivering a good product earlier to market may be extremely high.

The good news is, however, that many companies are trying to improve their internal processes. Enhancing systems engineering across an enterprise is a 'process not an event'[79] that involves far more than just buying tools, and the real investment is in improving enterprise discipline. This change has to be treated as a project that will take several years (Figure 14.1).

Changing the enterprise culture requires a good engineering approach, matched by a similar process at the management level. Systems engineering must make economic sense, or funding will not be made available. The chance of failure must be low – management is nervous of looking foolish. You cannot hope to get everything right the first time you handle new tasks. Yet the first projects cannot be allowed to fail, because this will spread the wrong message. A low-risk approach is therefore necessary, so start small, get support for the initial projects, and buy in the skills you do not yet possess.

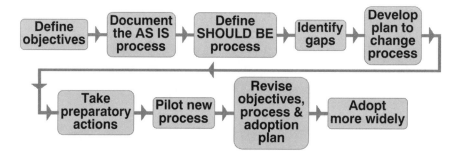

Figure 14.1: Improving the systems engineering processes

14.2. Success factors for process improvement

A range of factors increases the chance for success at process improvement. process. At the start of the improvement process, you are probably faced with a host of simultaneous problems. The emphasis has to be on reducing complexity to have any chance of success. Do the easy, high-reward parts first, notably getting the system processes (especially the front-end process) under control, applying strong and consistent management, and making the product competitive with rivals.

Defined and measurable objectives for the improvement are essential. 'User requirements' are the foundation to help system development become a measured process. Improvements to development efficiency, product development time, delivered quality, measures of schedule, resource predictability, time to implement user requirements, and the amount of re-usability can be assessed against requirements. These values are not normally measured for system projects, and as a result measurement of improvement is initially impossible. A goal for the first projects is to **define and apply a set of metrics** (see previous chapter). Process improvement and comparison between projects becomes possible on the next set of projects.

The **development processes** have to be good enough to handle the pilot projects. In practice, some kind of engineering processes will always exist already, so the task is one of improvement rather than introduction. Without an established process, the enterprise cannot ever know the real status of any of its projects. Do not try to write new processes and hope to apply them immediately. Good processes, especially for the front-end parts of the life cycle, are already available – use them and do not re-invent the wheel. Consistent processes for software and systems are needed, because of the overlap between the two disciplines. In many companies there is a huge gap between marketing and development, and the defined processes must ensure that any gap is reduced. Marketing should take responsibility for user requirements, putting themselves in the driving seat for developing new products. If the enterprise needs to tailor existing processes because its development needs are fundamentally different, then it should be done in a structured way, starting by defining the requirements for that process.

The **gap between the current and ideal** processes can then be identified, and a **plan generated to bridge the gap**. All necessary elements of the current processes should be accounted for in the new process. The plan should cover:

- *deciding what training & consulting is necessary;*
- *deciding how to acquire the skills and resources;*
- *deriving criteria for pilot project selection;*
- *identifying potential resources;*

      – *identifying the techniques for monitoring the pilots;*
      – *allocating the tasks to individuals.*

The plan then needs to be implemented, and **preparation performed** for choosing and implementing the first pilot projects.

Good staff with a balance of enthusiasm and experience are needed for the pilots. They should not be cowed by too many experiences of failure, or naive enough to expect instant success. The quality and commitment of people are the biggest single determinant of success. Good people will always turn in successful results – but they will probably have changed the product you imagined in the first place. But you can throw away good people by not treating them properly, so **getting a good working atmosphere** is crucial. System engineers are paid for their brainpower, not for occupying a desk from 9 till 5. People are your greatest asset[80], and an enthusiastic workforce will suggest improvements that will help make it happen. During the transition, staff will steadily gain experience and confidence, and so stability in the team is highly desirable.

One risk is enough in a project – choose it carefully

A good process for product management by the organization acquiring the product is critically important, but often neglected. Obviously this is important because the newly changed process will usually be introduced at the start of a new development. If the customer does not define a set of enterprise objectives and manage the user requirements well, the development is lost in fog. Without these objectives, a project can have little hope of providing a satisfactory product, nor can the development be controlled. The product manager must define clear strategic objectives, but not micro-manage projects. The product manager must perform systems engineering work to initiate the development sensibly, and make sure that the requirements, budget and schedule are consistent. This may involve design work without commitment to a specific design.

The **program initiation process** is a critical success factor. The enterprise must encourage an abundance of ideas, and have a solid process to improve the best of them and take them seamlessly into development. In many companies, the innovation process is somewhat ad-hoc. Even with the stage-gate process, some organizations evaluate on a purely marketing-based approach, without considering the systems engineering issues. New projects must be simultaneously affordable, practical, have a good market potential and be manageable. They have to be approved, rejected, or modified on this basis.

A low-risk approach is essential, because improving the systems engineering culture always involves more novelty than is desirable. Whenever possible, avoid taking risks. Like most things in life, the first time we do something, we fail. These capabilities have to be slowly acquired. You can always take one risk in a project, but taking more than one is foolish.

Previous successful experience in front-end system processes is a real help. Teams must be knowledgeable in early systems engineering tasks such as requirements management. Capturing and organizing requirements requires a blend of experience and human skills (see chapter 2). This role involves theatricality as well as technical skill, not too difficult to learn, but as with anything else we (mostly) get better at doing it with experience. You cannot write unless you have read, and so you can hardly be expected to write good requirements until you have read good examples. We repeatedly see engineers writing poor requirements documents, and the lack of high-quality example documents must be a contributory factor.

Pilot projects are essential to try out changes to the enterprise process. A discrete sub-project of a larger project is a good compromise. **Choose the pilot projects carefully**, making sure they are challenging, small enough to be manageable, yet large enough to be meaningful. As the pilots are completed, *process improvement* becomes possible. The enterprise can re-set the metric for the development process. The people involved in pilot projects are usually high-quality and enthusiastic enough to overcome the problems that will inevitably occur. Pilot projects provide proof of the benefits of process improvement, and positive feedback often starts long before the project is finished.

Never enter a battle you will lose – Proverb of Japanese Go

Management commitment and engagement are required to cover at least the pilot project. This means converting management from neutral observers (or worse) into involved participants in the improvement process. Make them work hard, ensure they define the management goals, and make any essential decisions. Employing external specialists can often be helpful in encouraging management to be responsible. You should always define the business case for improving the process. The business case could, for example, predict the impact of cutting the development cycle or of developing products with twice the current reliability. The enterprise must eventually own the improvement process or it will fail. This will involve financial support, plus access to the right areas for information. For instance, you will need to talk to the marketing department and operational staff to find out their requirements. Talk to managers in management terms, and convince them of the business case for improving systems engineering.

Management commitment is crucial

The gap between marketing and development must be bridged. Marketing needs to become much more organized, to own the user requirements and adopt a disciplined approach product management.

The enterprise must be willing to support pilot projects both financially and emotionally, but it would be unrealistic to ask for total engagement from management, because it will rarely be provided. All you need is enough support to get the pilot projects done without too much interference. Keep up a stream of publicity to sell the pilots – in the company newspaper, presentations, or organize celebrations on reaching milestones. We have to understand the enterprise and its foibles, and persuade it to change. A head-on charge at management, based purely on technical concepts, is certain to fail. Top-level management is often committed to change, but middle management is crushed between making their personal profit targets, improving the processes and the resources needed for re-training, expense and experimentation.

Trying to impose better system processes top-down on project staff leads to certain failure. It is essential to **convince the engineers** that the change will go through (and is not just 'management bluster') and that it is intellectually acceptable. 800–page procedures are just too long. Words that are not read might as well have never been written, however excellent the advice may be. Get engineers involved in the process definition, because they will keep it small and practical. Engineers principally learn from other's successes and failures. Moreover, they do not have the slightest problem in merely pretending to follow rules, even when those rules are impractical.

If you think education is expensive, try ignorance

Training and education for the people involved is critical to spreading the improvement process. You will have to grow the majority of your system engineers. Successful **systems engineering training** requires solid material, experienced teachers and good presentation skills. General-purpose trainers are inappropriate for these courses, because the presenters must have real project experience to be accepted by participants. Good young system engineers may find it hard to succeed in presenting systems engineering material, because of the perceived need for experience. You must monitor the ratings given by the course participants, and train the lecturers in presentation skills to get them up to standard. Course material takes a long time to evolve to an acceptable quality, and buying in and modifying existing material is much less expensive. By its very nature, the subject material is dense and intricate, and can easily be boring. It has to be made as attractive and interactive as possible, with real world examples incorporated into the material. The first version of the training course will be inadequate and require updating over another couple of years. You must use experienced, successful people for the improvement process.

The best form of education integrates methods training seamlessly with the work of the project – as the proverb says *say, do, learn*. Workshop-style learning provides a small amount of training, followed by an immediate working session to apply that knowledge in capturing and organizing the information. Little time is lost on training with this approach. Impractical ideas get ruthlessly exposed to the cleansing power of reality. Young engineering staff will learn rapidly through mentoring, i.e. working closely with experienced system engineers.

Training must cover managers and marketing staff as well as engineering staff, because they are often performing a systems engineering role. Their training material needs to be different to that of the engineers, and should use management terminology. Training is always bi-directional – as a presenter, you will learn as much as you teach if you give the material. You will often find that training will generate 'messages' from one staff group to another – e.g. from working engineers to middle management, or from middle management to the company executives.

Tools for requirements and systems engineering should be simple to use. A naive user should be able to operate the tools after a few minutes, but as with any new tools, mastering the subtleties can take several months. **Tools for systems engineering** have to be good enough for the job, the best commercial software tools are now excellent, and sensible companies have largely abandoned 'do-it-yourself' tools after counting the real costs. At the early stages, engineers are simultaneously trying to learn methods, tools, and techniques and organize existing fragmentary information. Wherever possible, tools should support and enable the chosen methods to be instrumented more easily, not impose their own method. Requirements and decision management tools provide the foundation for systems engineering. But however good the tools, we have to adjust ourselves to the 'mental model' behind them. This approach gives you the skills to overcome the inevitable 'finger-trouble' of first use of any tool. Training, especially workshop-style, in using the tools is essential. The tool must be expandable by the enterprise itself, because each project has its own needs, and because requirements are linked into so many (perhaps all) areas of a project. Tools should be bought only when there is a plan for training and time scheduled for applying them. Again a business case for tool investment should be produced. While processes come first, tools are often the enablers of change by making information-handling easier. Methods are not exciting, but people get more enthusiastic when they see the method made more visible through a tool.

Someone in the company must own the process of change, both at the technical and managerial level. The **internal champion** for change has a tough job especially in the initial stages, because mistakes are inevitable. This person is a technical reference point, and supports the younger staff. Resilience, intellect, commitment and an awareness of risk are all essential. However good this person is technically, he or she will not survive long without some management support. A champion may be needed at both the technical and the managerial level. The management champion must therefore have some access to funds, and some leverage within the enterprise to protect the innovators.

Tying into external certification such as ISO 9001[81] or a capability maturity (CM) model for systems engineering provides a public stamp of quality. The enterprise is no longer just claiming to meet some standard, but has been certified or assessed by some external body. This concept is highly visible and often easy to sell to management – there is a plaque to put on the wall and a logo for the company notepaper. External certification can mean a lot or nothing, and it is possible to go through the motions and obtain the certificate without actually having a good process. Everyone loses when this happens, and so the certification process should be used to drive real improvements in the processes.

Metrics and process improvement

Inevitably you will be asked to 'prove' that the expenditure on improving systems engineering can be justified. The only sensible response is to pose another question:

How efficient are our current processes?

While a business does not have a measurable process, this question cannot be answered. Improving the systems engineering processes should enable us to start to gather metrics, and to improve the process, and measure that process. One of the goals of the pilot projects should therefore be to define metrics that can calibrate the current process.

If you pretend to be something long enough, you eventually become it – Colette

Public relations to encourage management commitment

The business case is necessary, but not sufficient, and the rest of the business needs to be kept enthusiastic about the pilot project. This may involve presentations, good articles in the house magazines or seminars for management. Be enthusiastic, but tell the truth, with details about what is successful and what has failed. Public relations efforts are needed to sell the improvement process.

14.3. Likely causes of failure

The likely causes of failure are somewhat complementary to the success factors:

- *too technical an approach;*
- *trying to do too many new things at once;*
- *trying to do too much in-house;*
- *failure to get internal commitment;*
- *lack of intellectual acceptance from engineers;*
- *trying to make the change on the cheap ;*
- *trying to make the change before the enterprise is ready;*
- *trying to do too much too quickly.*

Treating the improvement process as a purely technical issue almost guarantees failure. Innocents may believe that purchase of tools is sufficient, but unless the entire process is tackled simultaneously, this can actually be a backward step.

Inevitably, attempting to introduce more discipline into an organization's development processes has to be evolutionary. Any attempt to improve the systems engineering processes in a purely top-down manner will fail. Working engineers need to be convinced that the proposed change is technically sensible and that management is really going to follow through the whole process. The biggest killers of enthusiasm are arbitrary, impractical standards and lack of management commitment. The biggest sign of the latter is unwillingness to release sensible amounts of resources. A half-baked approach is worse than not starting.

What should be out-sourced?

Many roles in process improvement can be out-sourced, but some tasks are so critical for success that they have to be handled internally. For example, the enterprise objectives represent the future direction of a company and therefore they must be 'possessed' by the company management. The business must control these, even if someone else assists in defining the enterprise objectives. Time and adrenaline are the major gains in out-sourcing some of the work of improving the system process. Both are invariably in short supply.

Another case which can leverage advantage from external specialists is by using them to import or transform data from one form to another (typically more structured). This effort can be quite large and is perceived as non value-added by the pilot team. Also by getting their data in place prior to workshops, participants can see their own data and rapidly become effective in applying the tools.

14.4. Making the business case

Potential savings = The current costs of non-quality

The cost of improving the systems engineering processes must be justified in business terms, taking into account the current costs of 'non-quality'[82]. When a product fails, it must be replaced or repaired, leading to extra resources for documenting the faults, handling the problems, spares, and transportation. You have to apologize to the customer, but you never recover the loss to your reputation[83]. The cost is far more than the cost of manufacture. The company is in repair mode, instead of designing improved products. What does it cost the company to deliver a product three months late? What does it cost if that product has a host of faults that require field replacement? How does a poor quality product affect future orders? The answers to these questions define the current financial cost of weak processes. If they cannot be quantified, the company is essentially flying blind. Decisions that result in a lower quality throw away the wealth of society.

To deduce the current costs of non-quality, take some typical recent projects and analyze what went wrong with the market research, requirements, front-end decisions, and the product development and introduction. These values enable us to predict the likely cost of non-quality for the current development. This will involve analyzing the likely cost of delays in delivering the right quality product, faults in the product when introduced, dissatisfaction of customers or inability to upgrade a product rapidly. A cost estimate needs to be made of these hazards, and the likelihood of them actually occurring. Thus it is a form of risk management (see chapter 6). The highest losses usually arise from delays in product introduction, which cause a loss of market share.

Management (rightly) is not concerned with systems engineering – it is merely a means to an end. Managers have to focus on the managerial issues of cost, business value and risk. The business case for improving systems engineering has to be cast in managerial, not technical, terms. We have to construct a business case based on the cost of improving systems engineering, the added value of the process changes and the risks to that business. Figure 14.2 details some of the key questions that need answering at the enterprise level.

The business case should ideally be comparative, i.e. it should show that the proposed policy is cost-effective compared to any other option. Of course, direct proof is impossible, because no-one is likely to develop a real system in two different ways to see which is better. The most normal form of

Questions	*Answers*
How much will it cost?	See the plan
What will it be worth to the project?	Estimates of savings due to shorter integration time, less re-work and operational failures
What will it be worth to the company?	Estimates of business loss for continuing current policy compared with savings and gains from changed policy (e.g. new business won)
Can you demonstrate that it really will work?	Show examples in other companies, do a risk evaluation
How much will it cost if it fails?	Reduce this value by pilot projects and copying from the experiences of others
Do you have a plan?	Yes, we have a full & costed plan for the next two years
What else do you need beyond finance?	We need management support for what we are doing - we will provide full information

Figure 14.2: Key questions for process improvement

comparison is between improving systems engineering and doing nothing (i.e. carry on doing what we are doing). Introducing new processes will involve spending money, so we have to estimate inefficiencies in the current system and project their likely cost into the future.

Figure 14.3 estimates the costs of weak processes (and hence the potential savings) on a real industrial project for a software tool[84]. The total losses due to late delivery were more than $700k, and an estimation was made that half of this could be saved in the next release. The loss of market share due to delays in introducing the product is the dominant factor in the cost equation. This delay allowed rival companies to produce better products, cutting the market share for the product. These figures led to a large investment in the next release cycle to make the test process more automatic and intense. While the figures in the diagram are estimates, they clearly show the scale of potential savings, even for a small to medium-size software product. For a huge market such as cellular phones, these figures could be multiplied several hundred times.

Costs at the project level

The costs of improving systems engineering within an individual project are:

- *staff resources involved in systems engineering;*
- *cost of tools;*
- *costs of support consultancy;*
- *disruption of projects;*
- *training of project staff in methods and tools;*
- *mistakes made in applying new methods.*

Why projects fail is as important as why they succeed

Potential problems	Likely impact	Estimated cost	Contingent cost
Cost of additional development through unplanned problems in integration & test	12 weeks	$16k/week of delay	$192k
Market share loss through delay	12 weeks	$25k/week of delay	$300k
Effort lost in repair of faults in delivered product & re-release	8 weeks	$25k/week of delay	$200k
Loss of future customer orders due to faults in product	Minor faults 12 week delay	$30k	$30k
		Most likely cost of systems engineering problems	$732k
	Potential for correction	50% *Likely saving*	$366k

Figure 14.3: Potential savings through better systems engineering

Costs for the enterprise

Logically, costs that apply across multiple projects should be borne by the business. These include costs in developing standards and training material, process development or acquisition, certification, and the contingency of correcting problems. Inevitably the first projects will make mistakes, and the resources have to be available for correcting them.

Benefits for the enterprise

Good processes at the enterprise level can deliver the following:

- improved time to market;
- more satisfied customers;
- earlier delivery of an operational product;
- management visibility and control over the development;
- a measurable (and hence improvable) process;
- a process where progress is visible to management;
- interoperability, re-use and communication across projects.

14.5. An example of costs and benefits

You must estimate the likely cost of non-quality

As an example, consider the costs and potential benefits for a real pilot project. This is drawn as anonymously as possible from our own experience, and concerns the introduction of digital television into a business experienced in analog television. The company was well organized, had high quality engineers, good technical quality, but little experience of systems engineering

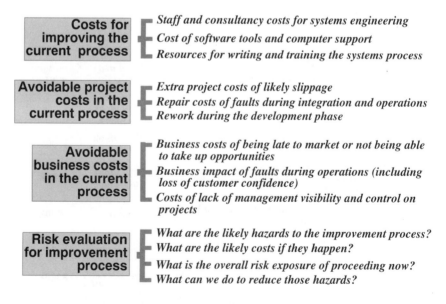

Figure 14.4: Key cost components in the management plan

processes, and with a large gap between the technical and managerial staff. Figure 14.4 shows the cost components for a management plan for the improvement process.

The visible expenditure on support, tools, consultancy, and training was approximately $90k. This was spread over a 3 month period, after which the project team was reasonably self-sufficient. The true internal cost of change for the project was approximately 3–4 times as much as the visible bill, i.e. $300k–$400k. This estimate takes into account staff time, training, and the costs of problems in applying new skills. These costs would have to be spent for any disciplined approach.

The value of the systems engineering effort is much less tangible than the costs (Figure 14.5). The deliverables were a good set of requirements, in which senior management became strongly involved. A cadre of trained staff enabled the enterprise to manage the evolution of these requirements and ensure traceability to the proposed designs. The net result was that the enterprise was able to mount a coherent attack on the problem, and not just view it in technical terms.

The value of the example project

Calculating the predicted value of the improvement process is difficult, although sometimes it is relatively easy to calculate some extreme limits. The project was a life-or-death issue for the enterprise. The future of the company depended on a successful transition from analog to digital television, which would inevitably dominate the whole market in a 5–10 year timescale. Time-to-market was absolutely critical because of the cut-throat competition. As the turnover of the corporation was approximately $3bn per year, the cost of the systems engineering effort was trivial – providing that there was any real benefit. The systems engineering resources therefore offered the opportunity to reduce future risk for only 0.0015% of the annual turnover of the company.

Figure 14.5: Benefits of improvement

Another way of examining the financial value delivered by systems engineering is to consider the cost of the project itself. The successful introduction of digital TV is likely to cost the corporation at least $150M. If requirements work led to only a 0.2% better chance of making the project successful, then again the expenditure would be worthwhile. These two figures indicate that systems engineering would be certain to be worthwhile, providing it has any sort of positive influence.

The business had a history of being engineering-driven in introducing new technology. A good proportion of previous projects had not been too successful, since they were not market-driven. Sometimes this had produced brilliant technology that was eventually successful, while at other times the net product had failed, cost too much, or been only partially successful. The major risks in this specific project were the conservatism and lack of commercial awareness of the world outside broadcasting. Improving systems engineering will not cure all existing problems, nor will it work immediately. All of these risks have to be factored into the potential benefits.

14.6. Business experience

Many businesses are currently trying to improve their system and software processes. The following examples are taken from real experience, and written by people deeply involved in trying to make such changes in a range of companies from aerospace, research, software, IT, telecommunications and medical devices.

Defence Evaluation and Research Agency – by Peter Brook, DERA

Research organizations are increasingly subject to market pressures which have traditionally driven the production sectors. Competition for funds has fuelled the need to produce advice and research reports on time and to the satisfaction of customers, in the face of rapid technological change. Research organizations are also customers for large system products, often at the leading edge of complex functionality and risk.

Underpinning any high technology enterprise is the absolute dependence on software-based processes. These processes generate its most important commodity, i.e. knowledge, as research results, as well as supporting its operation. Although the biggest short-term financial exposure comes from a small number of large projects, a greater cumulative risk may attach to the totality of the small and medium-sized projects. These are conducted by scientists themselves, rather than specialists.

The starting point for the UK's Defence Research and Evaluation Agency (DERA) was to attack the software issue. Software had been developed with a twin-track approach of enthusiastic amateurism, supplemented by instances of ad-hoc tool support, for the majority of the scientific computing. 'Real' projects, i.e. those requiring more than six to twelve staff-months of effort, had tended to call on outside support. The science base had been built on largely undocumented, unmaintainable code. For example, some large simulators were the combined efforts of multiple contractors, with no overall design and consistency, and were threatened by obsolescence and decay.

Software engineering processes were rapidly put in place, based on the European Space Agency Standard PSS–05–0, since published in book form[1]. This provided fairly formal software engineering development processes for medium-sized projects, and they were modified to deal with smaller projects and those of high criticality. In parallel, an internal software engineering center was established, to act as a focus for producing documentation, training and generally managing the roll-out process. The center was also charged with setting up an internal operation to undertake a proportion of the software engineering development projects. This was capped at 10%, sufficient to provide the essential 'hands-on' experience necessary to give the software group real expertise and credibility, and thus allow them to maintain the whole project in the longer term. Roll-out started with a small group of highly-supported projects and was rapidly spread to the population at large. ISO 9001 certification was obtained on time for the leading business sector and progressively for others.

A journey of a thousand miles starts with a single step – Chinese proverb

When this process was safely under way, a second major phase to address systems engineering was launched. This involved significant investment in the underlying standards themselves, and development still continues (this book represents work in progress). The aim is to produce a self-consistent suite of system and software engineering practices, integrated with the business's project and business management processes. An overall architecture for a document family for the business is shown in Figure 14.6. Development and implementation will probably take about three years. The early stages involve one-to-one mentoring and consultancy with individual projects, with central support provided from the engineering center, whose role now includes systems engineering.

The lessons[85] worth emphasizing are starting with a sound existing standard, employing committed experienced consultants, both in the formative stages and as trusted advisors later, and to use pilot projects to gain early success and champions.

With hindsight, the initial stages were rushed to meet the business needs for ISO certification. A balance has to be struck between maintaining the momentum that rapid change can bring, and putting all the pieces together systematically before large-scale roll out. Nevertheless, many staff welcomed the undoubted commitment of the organization and responded well.

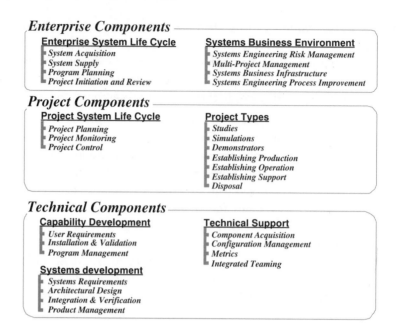

Figure 14.6: Architecture for systems engineering practices

In the rush, two particular groups were somewhat overlooked. The first were the scientists who write software routinely during their work, but are not specialists. For them, even the informal standards were too prescriptive and heavy. The standards were therefore cut down in size for those projects, with the active involvement of representative users.

The second group were the middle-ranking managers, for example those who manage projects with significant engineering content, but are not themselves practitioners. Insufficient attention had been given to bringing them into the project, and junior professional staff attending initial training courses made it clear that their managers needed education too. One-day courses were developed specifically to give them an appreciation of the underlying engineering processes being taught to their staff, with guidance on how these might be incorporated into project management plans.

Looking back, there has been a radical improvement in the business culture, with systems and software engineering more widely practised than previously seemed feasible. Measuring the benefits precisely is difficult, but larger and more complex projects are now routinely and successfully undertaken in-house. Work previously denied by major customers is being won directly and market-leading contractors are happy to engage in collaborative projects, often for third parties. DERA is also helping its major customer, the UK MOD, to think through the applicability of systems engineering principles to its own role in the acquisition process. Outside the world of big projects, user requirements documents are now routinely produced for activities right across the business. Even small engineering and research projects are seeing the benefit that comes from modest application of the principles of configuration management, phase reviews and metrication. Perhaps the biggest achievement has been the demystification of the field by the application, through training material and process documents, of the principles discussed here.

QSS Inc – by Richard Stevens, QSS Inc

The experience of QSS Inc. represents that of a smaller kind of business in a rapidly changing environment. This company produces the DOORS requirements management software, and during 3–4 years has grown from 3 to 30 software developers.

At the start, the development team was small, formed of colleagues who had known each other for years. A solid set of user and system requirements was generated. This group had intuitive communication and required little process infrastructure to partition and merge individual contributions to the product. Many design decisions were only captured as they appeared in the source code. This was a workable solution for an experienced small team well versed in each other's previous work, and driven by good user requirements.

As the software grew in size and the number of developers increased, the design and implementation approach needed to become more formal. Process certification also became an issue for the team, and so steps towards formalizing the development processes were made. The development team began by documenting existing policies, procedures and standards, starting with a detailed programming standard for the requirements tool's extension language. This document became immediately useful in helping control the quality and maintainability of add-on tools being developed by third-party contractors. Internal development processes were formalized using the ESA PSS–05–0 standard as a basis. The test process was automated, with code builds and testing occurring each night. All documentation, including requirements, specifications, tests, bug reporting and project management, was put under the control of the very tool (DOORS) the team were developing. This was extremely useful, as it made the developers users of their own system (*eat your own dog food*). The whole process was driven by the developers, and encouraged, but not imposed, from the outside. ISO 9001 certification was achieved for the software development process.

As the number of users increased, suggestions from customers quickly became the dominant source for providing enhancements. User group meetings were a particularly fertile ground for suggestions. However, some kinds of requirements (primarily system requirements) could not come from users. Users do not directly specify changes to the user interface or novel products. A system was set up to flow these requirements into the different products, and enable the support organization to query the status of any customer request. The same database acts as the source for marketing information.

Suggestions and complaints from any source are poured into a requirements database. These inputs arrive in random order, are of variable quality, and contain descriptive material. The same suggestion may be repeated several times. The requirements manager handles the requirements set from a customer viewpoint, and is responsible for prioritizing them. Anyone (including developers) can suggest a requirement, but the user representative must confirm it.

The first steps are to separate the 'non-requirements' information, descriptive material and design issues. The original source material must be still available and links retained to the material as it is transformed. Repetition can then be detected, and requirements which are essentially the same are electronically stapled together, so that one decision can be made which affects multiple requirements.

The company added its own business objectives at the same time. Structuring the user requirements then became possible, typically around user scenarios. Structure reveals omissions, inconsistencies, and duplication and again reduces the overall size of information.

QSS Inc then started to handle multiple projects, and a more complex approach to handling requirements became necessary. Perhaps not surprisingly for a requirements company, a requirements director was appointed to handle all of the requirements. This involved organizing requirements into a coherent set, and then partitioning them into the individual projects for review. Requirements capture became a continuous process instead of being tied to the start of any project. Figure 14.7 illustrates the information needed for decision-making. On the left-hand side of the diagram, requirements flow in from any source, from users, workshops with key customers, and suggestions from engineers working with the customers. They are cleaned up and structured into a coherent set for review by the requirements manager. The development side supplies resource estimates for each requirement. Both costs and benefits must be available to allow sensible business decisions on which requirements to implement or postpone. Thus the process can be seen as customer-controlled on the left-hand side, developer-controlled on the right-hand side, and mitigated by business decisions taking both costs and benefits into account. Individual product managers control the packages on the right-hand side. Product managers use the same concepts and terminology as the software engineers use for the core software. The process can be seen as a way of bridging the gap between

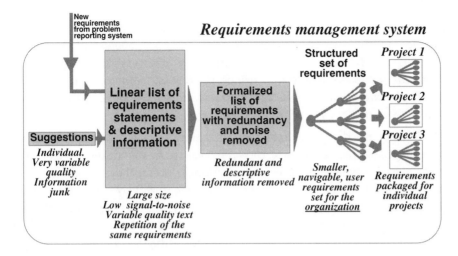

Figure 14.7: Requirements flow for multiple projects

marketing and development, putting a disciplined process in place to link the two.

The success of the main company product meant that many new spin-off products could be derived. A process for handling innovation became necessary. The company developed its own innovation process, elements of which were covered in the previous chapter. The major input to this innovation process came from customers, but in practice some kinds of innovation were expressed better from company-internal sources. A call for innovation across the company provided 35 ideas from a company of 110 people, mostly from sales staff or engineers working closely with the customers.

AT&T, Lucent Technologies and NCR – by William Miller, AT&T

The systems engineering discipline at AT&T, and now Lucent Technologies and NCR as well, emphasizes the specification of system requirements, architecture design, and detailed design. Marketing and product management businesses are responsible for documenting user requirements. Detailed test plans are used to verify component designs, architecture validation and service readiness tests in the field. Systems engineering, in effect, is highly distributed throughout businesses that have evolved a large number of 'stovepipe' functions that are functionally strong in contrast to project-driven businesses. Hence the organizational model is that of a 'factory' through which bits of projects are processed toward the offering of telephone service.

As competition has been introduced into previous monopoly or oligopoly markets, AT&T and its new offspring must become more adept at understanding user requirements and having them drive the systems engineering process. The *new* AT&T, Lucent Technologies and NCR are migrating to a stronger program management model driven by customer satisfaction and time to market considerations that are influencing the ways of performing work. The program management charters are beginning to institute the discipline of systems engineering that ties requirements, schedule and cost considerations into an information model using state of the art tools to efficiently and effectively manage the programs.

The heritage of designing telecommunications equipment and providing service has tended to emphasize the later aspects of the systems engineering process. User requirements were traditionally compactly encapsulated in terms of 'universal telephone service' that has relatively few performance requirements and a major constraint that new systems be interoperable with legacy systems. Hence, systems have been managed at the detailed interfaces to deconflict sub-system 'clashing' and reduce the testing that otherwise would occur.

As one might expect, the emphasis in development and services has been technology-driven, with less emphasis on the user requirements. New technology was only introduced to improve the cost basis of the service and had to meet regulated parameters for rate of return and long, e.g. 40–year depreciation rules for apparatus. The long lifetime of the technology as specified by regulators also set the pacing for introducing new technology as opposed to competitive market forces setting the pace.

The essence of the systems engineering process in the monopoly era is wonderfully captured by Arthur D. Hall's 1962 book, *A Methodology for Systems Engineering*[86]. That text cites a reference by Schlager[87] attributing that *The Bell Telephone Laboratories, Incorporated, was probably the first organization to use the term systems engineering.* The use of the term with roughly its present meaning began in the early 1940s, although its functions were performed in the Bell System from its very beginning. Hall identified the following pattern of systems engineering work: System Studies (Program Planning), Exploratory Planning (Project Planning I), Development Planning (Project Planning II), Studies During Development (Action Phase I), and Current Engineering (Action Phase II). Chapter 2 of Hall's book provides a case history on the TD-2 Microwave Radio Relay System to transmit television programs and telephone conversations across the North American continent that was developed and deployed into service in the 1950s.

AT&T has provided major support to the United States government and its allies during World War II, the Cold War, and continues to do so to this day[88]. This work was originally performed at the request of the government to leverage AT&T's knowledge competencies in systems engineering, basic research and technology development. Unlike systems engineering in the commercial sector during the monopoly era, AT&T honed its system integration skills, both as a supplier and as a prime contractor.

Significant contributions were made to nuclear weapons safety by Sandia Corporation as well as air defense, missile defense, and underwater surveillance systems by Bell Labs and Western Electric. AT&T also established Bellcom at the request of the U.S. government to serve as the systems engineering organization for the Apollo space program[89].

In the last decade, the units of AT&T were challenged by their government sponsors to improve their program management and systems engineering competencies as design to cost criteria and accelerated development timelines were introduced into the special sectors served by AT&T. These challenges from sponsoring government agencies were addressed in a new Systems Engineering Process described by James Martin[73] and used by the Advanced Technology Systems business unit of AT&T, now Lucent Technologies. This systems engineering process was the first internal company policy compatible with the EIA 632 and IEEE P1220 systems engineering standards. This copyrighted process was freely distributed throughout industry and became the AT&T standard before the 1996 trivestiture. Figure 14.8 shows an example of systems engineering practice; a standard template distributed across new projects within areas of Lucent Technologies.

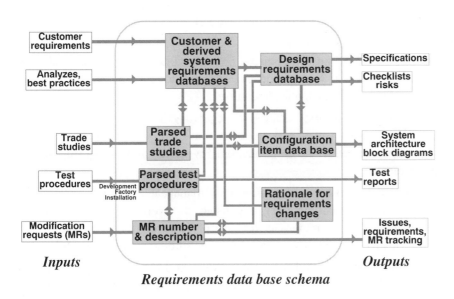

Figure 14.8: Default system model for Lucent

The financial sector – by Bruce Pinnington, Barclays plc

The financial sector as a whole, and banking in particular, is undergoing a revolution. Globalization, increased competition from new entrants, and reductions in the cost of delivery of services all contribute to force banking organizations away from their introspective, product focused nature of years gone by, toward a highly customer-centred, lower delivery cost focus today.

In the industry as a whole, about 50% of the profit comes from only about 5% of the customers. New entrants in the market place, such as supermarkets, telecoms companies, such as Virgin, tend to sell only to the most profitable niches. The larger 'total market' players therefore have to be particularly efficient at providing high value services to customers at low cost.

Exploitation of technology capability is crucial both in providing the expected level of service and reducing delivery cost. Industry figures in the US put the cost of a transaction in a branch at $1.08, over a telephone at $0.54, via an ATM at $0.26 and over Internet banking $0.13 or lower.

Customer loyalty has also changed, and can no longer be assumed. Customers are much more discerning and knowledgeable. To retain market share, financial institutions have to be able to deliver new services to market, and/or to react to moves by competitors in short timescales.

Consequences

The paramount need for a quick time to market has meant that institutions can no longer afford the luxury of large custom-made system developments, and now look instead to integrating established best-of-breed products with existing systems.

To rapidly deploy new products, whilst containing operational costs, organizations need a flexible and scaleable IT infrastructure, based around 'open' standards and flexible architectures.

A major institution cannot change its legacy systems overnight. Companies have to ensure that third-party products based on these new architectures will interoperate with existing business systems, and integrate with the infrastructure.

Flexibility has also to be controlled against manageability. If the infrastructure proliferates it will become very expensive or even impossible to manage operationally. The Gartner organization reports that in many large organizations the IT systems are on the verge of being unmanageable[90].

Large organizations also find that strong Policy and Governance of IT is vital in maintaining this balance. The requirements processes have to detect and evaluate possibly conflicting business requirements and policies, to ensure that today's IT growth does not compromise tomorrow's business development.

Systems engineering consequences

Does systems engineering have a role in this buy-it 'n' bolt-it-in-quick modern information system world? Many in the information system world may think not – indeed the term 'engineering' often invokes immediate suspicions of a long, in-house build-it-all mentality. So what processes do we still need?

The cornerstone to everything else is a good requirements engineering process, which is needed to ensure that:

- *business requirements drive technology requirements;*
- *all aspects of requirements are captured (from constraints such as performance and availability, through to operational and strategic considerations);*
- *requirements are specified over a timeline, so that business visions and strategies are captured and developed, and that consequent IT strategies can be developed;*
- *the right stakeholders are identified and involved in specification of requirements relevant to their role.*

Requirements engineering must no longer be seen as a project phase, running with limited scope for a few months, then stopping until the next project starts. It should be a continuous pan-project activity covering both immediate and visionary requirements gathering (see the earlier section on QSS Inc). Immediate requirements will feed projects (wherever they are), and longer term requirements will feed visions and strategies. All requirements must be regularly maintained.

The requirements engineering processes provide the information necessary to develop information technology strategies. Requirements engineering tools provide the means for collating all this information and ensuring the traceability between the IT requirements, and the business requirements and corporate policies.

Strong user requirement specification is particularly necessary where third-party products are being bought. Weak requirement specification at the start of a custom development can be addressed later – albeit expensively. But where third-party products have to be selected, weak user requirements will result in products being selected on superficial functional requirements only. The detailed requirements specification will then end up being driven by the product specification. Most crucially the evaluation against non-functional requirements, performance, availability, capacity and its interoperability with other business systems, and the infrastructure will be underplayed and the organization can be left committed to a non-optimal product.

Architecture, both for the business design and the information technology under-pinning it, has to meet conflicting demands for flexibility and manageability, providing the maximum interoperability between new distributed applications and older legacy systems. The more controlled this process is, and the more effective the Policy & Governance function is, then the nearer organizations will get to achieving plug-and-play for new bought-in applications and infrastructure.

In our 'service' focused world, testing and deployment have had to move up a level. Organizations can no longer perform isolated User Acceptance Tests (UAT) on the parts of IT which make up a service, but have to test the whole new business service, including all the non-IT processes. Parallel operational pilots may have to be planned and controlled.

New 'customer focused' services may require changes or additions to many of the components which deliver that service, both IT and non-IT. This will often result in a large number of sub-projects being created, possibly in widely dispersed parts of the organization, and increasingly including external suppliers. Projects will vary from technology building, to operational process design and documentation, and including activities from traditional IT project management though to supplier management, Operational Risk Analysis (ORA) and Business Resumption Planning (BRP). Management and co-ordination of these activities are intimate and crucial aspects of the systems engineering processes.

Conclusion from financial services

What we are seeing here is not a diminution of the systems engineering role at all, but quite the opposite. What is possibly diminishing, at least in relative significance, is the role of software engineering. As the financial industry moves away from building new software, and toward end-to-end service delivery, those who survive will be the ones not just looking to buy 'best of breed' products, but those who have the 'best of breed' systems engineering processes capable of delivering and supporting those products in the market place.

Motorola, Inc. – by Gary DeGregorio, Motorola, Inc., Land Mobile Products Sector

In an increasingly competitive environment, building complex systems in shorter timescales demands dramatic process improvements. Four critical elements provide the foundation for these process improvements:

- *an information/knowledge architecture to support our business, marketing, system, software and product development processes across the enterprise;*
- *information structures, within each architectural component, optimized by domain (e.g. marketing);*
- *improved thinking, decision-making, and planning methods; and*
- *a set of tools that make these methods possible at an enterprise level.*

Motorola and many other companies have pursued business process re-engineering to drive critical process changes. The goal is quicker delivery of systems and software to market, while improving overall product quality and market acceptance. While these initiatives have netted solid improvements, they appear destined for long-term failure unless serious attention is paid to the quality of the data. A recent ACM paper on data quality[91] illustrates the situation:

A leading computer industry information service firm indicated that it expects most business process re-engineering initiatives to fail through lack of attention to data quality. An industry executive report noted that more than 60% of surveyed firms (500 medium-size corporations with annual sales of more than $20 million) had problems with data quality. The Wall Street Journal also reported that Thanks to computers, huge databases brimming with information are at our fingertips, just waiting to be tapped. They can be mined to find sales prospects among existing customers; they can be analyzed to unearth costly corporate habits; they can be manipulated to divine future trends. Just one problem: Those huge databases may be filled with junk .In a world where people are moving to total quality management, one of the critical areas is data.

Document-based processes (where the process is defined through document artefacts produced at each stage) tend to focus attention on the format of the document rather than on information quality. Paper documents promote a 'stream of consciousness' approach, leading to an inconsistent mixture of information types (everyone behaves differently, even the same author at a later time). This blends attribute data with object data (e.g. the requirements text is blended with comments about design, priority, schedule, etc.). Data held in documents also tends to lack essential attributes such as ownership or technical risk, and many if not all linkages to where the information came from (e.g. markets, decisions, features, etc.).

Motorola, Land Mobile Products Sector (LMPS) is actively pursuing a project to address these critical elements[92]. The need for building this capability has grown over the last year with the phenomenal growth of the Intranet/Internet and the access to tremendous amounts of data through the World Wide Web. While this data provides an exciting research opportunity[93], it is largely unstructured. Sources must be qualified before their information can be used as part of the decision-making process.

Information and knowledge architecture, methods and tools

The following sections provide an overview of progress in defining and implementing an architecture that can hold both information and knowledge. This involves capturing and organizing essential information/knowledge, and providing methods and tools to make this possible at an enterprise level.

Motorola LMPS is developing an information/knowledge architecture for the essential data for both the business and engineering processes. Bridging the gap between engineering, business, and marketing through the use of a common information/knowledge architecture is key to success. A key goal for this architecture is to define the essential data, clarifying attributes and valid relationships between the data. This provides the 'glue' between the core data such as requirements, decisions, and technologies/capabilities.

The initial LMPS enterprise-wide information/knowledge architecture was defined over a two-year period, driven by the user input (200+ people) we have received from focus groups and on-going pilots. This architecture was implemented using the DOORS database, and used pilots to validate the architecture using data from real projects. We found that the definition of the initial architecture design was stable (one of our design goals), with only minor changes needed to address user or organizational issues over that period.

A Schema Development and Management Tool has been developed as part of this effort. This tool defines and propagates global attribute definitions, users, and access control. It holds and propagates the master definition of the information model (schema) and detects changes conflicting with the master definition, thus maintaining consistency in the database. Schema templates enable us to share an architecture definition with other organizations. In addition, a Viewer allows browsing of the schema in a "learning mode", to understand the purpose for each of the data elements, structures and relationships.

Information structure

The information architecture defines twenty-nine unique types of data that are essential to support system and software development. Each of these unique types of data is held separately within a module, since it uses a unique set of the globally defined attributes. Each module has an information structure optimized for the specific kind of data that it holds. The ability to organize complex sets of data into structures is one of the defining skills in the information age. Efficient structure is essential in identifying omissions, redundancy, and inconsistency. For business data, examples of the types of data include Markets, Customers, Business Requirements, Market Research, and Features. These different types of information must be kept separate from one another from a responsibility point of view, but linked to one another to communicate the information to one another.

Methods that drive the information/knowledge architecture

Three new methods being introduced into LMPS leverage and drive the Information/Knowledge Architecture:

- *requirements structuring methodology*[94];

- *structured decision-making and risk management methodology*[95];
- *technology, capability, and product roadmap planning methodology developed within Motorola.*

These are each critical in assisting managers, engineers and marketing professionals in making the transition from the inefficient document-based world to a highly content-focused information and decision-based process.

Effective management of complex system development **cannot** happen without a structured approach to Requirements and Decision Management (RDM). RDM provides the basis for integrating requirements and decisions to promote traceability, control and re-use. These capabilities support the 'Learning Organization' concept[96]. In support of capturing and manipulating decisions and its related data, Motorola has produced decision and risk management tools that run directly on the real project information.

Structured requirements

A structured approach to requirements focuses on how to organize information into highly effective hierarchical structures optimized to hold specific kinds of data. At the same time it defines the essential attributes (e.g. priority, risk, etc.) of the objects in each structure.

This method defines how to identify and segment different information types such as user, system, business, customer, architecture, and design. This segmentation is critical to reducing wasted effort and allowing for broader re-use of the requirements over time. Critical relationships are formed between different classes of requirements and the decisions they drive, to show the evolution of the requirements during system development.

Structured decision-making and risk management

Decisions are central to all effective systems engineering processes (see chapter 6). The Structured Decision-making method brings all business, marketing, and engineering data together for the first time, in a way that makes sense to each discipline. Decisions are the primary consumers and creators of requirements. The requirements for a product or system are the sum of the derived requirements from all upstream decisions. Tying decisions and requirements together in this manner enables true impact and trace analysis. Since decisions are central, we must capture key relationships to other essential data such as enabling technologies and product architectures. These tend to drive the alternatives that are being considered within a specific decision.

Technology planning

At technology intensive companies, technology, capability and product planning is a critically important activity. Companies that have been identified as having "best practices" in technology planning have established a structured process and fostered involvement between R&D and the business and marketing teams[97].

Technology planning, at Motorola, is a systematic process for forecasting and controlling the evolution of core technical competencies. Technology planning allows us to:

- *forecast critical competitive trends;*
- *build core competencies to gain/maintain competitive advantage;*
- *build a Technology Shelf of available technology to reduce risks to business and product plans;*
- *communicate viable solution options to product planners.*

This is done by building technology structures (three different types: availability, development, product) and planning technologies visualized as a roadmap looking similar to a stacked Gantt chart. In addition, technologies, capabilities and product roadmap elements are linked to each other to capture dependencies to competitive technology objects, and to related issues, decisions and plans. This process has been implemented into tools for technology capability and product planning, again working directly on real project information (see chapter 13.6).

Requirements management tools

When moving from a document-based to an information-based approach, navigation aids, views, and other supporting tools are needed to help users locate, enter, use, and update information and build knowledge related to their expertise. The DOORS tool provides the core capability, but several tools have been added to supply additional functionality and support the process. For example, the Document Generation Tool defines and maintains document templates for a varied set of documents. This pulls hybrid information from a variety of sources into a single coherent document. In addition, a number of market research and analysis tools have been specified.

Training

Training and education is critical to move an organization from a document-based approach to one that leverages the information/knowledge architecture. Tool and method courses have been generated for each of the key methods described in this section. In addition, a new course will be developed to support understanding of the information architecture itself. It is strongly recommended that all training be done "Just-in-Time" and be workshop-based within projects to minimize time lost and maximize understanding by using the real project data.

Conclusions

In a market-driven environment, achievement of enterprise strategies for rapid system development requires fundamental changes in commercial systems engineering. Process improvement efforts at the individual project level do not have the necessary scope. A company-wide architecture for information and knowledge is required for the revolutionary changes necessary to realize the strategies. Additional requirements push the organization toward becoming an information/knowledge-based enterprise, rather than document-based. To address the concerns about data quality, processes must also become focused on content instead of format.

Based on our actual pilot experiences, user feedback, and the large amount of interest being generated inside and outside of Motorola, we are sure we are on the right track. Our content focus has been found to be refreshing, yet challenging by the pilot users. Once they clear the conceptual hurdle of working outside a 'document', they become extremely energized and productive, especially on discovering that they can relate their work to others and understand where it fits in the big picture.

The medical device industry – by Brian McCay, QSS Inc.

The medical device industry (MDI) develops life-critical devices that are used worldwide. MDI users potentially include every person on the planet. The purpose of medical devices is to improve the quality of every user's life, and in the extreme, save and prolong their lives. This reality sets the MDI apart from other life-critical system industries such as the military or the aerospace industry, although there are, of course, many similarities such as:

- *use of high technology as a competitive edge;*
- *increasing use of information technology, especially software intensive solutions;*
- *development of more complex devices that interact with other systems, resulting in emergent behavior;*
- *high risks to the company and its executive management if product failures occur;*
- *large rewards when the devices function correctly, especially in very public situations;*
- *ever-increasing constraints from government regulatory bodies.*

In the MDI area, the risk of death or serious injury due to the misuse or misbehavior of these devices led to Government regulations to protect the public interest. The resulting systems were more complex, no more functionally effective, but much safer from a consumer's perspective.

The MDI is currently undergoing dramatic change fuelled by:

- *global competitive forces;*

- *rapidly evolving technology in the IT, pharmaceutical and biological arenas;*
- *new quality system regulations now in effect in all major countries where their products are sold.*

For example, the Federal Drugs Administration (FDA) in the United States is now mandating 'Design Control' as part of their Quality System Regulation. Previously, the FDA Good Manufacturing Practices Regulation focused primarily on manufacturing. Now the FDA has traced the vast majority of all deaths related to medical devices back to the design phase of the device, not the manufacturing phase. As a result, the Design Control approach mandates many of the best practices of systems engineering.

ISO 13485 quality systems medical devices

Along with ISO 9001 are international standards (ISO 13485) that specify the quality system requirements for the design, development, production and where relevant installation and servicing of medical devices. FDA's Quality System Regulation harmonizes with these standards. Many countries demand compliance with these regulations before medical devices can be sold within their country. For example, the European Community has specified EN 46001, the application of ISO 9001 and also demands CE Marking to signify the safety of a medical device.

Design Control within FDA's Quality System Regulation has the simple goal of reducing the number of lives lost due to the use of medical devices in the United States. From its own perspective, the MDI is facing unprecedented challenges, but analogous solutions to Design Control already exist, and need only be tailored to meet MDI requirements.

Many MDI companies view FDA's Design Control and Europe's CE Marking requirements as a business opportunity to:

- *enhance business processes;*
- *evolve company culture;*
- *take advantage of technology investments;*
- *develop derivative products more cost effectively;*
- *comply with regulatory constraints.*

Of course, all companies want to perform these activities within the context of improving the bottom line. With the view that systems engineering is a risk reduction activity and that MDI risks are quite high, the application of proven disciplines such as requirements management makes perfect sense.

The need for systems engineering in the MDI

Systems engineering, particularly requirements management, is no longer optional, but is mandatory for business survival. The issue facing the MDI is to rapidly understand systems engineering and requirements management to ensure a good return on investment. The challenge to systems engineering professionals is stepping up to meet the concerns of the MDI.

The real issue facing the MDI is a question of how to institute best systems engineering practices. The peace dividend of the early 1990s and the maturing of proven systems engineering tools offers the MDI an opportunity to take full advantage of what the systems engineering community has to offer. Thousands of experienced system engineers have become available in today's marketplace. These professionals are finding their way into quality organizations within the MDI. These system engineers will have to apply their trade in a much more competitive environment. Their biggest challenge is to understand the MDI and what 'tools' to apply within their company to yield the greatest return on investment. They are being asked not simply to institute a sound systems engineering practice but to satisfy business objectives as well.

Systems engineering tools, and specifically requirements management tools, are becoming commonplace. Examining the needs of the MDI, one quickly sees that senior management, research and development departments, marketing, product development teams, manufacturing organizations, maintenance teams, as well as quality and regulatory professionals are all involved in assuring compliance with Design Control requirements. In addition, many MDI companies use suppliers of device components, including off-the-shelf software, in their end products. Each component must comply with regulatory constraints as well. These business relationships force tool vendors to offer solutions that work just as effectively across the Internet, as they do across Intranets, WANs, LANs, on the desktop, or on the road.

Design Control will impact across the whole company, and all device development, manufacturing, and maintenance personnel must conform to Design Control standards. Thus, the second challenge facing systems engineering success in the MDI falls directly on the tool vendors. They must solve complex engineering problems by developing, supplying and supporting easy-to-use tools that meet the document-related requirements of MDI initiative.

14.7. Summary

Most companies that try to improve their processes seem to be successful, but most of them find that the process of change is much slower than they might expect. The key factors for success are the same as with any other process of change – willpower, good objectives, planning and organization. The process may take several years; at a time when many companies are operating on a shorter and shorter horizon, this needs some vision from the top of the company.

An acute awareness of the underlying risk in the improvement process is indispensable. Changing the behavior of an organization is inherently dangerous and the failure rate is high. Success depends on good relations with management, overall atmosphere and a low-risk approach. Change is a marathon, not a sprint, so define your goals and establish the rules to ensure success. Make sure the change is connected to the marketplace, and to customer satisfaction. People will have a different attitude if their jobs and security are tied to the success of the improvement. The industrial tide is flowing in your favour, but you can be too early in your efforts, and failure will set back the cause by years.

Success in the first pilot projects is the beginning and not the end of the improvement process. Once these initial tasks are running well, the challenge moves to spreading the improvement across the company, while simultaneously improving the underlying process. At this point, the internal champion becomes more respectable, and has a public relations task of getting the message to the rest of the company. This clearly requires managerial and public relations skills.

The correct approach is to generate a follow-on management plan in advance at least to some level of abstraction. This plan must cover roll-out to a much larger fraction of the enterprise. Even this initial plan needs to be sold to management, again in business terms, but the success of the pilot projects should make this easier. By the time that you are ready to implement this, the risk is much smaller and you are much more likely to get some support. However, the investment is higher. For the product champion, the main danger is that the rewards of success will be taken away, and this is partly inevitable. The next step is scaling-up from the pilot work to spread the results across the business, and the product champion needs to grow and change with the organization.

Exercise for Improving the systems engineering processes

Exercise 51: No standards, please

You are in charge of several projects. A project manager working for you tells you that he/she does not want to follow the standard development processes of the organization.

The manager says that the increased documentation demanded by the processes will cost '50–100% more' and the 'customer is unwilling to pay for this'.

The manager wants to get on 'with the real work' of the project.

What do you say to this project manager?

Summary

fifteen

15.1. Concepts of systems engineering

This book has presented an array of related concepts that make up systems engineering. This last chapter brings together the essence of the subject and looks to future developments.

No single, simple definition seems to encompass the multi-faceted nature of systems engineering, which is perhaps why so many are in current use. Simon Ramo, Nobel Laureate and co-founder of TRW (also considered by many as the founding father of the subject) may come closest, by emphasizing the holistic aspects of the discipline:

> *Systems engineering is a branch of engineering which concentrates on the design and application of the whole as distinct from the parts... looking at a problem in its entirety, taking account all the facets and all the variables and linking the social to the technological*

What is not good for the beehive cannot be good for the bees – Marcus Aurelius

The principles behind this book have been extracted from industrial experience, from engineers who have specified and built planes, radars, telecoms systems, weapons, information systems and spacecraft. The underlying concepts of organization would have been familiar to the ancient Romans or Chinese. Before anything else, consider what is wanted. Only then choose and optimize the solutions to meet those needs, implement those solutions, then test them against your needs (Figure 15.1). Repeatedly go round the loop to improve everything, considering the whole problem before leaping to solutions. Nothing could be simpler or more obvious, but this does not make it easy. The book explores these deceptively simple tenets from a variety of viewpoints, but makes no claims to an underlying theory, nor does it suppose there is any.

Systems engineering embraces the following concepts:

a holistic, balanced approach: *systems engineering treats the problem, its environment, and the solution as a whole, not as a set of disconnected parts. The system and its environment have to be considered as an entity. Trade-offs between requirements, costs, and timescales are an essential part of the work.*

creativity and domain knowledge: *systems engineering demands intense creativity, particularly in the system requirements and architectural design processes. The role is far more than coordination and management of other*

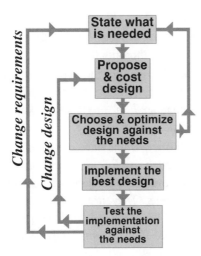

Figure 15.1: The essence of systems engineering

people s work. Systems are made by people, and are the product of clever minds. Indeed success or failure often turns on the ability of a single brilliant person. The system engineer must also understand the design domain in some detail to make logical decisions. We need to immerse ourselves in (but not dictate) the detail of systems, and be sensitive to changes that might affect us. Committee-driven approaches will not work. At different stages, we need visionaries, inventors, makers, negotiators, organizers, and implementors, acting as part of a team. Process and tools are essential, but we must allow room for creativity, and sometimes use intuition instead of apparently hard facts.

coping with risk and change: *risk and human fallibility are constants in system development and operations. We have to predict the operating environment of the system we are constructing. The perfect design is beyond our reach, reason has its limitations, and life is not predictable. Yet the systems must still work reliably and safely. Continuous change is hard enough to handle and requires constant awareness of the business environment. Discontinuous change is even more difficult to survive. Although systems engineering is about prediction and direction, the future is only partially discernible. We cannot anticipate every problem, but we must build systems which can cope with change.*

managing complexity: *modern systems are large, intricate and difficult to develop. They need discipline, organization, traceability, planning, and allocation of responsibilities to ensure efficient development. Systems engineering processes and tools help contain the problems which result from this complexity, both in product and development process.*

re-using experience: *an intricate system like a car is built on a century s work by a million engineers. Few core concepts need be invented, and we must* be humble in learning from the past. This requires sharing of what we know, in the form of best practice for products and processes. This should be based on reality more than dry theorizing.

a user-driven approach: users are the experts at using the system. We have to build systems which satisfy them, or risk product or even business failure. Requirements management is therefore a key activity for the system engineer, pervading the whole life cycle.

whole-life consideration: systems have a natural cycle, from conception and birth, and then through useful life until disposal. They may live on, transformed through evolution, or spawn successor products, reusing parts of the original blueprints. They are often coupled to other systems with which they must co-evolve to survive. Early decisions may impact much later in a product life cycle, and systems engineering must be aware of the downstream consequences.

comprehension of multiple disciplines: system engineers inevitably interact with many specialist disciplines. They must understand enough about these specialist skills to know what is vital for success, and how to deploy them. Although system engineers are generalists, they must never imagine that they can do what they want or succeed on their own. Systems engineering is a service to others, providing a realistic framework for specialist knowledge.

Not everything that comes apart can be put back together

improving the performance of the team: systems engineering involves many different roles through the life cycle. Developing a complex product is always a team effort, and methodologies must always take account the interactions within a creative team. We must improve the teamwork, to conquer difficult problems that no single person could have solved alone. The customer and the supplier must share risks from an early point, or the customer needs to take the systems engineering work to a point where risk is acceptable. The last few years have seen an increase in integrated stakeholder teams and concurrent engineering, based on partnership and information-sharing.

management of information: systems engineering is not a technical discipline like software or mechanical engineering, because it defines the products to be implemented by others. Information modeling and management are essential to direct the system development.

linkage to business goals: engineering of complex systems can succeed only within businesses providing trained staff, finances, facilities, practices and tools. Market-leading system businesses (such as Hewlett-Packard and Motorola) commit to continuous system improvement, and spread these concepts through their supply chain. Systems engineering principles also apply to the building of those organizational support systems.

15.2. Wider scope of systems engineering

Systems engineering is part of everyday life, not just an exotic discipline for specialists. For example, two cornerstones of systems engineering are separating requirements from solutions and treating the customer with respect. Yet we see commonly children working hard to answer the wrong question in their homework or exams, and engineers saying 'users don't know what they want'. Politicians constantly intrude into the detail of solutions without having any defined objectives.

The commonsense principles of systems engineering can be applied far outside conventional engineering domains. In government legislation, we continually see requirements and solutions completely mixed up. Imagine that laws had clear, separated objectives, that the proposed legislation was then checked against those objectives, and checks were performed later to ensure that the objectives had been met. Sometimes this has happened but it is rather uncommon. Even bigger challenges face governments in areas such as welfare reform and the re-building of legislative systems. Separating requirements from solutions allows non-specialists (such as politicians or even voters) could control complex areas much more coherently.

Uncertain, global risks

Systems engineering is particularly important in handling risk, especially where the level of risk is uncertain. There are plenty more potential disasters lurking in genetic engineering, nuclear engineering and global environmental problems. For example, in a problem such as BSE in cattle, failures in numeracy and risk management allowed an agricultural problem to grow into a multi-billion dollar health disaster. Globalization means that ideas or new products spread world-wide almost instantly; but so do pollution, genetic engineering mistakes, or viruses. In the 14th century, the Black Plague took several years to spread from East Asia to Europe when land trade was opened with China. Now a jet plane can carry cholera-infested people 3,000 miles in one day[98] or a whole population can be exposed to dangers such as BSE through a single supermarket chain. Pollution is now causing problems on a world scale, and so environmental issues are clearly becoming more important. Usually the potential cost of failure (as in genetic engineering) is enormous, but the level of risk is not understood at all. Previous experience with nuclear hazards, the introduction of X-rays, or the way in which bacteria have quickly become immune to antibiotics should teach us extreme caution in such situations. These problems typically involve global issues, uncertain risks, intense politics, groups with different interests, many possible solutions, huge potential damage consequences, and high implementation costs. In all of these areas, problems have to be considered as a whole, risk management must be handled professionally, and solutions must be separated from requirements.

The limits of systems engineering

Systems engineering is always in danger of 'reductionism', in particular imagining that the world can be dissected, predicted and controlled by analysis. The reductionist considers the behavior of a system only through its parts, rather than concentrating on the properties of the whole. Systems built by those that think this way often fail because of unsuspected emergent properties – an airport is shut down because of a restaurant fire, or a fishery becomes polluted through agricultural run-off. In practice, few system engineers have ever suffered from the delusions of reductionism. They are only too well aware of the intricacy and unpredictability of the real world, and how poorly it can be modeled. The properties of the whole must not be neglected, to meet the goal of an integrated entity meeting user needs.

Even so, the very act of decomposing a system into components – either for the purposes of design, or just explanation – still attracts the charge of reductionism in some quarters. In response, Dawkins[99] discusses the nature of complexity in systems, including biological systems (the most complex of all):

Always ask: What are the objectives for this?

The hierarchical reductionist, on the other hand, explains a complex entity at any particular level in the hierarchy of organization, in terms of entities only one level down the hierarchy; entities which themselves are likely to be complex enough to need further reducing to their own component parts, and so on. ...explanations which are suitable at high levels in the hierarchy are quite different from the kinds of explanations which are suitable at lower levels. This is the point of explaining cars in terms of carburettors rather than quarks. But the hierarchical reductionist believes that carburettors are explained in terms of smaller units ...which are explained in terms of smaller units ... which are ultimately explained in terms of the smallest of fundamental particles. Reductionism in this sense, is just another name for an honest desire to explain how things work.

15.3. User-driven system processes

Systems engineering transfers power to users, making development a market-driven, not a technology-driven process. Systems are becoming subject to the discipline of requirements, which drive all the end products. A focus on user needs pervades the whole process, and must never be distant from the developers. Requirements engineering is therefore an intimate part of systems engineering. At the enterprise level, it must become a continuous activity that spans all projects. A continuous flow of requirements derived from current projects is an essential task for a customer organization.

Information on customer needs almost invariably exists already within the business, hidden in desks, on cassette tapes of interviews, or customer problem lists scattered through the business. For mass-market products, market surveys and other relevant information are documented in the returns from service engineers and sales staff. The strategic aims of the business, and possibly the intuition of the chief executives, guide the project shape. Large corporations often have operational or marketing departments establishing their future requirements, frequently guided by cost-benefit analysis and operational research.

Whatever way the requirements are captured, there must always be close interaction between deciding what to ask the developers to produce and being assured that it is feasible, affordable and the risks understood. There is a transformation in the early stages from an ill-specified user need to a fully validated design.

Risk and costs are clearly tied together, and both must be fairly transferred between customer and supplier. If an organization wants to have fixed-price developments, then it has several choices:

- *work in partnership with the implementors at the front-end of the process;*
- *perform the systems engineering work itself to reduce the risk in the project (this may involve building prototyping equipment);*
- *paying for pilot projects between competing contractors;*
- *wait for the market to supply the system.*

Understanding the need for feedback and a tailored development approach can lead to a more mature relationship between acquirer and provider. In practice, deriving a specification wholly in the customer environment before handing developers a fixed-price contract, with punitive penalties for problems is completely unsustainable. It may work at the contractual level for one contract, but it is an amoral attempt to have power without responsibility.

If there are no requirements then any solution is satisfactory

Systems engineering and project management

This book has illustrated the close links between the functions of systems engineering and project management. The roles are overlapping and inseparable throughout all stages, and need to be closely bonded.

The system engineering role interacts with management and company politics. The most valuable messages that have to be preached – discipline, up-front investment, the need to consider the whole project – will inevitably draw criticism. During a crisis, under excessive time or competitive pressure, core systems engineering principles are often jettisoned to 'get things done quickly', only to compound the problems downstream. As a result, technical issues are not always given due weight in managerial decisions.

A recent survey of the UK's national systems engineering capability[100] found weak appreciation of systems engineering principles among project managers, contributing to failure on large projects. It reported that:

Engineers consider systems engineering is the obvious approach and believe that project and senior managers only need to be told. Project and senior managers assume it is already done. Only experience of failure brings home the message that all parties have to work hard to make systems engineering deliver the benefits

In the 1960s, project management leapt forward in methods and tools, particularly in scheduling and resource control. Systems engineering (and particularly requirements management) were neglected, perhaps because the disciplines are even more difficult intellectually. Consequently we live with a culture where schedule and resource control are sometimes seen as sufficient for management, as exemplified by so-called 'project management' tools.

These omissions are now being corrected with the recent huge rise in interest in systems engineering. INCOSE (the International Council on Systems Engineering[101]) has been the key agent for change. The methods of systems engineering can now influence project management considerably, and there is a window of opportunity for both professions to move ahead together. However, to spread the concepts more widely, systems engineering needs to present its most important concepts as simply as possible.

15.4. Realistic system processes

The first half of this work covered the system life cycle from a simplistic, sequential perspective. While this is unrealistic, it does introduce many valuable concepts. To cope with the complexity of the real world, a number of elements were then introduced one at a time:

- *repeated, staged, exploration of the whole life cycle at different levels of abstraction with progressive commitment;*
- *commitment to a design only when the risks are acceptable;*
- *decomposition into modules with defined behavior and interfaces;*
- *development of architectural components in separate projects, each with their own life cycle;*
- *organization of the system architecture into hierarchical layers of partially independent components;*
- *delivery of early but partial functionality to stimulate feedback from operations of the system;*
- *prototyping to explore risk before commitment to systems or components;*
- *intensive involvement of users at all times;*
- *a generic system development process for each sub-process;*
- *a generic enterprise process linking business issues, project management, and systems engineering.*

In practice, all of these elements may well operate simultaneously in a complex project. The development of a plane or a large information system involves multiple simultaneous developments, acquisition of COTS components, and feasibility studies spread across multiple levels. These concurrent activities are operating continuously under the visibility provided by the stage-gate process.

The separate processes of the simple lifecycle emerge almost unscathed from these changes. The concepts behind, for example, user requirements or architectural design, remain valid even in a complex multi-level development. The underlying need to obtain closure and maintain traceability between the elements of document structures is essential.

15.5. Becoming a good customer

If customers play their part well, implementation becomes much easier. Being a good customer organization involves a deep understanding of the operational environment, plus an ability to view and control developments at the right level of abstraction. The good customer must understand the development in some detail, but not micro-manage the implementors, or even the systems engineering work. This does not imply a passive role. Many organizations exist primarily to support customers, and must develop and propagate best engineering practice within their own organizations and those of their suppliers. In the space field, NASA and ESA provide clear models.

The concepts of product management are a starting point for a good acquisition policy. However, the pace of change for intricate systems means that the customer is having to become expert at handling problems, which include variety of systems engineering elements such as:

We shape our buildings, thereafter they shape us
– Winston Churchill

acquiring for upgradeability: *systems need updating more frequently than previously, because of the rate of change of technology and the business or operational environments;*

acquiring systems in families: *minimizing the logistics, re-supply tasks, maximizing interchangeability and minimizing development costs are important. Customers need systems with common subsystems components;*

acquiring systems of systems: *when systems are strongly mutually dependent in operation, systems engineering is needed above the individual projects. Examples include large-scale military information systems, air traffic control, and wide area transportation systems. The basic tools are the framework architecture (possibly customer-owned), linked to overall user needs and clear, open interfaces between the system components. Integration testing and configuration management of such complex meta-systems provide new challenges for customers and suppliers;*

evolutionary acquisition *customers may be procuring systems which are first of a kind or high-risk. An iterative development approach can reduce risk, but requires much stronger customer-contractor interactions than has been traditional for custom developments;*

making use of advanced simulation technology: *simulation technology is* *providing tools of unprecedented power to support much of the early requirements, design and trade-off analysis, which may be conducted jointly between customers and suppliers;*

acquiring for minimum whole-life costs: *it is well known that decisions made early on in the life of a system may come to dominate its eventual costs. The linkage between whole-life costs and system design principles is still a mysterious area;*

linking to business processes: *many complex systems tie in closely with the processes of the business they serve. Their specification and eventual integration require understanding of the customers internal operations, which may be transformed as a result;*

acquiring at service level: *to avoid the more challenging problems of acquiring systems, organizations are increasingly contracting for a complete operational capability rather than for equipment. To take an extreme case, why get involved in the detail of procuring planes, when you can procure an airline, complete with pilots, maintenance, logistics, and air traffic control? As far as systems engineering is concerned, the same work is necessary, although responsibilities, risks, interfaces and ownership will have shifted.*

Organizations that acquire complex systems increasingly need skills similar to those of the large system integration corporations, but emphasizing the user and customer roles. The new challenges mean, however, that customer and supplier processes can no longer sit in isolation. The growth of integrated product teams in the defense community are witness to this. Many large commercial companies have already partnered with their suppliers to create extended enterprises, linking through the supply chain. In the future, we are likely to see the same principles re-applied to the customer-service provider interface.

15.6. Systems engineering and the business

Systems engineering defines the future of the modern business. Good systems engineering processes are a real advantage, enabling companies to satisfy their customers with competitive products. It helps them cut the calendar time for development. Companies that optimize new product innovation will be at an overwhelming advantage.

Automation of the systems engineering process through better tools is inevitable, but must necessarily trail behind an increased understanding of the process. Reality dictates everything, processes can then be defined, followed by methods, and only then can tools be sensibly implemented. This may seem patently obvious, but hundreds of millions of dollars have been wasted attempting to build 'systems engineering environments' with weak or non-existent processes and information models. These were technically-driven around database theories – and more recently synthetic environments – not as implementations of a well-understood systems engineering process.

Synthetic environments

Developments in advanced simulation technology present both an opportunity and a challenge to systems engineering. Chapter 11 discusses the way in which prototypes in various forms are already integrated with the engineering process, but the sheer scale of computer power on offer will probably transform how engineering is undertaken.

The availability of simulated environments is unlikely to change the 'what' of systems engineering. But 'how' it is done could be radically different as the virtual computer-created world becomes more realistic, the boundary between prototypes and operational equipment becomes unclear and feedback becomes more immediate and rapid. The whole development will still need to be supported by a strong process and information models to be held together and controlled. At the time of writing, a new synthesis is under way with simulation and systems engineering on a rapid convergence path, with the potential for even bigger competitive advantages.

Transition from paper

We have become cynical about the repeated predictions of the 'paperless office', but in systems engineering the transition from paper to computer control of information is well underway. This goes far beyond word processing. Project information is managed electronically as an information set, even though paper documents are still extremely useful. This approach maximizes the value produced by information – 'write once, use many times' and is the harbinger for how to manage intellectual assets. However, this approach requires much more discipline than the older document-based approach, starting with process definition and the production of information models. The system engineer needs to create, organize and interlink information to direct the development. Significant improvements in systems engineering tools in the last decade are making them more capable of fulfilling this new role.

15.7. Future system life cycle processes

The system life cycle is the foundation for most project activities, and success will often depend on a sensible choice of process. However, the lack of commonly agreed process standards has restricted the wider adoption of systems engineering, outside a small number of customer and supplier organizations. Process models must be rich and meaningful enough to bring the communities together, and general enough to meet the needs of a wide range of industries. They must cover the system development from initial conception to useful deployment ad eventual disposal.

A good process model helps:

open trade *by defining a widely-accepted language to enable collective action. This provides a basis for negotiation, agreements and contracts. It also defines generic actions and responsibilities throughout the life cycle, for use in acquirer/supplier transactions between enterprises and throughout the supply chain.*

organizational capability *by providing a common perception of the required skills, resource types and roles, and a starting point from which an organization can build specific policies, standards and procedures. It can also form a common basis for measuring and improving organizational capability.*

personal competence *by encouraging systems engineering proficiency and professionalism through norms for personal attainment and qualification. A good process model may lead to codes of professional conduct and even social responsibility, equivalent to those of more established professions.*

Standardization activities look likely to produce world-wide standards for systems engineering. Figure 15.2 shows the evolution of systems engineering standards. First in the field were the US DoD Military Standards (Mil Std 499), which codified the practices of the US defense industries during the 1960's and 70's. In retrospect, these standards were rather prescriptive and suitable only for large systems. They assumed a single-shot, 'big bang' development, not fitting well with thinking on evolutionary or staged development. However, a generation of system engineers was trained in their use, and many successful and intricate systems have resulted from their application.

The Perry Initiative broke the sequence of military standards development in 1994, with the DoD withdrawing from standards making, preferring those of the market place wherever possible. Attention then shifted to IEEE, with their

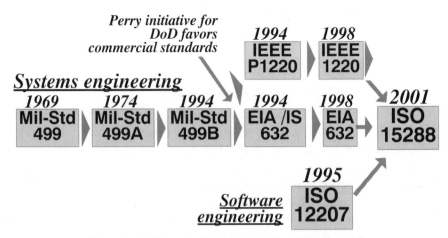

Figure 15.2: History of systems engineering standards

publication of IEEE 1220, a standard for the application and management of the systems engineering processes. It is currently the best and most extensively used international systems engineering standard and is referenced internationally by commercial industry. However, it fails to separate user and system requirements, and does not fully address recursiveness in the systems engineering processes. The origin of the standard has also led to it being perceived as too cumbersome for small projects.

The US Electrical Industries Association (EIA) has produced EIA 632. At the time of writing, key players are reviewing a new version of the document, aimed at release in 1998. A number of new concepts are more clearly depicted in this revision, including stakeholder requirements and recursive application of a set of basic systems engineering processes. The EIA 632 standard will eventually be accompanied by a compatible Systems Engineering Capability Model.

The first world-wide process standard may be that of the International Standards Organization (ISO) with their 'Systems Life Cycle Processes Standard' 15288 scheduled for completion by 2001. Early indications suggest strong support from leading industrialized nations such as Japan, USA, UK, France, Germany, Sweden, and Australia. ISO/IEC 15288 will impact on the existing 'Software Life Cycle Standard', ISO 12207, to harmonize the system and software engineering processes. One of the authors (SA) is joint editor of ISO 15288, and many of the concepts embodied in this book are being offered to the ISO for consideration.

If current progress is sustained, world-wide standards should emerge early in the 21st century, reducing trading barriers for global systems engineering and providing a common backbone for business processes. Suitably supported by information-handling toolsets, the vision of integrated global enterprises will draw a step closer.

15.8. Conclusions

The development of systems is one of the most challenging of all human activities, and driven by a need to cope with complexity. System engineers aim to take intricate problems and produce robust practical solutions. The techniques for coping with complexity can be reapplied to problems of any type. Systems engineering is a generic delivery mechanism for a customer-driven approach, and likely to spread far from its current technical niche.

Almost all businesses now understand the need to improve their development process. Systems engineering is crucial to the future of any customer or supplier organization. This book offers a disciplined approach to system development, based on commonsense concepts.

The world is moving rapidly to a knowledge-based economy, and the really successful economies will be those that manage their knowledge effectively.

Systems engineering is the core technology to wring value from this situation – it closes the loop between customers and developers. Businesses, and countries that cannot understand this will disappear from complex product development.

But we must never imagine systems engineering as a mechanistic process, certain to bring success. The book has shown many of the factors involved in handling complexity, but there can never be a set of rules – even if they were perfect – that will guarantee a good result. Systems engineering is a useful aid to human intelligence, but no process (or book) can ever substitute for professional judgement made with knowledge of the situation. You always need good players to win a game – however many lessons you give them before the game. In the end, human decisions and strategy drive the systems engineering processes, and not vice-versa. Systems are built by humans, and as the product of human culture, they are built first in the mind. The development strategy has to be chosen from deep knowledge and understanding of all of the issues involved. Systems engineering is the starting point for applying intelligence, not a set of rules that can be slavishly followed.

Systems engineering encapsulates what humans know about coping with complexity. This knowledge is spreading from specialized integration organizations to the broader marketplace and into customer organizations. The emergence of product and organization-independent process standards will reinforce the trend. Systems thinking combined with engineering practice is so powerful in addressing large complex issues that it has justly been called the problem-solving technique for the modern age.

Appendices

The Web site

Linked Web sites

A variety of Web sites are linked to this book, and contain related material.

www.complexsystems.com

The Web site www.complexsystems.com will act as a clearing site and pointer to other Web sites associated with the book. This will include references to the latest available system standards, a reference model for systems engineering, document templates, an example project, readers' comments on the exercises, and course material based on the book.

The Web site will also contain comments received on all the above material.

Viewfoils for all the images in the book

All of the images of the book are contained in Adobe Acrobat PDF format, and can be read by the free reader available from the Adobe web site at www.adobe.com

Answers to the exercises

Suggested answers to the exercises at the end of each chapter are provided. If you have any suggested improvements, please send them to the linked Web site.

Workshop plan

The plan covers an agenda for a five-day workshop to derive draft versions of user requirements, system requirements, architectural design, life cycle definition, cost analysis and risk management for a new project. The workshop combines teaching with immediate use of that knowledge to capture project information.

Glossary of terms

A glossary of terms for systems engineering is included.

www.dera.gov.uk/syseng

This Web site contains the DERA processes for software and systems, plus details of the current DERA work on international standards. This site will mirror all the issues raised in this book.

www.incose.org

The Web site for the International Council on Systems Engineering (INCOSE). This is an invaluable reference site for systems engineering, containing details of conferences, national and regional chapters, and the work of INCOSE technical committees.

Glossary

Abstraction A view of a system that has a consistent level of behavioral and compositional detail in each branch of the architecture and hides finer, lower level detail.

Alpha-testing Testing of a pre-production version of a system (or subsystem) by representatives of the customer organization in the environment as close to operational as possible. See also Beta-Testing.

Animation (of requirements) Examination of a set of requirements for completeness or consistency by invoking them in a temporal or logical sequence.

Applicability relationships The link, or traceability, between a high level performance or non-functional requirement and the implied (or stated) functional requirement imposed on a range of sub-systems or components at a lower level.

Architecture The structure of levels and/or branches that partition a system into its constituent parts or components.

Architectural design A clear definition of a system which is to be built, at a level of detail sufficient to allow reasoning about the overall system behavior.

Associated cost A concept in risk management. The cost associated with the occurrence of a hazard for which a risk has been identified.

Associated value A concept in risk management. The benefit derived from taking a specific risk.

Asynchronous processes Processes whose execution bear no fixed temporal relationship to each other.

Atomic requirement A discrete user or system requirement, capable of separate test in the implemented system.

Baseline A concept in configuration management. The software component versions and hardware modification states which form the basis for continued system development.

Behavioral model A system representation which expresses the inherent actions and the responses to external events that characterize a system.

Benchmarking Formal or informal comparison of (systems engineering) processes, best practices and performance with equivalent organizations.

Beta-testing Reduction of the overall cost and risk of system faults by enlisting friendly customers to conduct tests of a pre-production system in the operational environment.

Business An organization whose purpose is to profit by acquiring or supplying systems. See also Enterprise.

Business process re-engineering   The use of system engineering principles to define and (re)organize the processes of a business.

Business requirement   Those requirements introduced for the benefit of the business that is developing a system.

Capability   An integrated set of interdependent systems comprising operational products and the associated products and services necessary to sustain operation.

Capability development   The highest level view of development: the satisfaction of a desired user capability by the design and supply of products installed into the operational environment.

Cohesion   The degree to which elements or functions of a system interact and depend upon each other.

Component   A discrete, configured, essentially homogeneous part of a system that is supplied by a technology or discipline-specific organization.

Configuration management   A method of controlling storage, accesses and changes to discrete, defined, related parts, models or specifications of a system at any time during its lifetime.

Constraint   In the context of a requirement, a restriction on the acceptable solution opportunities (a type of requirement itself). See also non-functional requirement.

Coverage relationship   The traceability of requirements to implementation in system development processes.

Customer   A role having the responsibility for acquiring a specified capability.

Decomposition   The activity of identifying the constituent elements and relationships of a system or sub-system.

De-coupling   The minimization of interactions between system functions.

Design margin   The additional performance included in excess of the user requirement to cater for uncertainties in design knowledge, and operational, test and production environments.

Design to cost   The use of product cost as a paramount design goal

Development life cycle   A tailored set of processes by which a system is created to meet a specified requirement.

Development system   The organized set of resources enabling a system to be developed.

Downey cycle   A staged development life cycle for risk managed defense equipment acquisition favored by UK MoD.

End user   The user who benefits directly from a system when it is used in its operational environment.

End-to-end scenario A description of a system which specifies, exercises and measures system dynamic behavior between an initial stimulus or state and a final response or state.

Enterprise An organization that identifies a competitive market opportunity, or has a statutory obligation, to fulfil the need for a system.

Estimated cost A concept in risk management. The predicted cost of a system assuming that no hazards occur.

Evolutionary development Repetition of the basic development process to produce new versions of a product incorporating experience from operational use, technological advance and revised customer requirements.

Evolutionary life cycle A life cycle form in which knowledge from system utilization guides the development of the next generation of that system.

External system A system outside the control of, but interacting with, the system under development.

Formal requirement An unambiguous and quantitative stipulation of system functionality or performance.

Framework architecture A stable system structure that accommodates, without change, evolving or different components

Functional requirement A requirement for a specific system action or response.

Hazard An undesirable event which could arise to affect the quality, cost or schedule of the system under development.

Horizontal prototype A prototype representing a system across a broad range of functions but to a limited depth in detail.

Incremental development An approach to development in which an agreed user requirement is achieved in a series of systems with progressively increasing performance.

Incremental life cycle The enterprise life cycle incorporating the processes of incremental development.

Information model The structure, nature and links of all information sets transferred between life cycle processes

Key requirement A user or system requirement identified as determining one or more demanding or critical system characteristics.

Legacy system An existing system which events determine as being a given part of a current environment or solution.

Modular requirements Groupings of requirements, typically by functional area, to encourage cohesion in implementation and to simplify subsequent update or change.

Multi-level development   The creation of a complex system by a layered set of quasi-independent enterprises and projects.

Non-functional requirement   A requirement which stipulates a physical or performance characteristic. See constraint.

Object orientation   A method that views entities, e.g. requirements, artefacts, as being discrete, encapsulated with hierarchies of attributes and thereby encouraging modularity and re-use.

Operational capability   A set of products, i.e. a delivered system together with support product or processes, installed into an operational environment.

Operational environment   The conditions under which a delivered product is required to be operated by the end-user.

Operational requirements   Those requirements that pertain to the system's period of operation.

Operational scenario   A selection of user requirements organized sequentially or concurrently in a setting to represent some aspect of the required operation.

Procedure   A formally established sequence of actions.

Process   A set of actions that receives an information or material input and operates on it in a specified manner to produce an information or material output.

Product   The supplied output of a process or group of processes.

Product engineering   The process of technical management exercising control of all the technical issues leading to the creation of a single product.

Production system   The organized set of resources enabling a system to be produced and delivered.

Program engineering   A process of technical management exercising overall technical authority for establishing a capability.

Project   The structure of authorities, resources and controls within an enterprise organization in order to supply a product or service.

Prototype   The experimental implementation of all or part of a developing system in order to gain information or to assess risk.

Quality function deployment (QFD)   A proprietary method for tracing system design elements to user requirements.

Rapid application development (RAD)   A development method requiring continual user involvement that permits frequent small evolutionary stages.

Real-time system   A system required to respond within short, tightly specified time variant from sources external to the system.

Redundancy   Tolerance to faults in a system by use of multiple instances of hardware or software resources.

Regression testing   Testing conducted to ensure that the introduction of change, e.g. evolution, modification, has not devalued the results of earlier tests.

Requirement   An expression of need, demand or obligation.

Requirements engineering   The role of capturing and managing requirements.

Re-use   The implementation of an existing system or component in an alternative application.

Risk   The chance of a hazard occurring.

Risk management   The pursuit of cost-effective actions to minimize impact of hazards, were they to occur.

Safety-critical functions   System functionality, the failure of which can in result in loss or injury to human life.

Schema   See information model.

Sequential life cycle   A life cycle processes executed in a fixed, non-concurrent sequence.

Software-intensive system   A large system whose functionality and composition is dominated by software components.

Software-shaped system   A system in which software is the critical element in terms of cost, added value and risk.

Stage   A single pass through the development cycle terminating in a business decision about future development projects.

Stage-gate   A business-driven decision point between successive stages.

Sub-project   A subordinate project relative to a project of interest in a hierarchy of projects.

Subsystem   A subordinate project relative to a project of interest in a hierarchy of projects.

System   A human-made entity with a distinguishing and defined purpose that draws on integrated, constituent parts, each of which does not individually possess the required overall characteristics or purpose.

System design   The processes which create a specification for all the components from which a system may be produced.

System requirements   An intermediate step between user requirements and system design; an internally consistent definition of what the system will have to do.

System requirements document   A document or data-base in which the system requirements are captured.

Systems engineering   The technical and control actions associated with the processes in the system and capability development processes.

Tailored development   A development where the individual steps of the sequential life cycle are re-structured to suit the particular circumstances.

Time to market   Elapsed time between identifying a marketing opportunity and the availability of a developed product for supply to a customer.

Traceability   The ability within the system development to relate a feature of design or implementation to a parent requirement.

Trade-off   A decision making activity that selects from alternative solutions on the basis of overall benefit to the system.

User environment   See operational environment.

User requirements   An expression of the needs of all stakeholders in the utilization domain.

User requirements document   A document or data-base in which the user requirements are captured.

User scenario   See operational scenario.

Validation   Actions to confirm that the behavior of a developed system meets user needs

Value engineering   The exercise of judgement on cost-benefit issues during system development.

Verification   Actions to confirm that the product of a system development process meets its specification.

Verification system   The organized set of resources enabling tests to be conducted, recorded and assessed to ensure verification.

Vertical prototype   A prototype which represents a selected portion of system functionality in detail.

Visual metaphor   A familiar real-world object used as the basis for the design of the look and feel of the interface of a system with its user.

Walkthrough   A preliminary and informal review of documentation to eliminate errors before the requirements or design are fixed.

Working environment   See operational environment.

References

[1] Mazza C. et al. "*Software Engineering Standards* Prentice-Hall ISBN 13-106568-8 P March 1994.

[2] from the Standish Group Web site at www.standishgroup.com

[3] *Scientific American.* (Sept 1994).

[4] Cooper, Robert G. *Winning at new products* ISBN 0-201-56381-9 Addison Wesley (1993).

[5] Moody, J. A. et al. *Metrics and case studies for evaluating engineering designs* Prentice-Hall ISBN 0-13-739871-9 (1997) Van Nostrand, New York, (1990).

[6] Morris, P.M. and Hough, A. *Anatomy of major projects* ISBN 0-471-91551-3 John Wiley (1987).

[7] Checkland, Peter. *Systems thinking, systems practice* ISBN 0-471-27911-0 John Wiley (1993)

[8] Norman, Donald. *Turn signals are the facial expressions of automobiles* Norman, Donald ISBN 0-201-58124-8 Addison-Wesley (1992).

[9] Sabbagh, Karl. *21st Century Jet – The making of the Boeing 777* ISBN 0-330-32890-5 Pan (1995).

[10] Von Hippel, Eric. *The sources of innovation* ISBN 0-19-504085-6 Oxford University Press (1988).

[11] Jacobson, Ivar. *Object-oriented software engineering: a use-case driven approach* ISBN 0-201-54435-0 Addison-Wesley (1994).

[12] Gilb, Thomas. *Principles of Software Engineering Management* Addison-Wesley. ISBN 0-201-119246-2 (1988).

[13] Longworth. "*Realistic user requirements* ISBN 085-012-628 NCC (1987).

[14] Hatley, Derek & Pirbhai, Imtiaz. "*Strategies for Real-Time Systems Specification* ISBN 0-932-633-11-0 (1988).

[15] Fowler, Martin, Scott, Kendall. *UML distilled: Applying the standard object modeling language*. ISBN 0-201-32563-2 Addison-Wesley (1992).

[16] see www.scenarioplus.com

[17] *The Times*, (November 23, 1996).

[18] Coad, Peter. & Yourdon, Edward. "*Object-oriented analysis*" Yourdon Press. ISBN 0-13-629981-4. (1991).

[19] Edwards, Keith. *Real-time structured methods*. ISBN 0-471-93415-1. Wiley. (1993).

[20] Rumbaugh, James. *Object-oriented modeling and design* ISBN 0-136-29841-9. Prentice-Hall (1991).

[21] See the www.rational.com web site for a definition of the UML standard.

[22] Alexander, Christopher. *Notes on the synthesis of form*. Harvard University Press. ISBN 0-674-62751-2 (1964).

[23] Monroe, Robert, T. Kompanek, Andrew., Metlon, Ralph., and Garlan, David. *Architectural Styles, Design Patterns, and Objects* IEEE Software, (January 1997).

[24] Mozart, quoted by Mintzberg, H. *The rise and fall of strategic planning* ISBN 0-13-781824-6 Prentice-Hall (1994).

[25] The International Alliance of Interoperability – see www.interoperability.com and related sites.

[26] Jackson, Ken,. Boasson, Maarten. *The benefits of good architectural style in the engineering of computer based systems*, Proceedings of 1995 International Symposium and Workshop on Systems engineering of Computer Based Systems, Tucson, Arizona, ISBN 0-7803-2531-1 (March 1995).

[27] Perrow, Charles. *Normal Accidents*" ISBN 0-465-05143-X Basic Books (1984).

[28] Booher, H. R. (editor) *MANPRINT – An Approach to Systems Integration*, Van Nostrand Reinhold ISBN 0-442-00383-8 (1990).

[29] Oughton, Frederick. *Value analysis and value engineering* Pitman ISBN 0-273-40532-2 (1969).

[30] Petroski, Henry. *Invention by design: How engineers get from thought to thing* Harvard University Press ISBN 0-674-46267-6 (1996).

[31] Hauser, J. & Clausing, D. *The house of quality* Harvard Business Review. May–June 1988, p.63.

[32] see www.qssinc.com

[33] Petroski, Henry. *To engineer is human – the role of failure in successful design* ISBN 0-333-40673-7 St Martin's Press (1982).

[34] Clark, K.B. and Fujimoto T. *Product Development Performance"* ISBN 0-87584-245-3. Harvard Business School Press (1991).

[35] Christopher-Jones, J. *Design methods* ISBN 0-471-27958-7 Wiley (1980).

[36] US Air Force. Arrow, Kenneth J in M Szenberg *Eminent economists – their life and philosophies"*. Cambridge University Press.

[37] Babich, Wayne. *"Software Configuration Management – Coordination for Team Productivity* Addison-Wesley. ISBN 0-201-10161-0 (1986).

[38] Gilb, Thomas & Graham, Dorothy. *"Software Inspection"* Addison-Wesley ISBN 0-201-63181-4. (1993).

[39] Kepner, Charles H. and Tregoe, Benjamin B. *The New Rational Manager*. Princeton Research Press. (1981).

[40] Bernstein, Peter. *Against the Gods – the remarkable story of risk"* John Wiley ISBN 1-471-12104-5 (1996).

[41] Simon, H. A. *The Science of the Artificial* ISBN 0-262-69191-4 MIT Press (1996).

[42] Boehrn, B. *A spiral model of software development and enhancement*. IEEE Computer, Vol 21, no 5. (May 1988), p. 61–72.

[43] Dynamic Systems Development Method Group, see www.dsdm.org

[44] *DERA Software Practises Manual* DERA/COM/G9540/1.0. UK Defence and Evaluation Research Agency.

[45] ISO 9000. Contact the national standards organization e.g. American National Standards Institute (ANSI) NY, NY.

[46] Arnold, Stuart. *The DERA Systems engineering Practices Reference Model*, (see Web site at www.complexsystems.com)

[47] Alderson, A, Arnold, S, Brook, P, Jackson, K, & Stevens, R. *An improved systems engineering process* Proceedings of the 1997 Symposium on Systems Engineering of Computer-based Systems. Monterey, March 1997.

[48] *New York Times*, Nov 16, 1997.

[49] Douglas, Evan J. *Managerial economics: analysis and strategy* Prentice-Hall ISBN: 0-135-54346-0 (1992).

[50] Nuese, Charles J. *"Building the right things right*. ISBN 0-527-763000 Quality Resources (1995).

[51] McKinsey & Co. *Speeding up Product Development* from *Reinersten, D.G. Search for new product leaders* Electronic Business (July 1994).

[52] Utterback, James. *Mastering the dynamics of innovation*. ISBN 0-87584-740-4 Harvard Business School (1996).

[53] ESA/INFO(96)34 July 24 1996.

[54] Tufte, Edward. *"Envisaging information* ISBN 0-961-39211-8 (1992) and *The quantitative display of information* ISBN 0961 39210X (1992) both from Graphics Press, Cheshire Connecticut.

[55] Garland, Ken. *"Mr Beck s Underground Map"*. ISBN 1-85414-168-6. Capital Transport. (1995).

[56] Tschicold, Jan. *"The form of the book"* Hartley & Marks (1991).

[57] Piplani, Col. L. K. et al. *Systems Acquisition Manager s Guide for the use of Models and Simulations* ISBN 0-16-045161-2 Defense Systems Management College (Sept 1994).

[58] Casti, John L. *Would-be Worlds* ISBN 0-471-12308-0 Wiley (1996).

[59] *Financial Times*, Jan 9, 1997.

[60] Emmerich, W., Finkelstein, A., Montagnero, C. & Stevens, R. *"Standards Compliant Software Development"* in Proc. International Conference on Software Engineering Workshop on Living with Inconsistency, (IEEE CS Press), 1997, electronic publication.

[61] International Function Point Users Group. *Function Point Counting Practices Manual*, Release 4.0 IFPUG, Westerville, Ohio, 1994.

[62] DeGregorio, Gary. *An information architecture for systems engineering – progress examples and direction* INCOSE Conference, Los Angeles (1997).

[63] Modified from Gartz, Paul. *Avionics development and integration system methods"* IEEE AES June 1987 p.2.

[64] Farncombe, Andrew *"Tayloring (sic) systems engineering processes to project management circumstances* UK INCOSE Third Annual Symposium, (1996).

[65] Gorchels, Linda *The Product Manager s Handbook* ISBN 0-8442-3669-1 NTC Business Books. (1997).

[66] Report of the Steering Group on Development Cost Estimating Vol. 2. H.M Stationery Office (1969).

[67] DoD Directive 5000.2-R *"Mandatory Procedures for Major Defense Acquisition Programs and Major Automated Information Systems* (1996).

[68] Stewart, Thomas A. *Intellectual Capital* ISBN 0-333-69479-1 Nicholas Brearley (1997).

[69] Kleinschmidt, Elko J. *New products: the key factors in success* monograph for the American Marketing Association (1990).

[70] diagram used within QSS Inc for evaluating projects proposals.

[71] *"Maturity Model SE CMM-94-06, CMU/SEI-94-HB-05; SEI Appraisal Method Description, Version 1.1.* Software Engineering Institute (1996).

[72] CAWG-1996-02-1.50 INCOSE SECAM Assessment Model. Version 1.50. International Council on Systems Engineering (July 1997).

[73] Martin, J. N. *Systems engineering guidebook: a process for developing systems and products* Boca Raton, FL, CRC Press (1997).

[74] Pulford, Kevin et al. *A quantitative approach to software management* ISBN 0-201-87746-5. Addison Wesley (1996).

[75] Rich, Ben. *Skunk works* ISBN 0-316-74330-5 (1994) Little-Brown.

[76] see www.skandia.se

[77] Svieby, Karl Erik. *The new organizational wealth* ISBN 1-57675-014-0 Berret-Koehler (1997).

[78] Klein, David & Prusak, Laurence. *Characterizing intellectual capital* multiclient working paper for Ernst & Young, Boston, March, 1994 (from Stewart's book).

[79] Jock Rader, Hughes Aircraft. Personal communication.

[80] DeMarco, Tom & Lister, Tim. *"Peopleware – Productive projects and teams"* Dorset House. ISBN 0-932633-05-6 (1987).

[81] *"ISO 9000-3 Quality Management and Quality Assurance Standards – Part 3: Guidelines for the application of ISO 9001 to the Development, Supply and Maintenance of Software* (Sept. 1990).

[82] Spenkey, Paul *World class performance through total quality – a practical guide to implementation* ISBN 0-412-642270-0 Chapman & Hall (1992).

[83] Taguchi, G. & Clausing, D. *Robust quality* Harvard Business Review Jan-Feb 1990 p. 65.

[84] (private communication).

[85] Brook, P., Barnes, D, Arnold, S., and Stevens, R. *"Developing Software and Systems Engineering Standards by an Evolutionary Process* INCOSE International Symposium, Boston, July 1996.

[86] Hall, A. D. *"A Methodology for Systems engineering* , Van Nostrand Reinhold Company, New York, 1962 by Litton Educational Publishing, Inc.

[87] K. J. Schlager. *"Systems engineering - Key to Modern Development,* IRE Trans., Prof. Gp. Eng. Management, 3, 1956, pp. 64–66.

[88] Members of the Technical Staff, Bell Telephone Laboratories. *"A History of Engineering and Science in the Bell System, National Service in War and Peace (1925–1975)* Bell Telephone Laboratories, Inc., 1978.

[89] Members of the Technical Staff, Bell Telephone Laboratories, *"Where On the Moon? An Apollo Systems engineering Problem* Bell System Technical Journal, Volume 21, Number 5, May–June 1972.

[90] Keyworth et al. *Network systems management scenario: navigating the turbulence* . Strategic analysis report. Gartner Group (March 1997).

[91] Wand, Yair and Wang, Richard Y. *Anchoring Data Quality Dimensions in Ontological Foundations, Communications of the ACM*, Vol. 39, No. 11, November 1996.

[92] DeGregorio, Gary and Novorita, Bob. *Less is More: Capturing the Essential Data Needed for Rapid Systems Development,* INCOSE International Symposium, Boston 1996.

[93] Etzioni, Oren. *The World Wide Web: Quagmire or Gold Mine?, Communications of the ACM*, Vol. 39, No. 11, November 1996.

[94] Stevens, Richard. *"Structured Requirements Course,"* Quality Systems & Software Ltd., UK, January 1996.

[95] Fitch, John. *"Structured Decision Making and Risk Management Workshop,* Course Notes, Systems Process Inc., January 1997.

[96] Senge, Peter M. *"The Fifth Discipline – The Art & Practice of The Learning Organization* Doubleday/Currency, 1990.

[97] Metz, Philip. *Integrating Technology Planning with Business Planning, IEEE Engineering Management Review,* Winter 1996.

[98] Diamond, Jared. *Guns, germs and steel - the fate of human society* ISBN 0-393-03891-2 W. W. Norton (1997).

[99] Dawkins, Richard. *"The Blind Watchmaker* Penguin Books, London. ISBN 0-14-008056-2 (1988).

[100] *"Building Integrated Systems* , IEE, July 1997 ISBN 0-85296-935-2.

[101] see the INCOSE web site at www.incose.org

Index